The ABCs of

Microsoft Internet Explorer 3

The ABCs of
Microsoft® Internet Explorer 3

John Ross

SYBEX®

San Francisco - Paris - Düsseldorf - Soest

Associate Publisher: Carrie Lavine
Acquisitions Manager: Kristine Plachy
Developmental Editor: John Read
Editor: Marilyn Smith
Project Editor: Kim Wimpsett
Technical Editor: Jim Bonelli
Book Design Director: Cătălin Dulfu
Book Designer: Design Site
Graphic Illustrator: Patrick Dintino
Electronic Publishing Specialist: Stephanie Hollier
Production Coordinator: Amy Eoff
Indexer: Ted Laux
Cover Designer: Design Site
Cover Illustrator: Sergie Loobkoff

Library of Congress Card Number: 96-69669
ISBN: 0-7821-1885-2

Manufactured in the United States of America
10 9 8 7 6 5 4 3 2 1

Acknowledgments

Thanks to all of the Sybex editorial, production, and marketing folk whose labors are reflected in the quality of the book you hold in your hands.

Contents at a Glance

Introduction xvi

Chapter 1: How the Internet Works 3

Chapter 2: Where to Find Internet Explorer 19

Chapter 3: Connecting to the Internet 31

Chapter 4: Installing and Configuring the Program 51

Chapter 5: Browsing the World Wide Web .67

Chapter 6: Working with Interactive Web Pages 89

Chapter 7: Returning to Favorite Web Pages 99

Chapter 8: Downloading Files 123

Chapter 9: A Quick Guide to Internet Explorer Commands 143

Chapter 10: Using Multimedia Tools with Internet Explorer 189

Chapter 11: Internet News 215

Chapter 12: Sending and Receiving E-Mail 235

Chapter 13: Other Internet Tools 255

Appendix A: Keeping Internet Explorer Up-to-Date 273

Appendix B: Internet Explorer Keyboard Shortcuts 277

Appendix C: Some Major Web Sites 281

Glossary of Internet Terms 295

Index 343

Table of Contents

Introduction . . . . *xvi*

Chapter 1: How the Internet Works 3

The Structure of the Internet 4
Clients and Servers 6
Telnet 7
FTP File Transfer 9
News 10
Electronic Mail 11
Gopher 12
The World Wide Web 14
Welcome to the Internet 16

Chapter 2: Where to Find Internet Explorer 19

Which Version? 21
   32-Bit or 16-Bit Winsock? 21
Finding Internet Explorer on the Internet 23
   Downloading through the World Wide Web 23
   Downloading from Microsoft's FTP Archive 23
Downloading Internet Explorer from Microsoft Network 23
   Installing MSN 24
Obtaining Internet Explorer through Other Online Services 26
   Using the Microsoft Download Service 26
Using internetMCI 27

Chapter 3: Connecting to the Internet 31

What Kind of Connection? 32
Installing and Configuring a Modem 32
   Choosing a Modem 33

Installing a Modem in Windows 95 34

Installing a Modem in Windows 3.1 36

Choosing a Service Provider 36

Using a National ISP 37

Using a Local ISP 38

Connecting through an Online Service 38

Setting Up Windows 95 Dial-Up Networking 41

Loading the Software 42

Creating a Connection Profile 43

Connecting to the Internet through Microsoft Network 45

Changing the Default Connection 46

Windows 3.1 Connections 47

Using Alternative Connection Methods 48

Chapter 4: Installing and Configuring the Program 51

Installing Internet Explorer in Windows 95 52

The Desktop Internet Icon 53

Using the Internet Properties Dialog Box 54

Removing the Icon from Your Desktop 56

Changing the Name of the Icon 56

Changing Internet Explorer's Appearance and Performance 57

Options in the General Tab 58

Changing Type Fonts 61

Changing the Address Format in the Status Bar 62

Associating File Types to Programs 63

Chapter 5: Browsing the World Wide Web .67

Starting Internet Explorer 68

The Internet Explorer Screen 68

Changing the Toolbars' Appearance 70

Creating Your Own Quick Links 71

Moving around the Web 72

Typing an Address 73

Using Hot Links 73

Using the History Folder 76

Moving Forward and Backward 76
Using More Than One Window at a Time 76
Start Pages and Home Pages 77
Choosing a Start Page 78
Changing Your Start Page 78
Creating a Custom MSN Start Page 78
Using Internet Search Tools 83
Jumping to a Search Tool 84
Changing Your Search Page 85
Jumping to Favorite Pages 86
Jumping to Favorite Pages 87

Chapter 6: Working with Interactive Web Pages 89

Text Fields 90
Checkboxes 91
Radio Buttons 93
Drop-Down Menus and Scrollbar Lists 94
Submit and Reset Buttons 95
Interactive Games 96

Chapter 7: Returning to Favorite Web Pages 99

Working with the Favorites List 100
Adding Items to the Favorites List 101
Opening the List 101
Organizing Items in Your Favorites List 102
Changing the Appearance of the List 103
Adding Other Items to Your Favorites List 104
Creating New Subfolders 105
Cleaning Out the List 107
Importing a Netscape Bookmark List 108
Making Your Own Hot List 109
Creating a Hot List Page 109
Adding the Hot Link Page to Your Favorites List 109
Creating and Using Web Shortcuts 110
Creating a Shortcut to the Current Web Page 111

Creating a Shortcut to the Current Web Page 111
Changing a Web Shortcut Icon 111
Creating a Web Shortcuts Folder 113
Adding a Web Shortcut to the Start Menu 114
Opening Shortcuts from the Keyboard 115
Sending a Shortcut to Another User 118
Creating Shortcuts in Windows 3.1 118
Changing the Default Browser: A Warning 119

Chapter 8: Downloading Files 123

Associating MIME Types with Application Programs 124
Changing an Existing File Association 125
Adding a New File Association 128
Finding New File Viewers 129
Saving Web Pages and Reading Them Offline 130
Saving a Web Page 130
Viewing a Saved Web Page 130
Downloading Files from Web Pages 131
Downloading Files from FTP Archives 132
Moving around an FTP Archive 133
Finding Files with Archie 134
Working with Compressed Files 137
Downloading Files from Gopher Servers 138
Working through Gopher Menus 139
Exploring Gopherspace 140

Chapter 9: A Quick Guide to Internet Explorer Commands 143

File Menu Commands 143
New Window 144
Open 144
Save 144
Save As File 144
Send To 146
Page Setup 146
Print 149

Create Shortcut 150
Properties 150
Close 151
Edit Menu Commands 151
Cut 151
Copy 151
Paste 151
Select All 152
Find (on This Page) 152
View Menu Commands 153
Toolbar 153
Status Bar 153
Fonts 153
Stop 155
Refresh 155
Source 155
Options 156
Go Menu Commands 176
Back 176
Forward 176
Start Page 176
Search the Web 176
Today's Links 176
History List 176
Open History Folder 177
Favorites Menu Commands 178
Add to Favorites 178
Organizing Favorites 178
Favorite Web Pages 178
Help Menu 179
Right Mouse Button Commands 179
Save Background As 180
Set As Wallpaper 180
Copy Background 182
Select All 182

Create Shortcut 182
Add to Favorites 182
View Source 182
Refresh 182
Properties 182
Open 183
Open in New Window 183
Save Target As 183
Copy Shortcut 183
Save Picture As 183
Show Picture 183
Toolbar Commands 184
Back 184
Forward 184
Stop 184
Refresh 185
Home 185
Search 185
Favorites 185
Print 185
Font 185
Address Field 186
Quick Links 186

Chapter 10: Using Multimedia Tools with Internet Explorer 189

Embedded Audio and Video Files 190
Plug-in and Add-on Programs 191
What You Need for Audio 193
Sound Clips and Live Connections 194
Playing WAV, AU, and AIFF Files 195
Using the Windows Sound Recorder 195
Using the Internet Explorer Audio Player 197
Playing Compressed Audio 197
Using StreamWorks 203
Using True Speech 204

Playing Video and Multimedia File Formats 208
   Using MPEG Players 208
   Using the QuickTime Player 210
   Viewing Images in VRML Format 210
   Interactive Multimedia with Shockwave 211
   Viewing VDOLive Video 211
   Using StreamWorks for Video 212
Summary: Audio and Video Formats 212

Chapter 11: Internet News 215

What Happens in Newsgroups 216
How News Is Organized 218
Using Microsoft Internet News 219
   Configuring the Newsreader 220
   Reading News Articles 221
   Viewing Subscribed Newsgroups 222
   Sending Messages to a Newsgroup 223
   Hiding the Desktop Icons 225
Using Free Agent 226
Obtaining News from MSN 227
   Finding Newsgroups 228
   Reading News 229
Reading News on AOL 230

Chapter 12: Sending and Receiving E-Mail 235

How E-Mail Works 236
   Address Formats 237
   E-Mail Client Programs 238
Sending E-Mail from Internet Explorer 238
Using the Microsoft Exchange Client 238
   Configuring the Internet Mail Messaging Service 241
   Creating and Sending E-Mail through Exchange 243
   Receiving and Reading Messages with Exchange 244
Exchanging E-Mail with Microsoft Internet Mail 245
   Sending and Receiving Messages with Internet Mail 247

Attaching Files to Messages 248
Managing E-Mail with Eudora 250
   Configuring Eudora 250
   Receiving Messages with Eudora 251
   Sending Messages with Eudora 252

Chapter 13: Other Internet Tools 255

Using FTP Clients 256
   WS_FTP 257
   Other FTP Clients 261
Using Telnet Clients 262
   Windows 95 Telnet 263
   HyperTerminal 264
   Telnet Clients for Windows 3.1 266
Running Diagnostic Tools 267
   Ping 267
   Traceroute 268
   WS Ping 269
Time Synchronizers 270

Appendix A: Keeping Internet Explorer Up-To-Date 273

Appendix B: Internet Explorer Keyboard Shortcuts 277

   Moving around a Web Page 277
   Other Keyboard Shortcuts 277

Appendix C: Some Major Web Sites 281

   General-Interest Guides 281
   Guides to Downloadable Software 288
   Interactive Search Tools 289

Glossary of Internet Terms 295

   Index *343*

Introduction

Internet Explorer is Microsoft's entry in the competition to provide access to the Internet and the World Wide Web on every desktop in the known universe. Internet Explorer is a fine Web browser, but because Microsoft gives it away, it does not come with an instruction manual. This book contains the information you will need to understand how the Internet works, and how to obtain and install Internet Explorer, connect your PC to the Internet, and use the program to view Web pages and other Internet resources. If you're already using Internet Explorer, *The ABCs of Microsoft Internet Explorer* will tell you how to set up the program for best performance and how to find some of the best starting places for your Internet adventures.

Because a Web browser is not always the best way to navigate the Internet, the book also includes descriptions of some other programs (from Microsoft and other suppliers) that provide access to other Internet services, including e-mail, news, telnet (remote login to distant computers), and a handful of diagnostic programs. You'll also learn how to run faster and more efficient FTP file transfers than you can perform with Internet Explorer.

The ABCs of Microsoft Internet Explorer assumes that you're already up and running with Windows 95 or Windows 3.1, but you have little or no experience with the Internet. You might be a complete newcomer, or maybe you've poked a toe into the online world through America Online, CompuServe, or the Microsoft Network. Either way, you want to understand how the Internet works and how to install and use Microsoft's Internet browser.

How This Book Is Organized

The ABCs of Microsoft Internet Explorer opens with a general description of the Internet, and then shifts to more specific information about Internet Explorer. Following a complete description of Internet Explorer's features and functions, there's a guide to finding and using add-in programs for audio, video, and multimedia. The final four chapters of the book describe other Internet application programs that you will want to use along with Internet Explorer.

Chapter 1, "How the Internet Works," provides background information that will help you understand the internal "plumbing" of the Internet. It explains the basic structure of the Internet and includes specific information about major Internet services.

Chapter 2, "Where to Find Internet Explorer," contains instructions for finding a free copy of the Internet Explorer software.

Chapter 3, "Connecting to the Internet," includes step-by-step instructions for setting up an Internet account through independent access providers, America Online, or the Microsoft Network.

Chapter 4, "Installing and Configuring the Program," explains how to load the software and how to set the options that control the way Internet Explorer downloads Web pages and files, as well as how it uses file associations and MIME types to open and run downloaded files.

Chapter 5, "Browsing the World Wide Web," tells you how to use Internet Explorer to move around the Web. It also explains the uses of each of the program's controls and features.

Chapter 6, "Working with Interactive Web Pages," describes the ways that Web page designers allow users to send information back to them, to consult online databases, and to play games through the Internet.

Chapter 7, "Returning to Favorite Web Pages," explains how to create and use a list of favorites or a local hot list to jump back to those pages with just a few mouse clicks, and how to jump to Web sites directly from your Windows desktop or Start menu.

Chapter 8, "Downloading Files," provides instructions for moving programs and data files from servers to your own computer through the Internet.

Chapter 9, "A Quick Guide to Internet Explorer Commands," contains descriptions of all the commands in the program's menus and toolbars.

Chapter 10, "Using Multimedia Tools with Internet Explorer," describes plug-in and supplemental programs that many Web site designers use to add sound and video to their pages.

Chapter 11, "Internet News," explains how Internet newsgroups work and how to participate in them using Microsoft Internet News, Free Agent, the Microsoft Network, or America Online.

Chapter 12, "Sending and Receiving E-Mail," describes electronic mail and explains how to send mail from Internet Explorer, as well as how to send and receive messages through the Microsoft Exchange client, Microsoft Internet Mail, and Eudora.

Chapter 13, "Other Internet Tools," contains information about some additional Internet services, including FTP file transfer, telnet remote login, and diagnostic tools, and offers sources for the application programs you will need to take advantage of them.

Appendix A, "Keeping Internet Explorer Up-to-Date" contains instructions for obtaining the most recent version of the program from Microsoft.

Appendix B, "Internet Explorer Keyboard Shortcuts," is a list of keyboard alternatives to many of the program's menu and toolbar commands.

Appendix C, "Some Major Web Sites," is a set of pointers to World Wide Web pages that you might want to visit as starting points for your Internet explorations.

Glossary of Internet Terms defines key words and jargon that you may not understand.

Connecting Your PC to the Internet

If you're new to the World Wide Web, you might feel overwhelmed by the size and complexity of the Internet. There are millions (yes, *millions*) of people on the 'Net, and almost as many Web pages and other online services and resources. Do you need to understand networking and data communications before you can send an e-mail message? No—the inner workings of the Internet are complicated, but as a user, you don't have to worry about them. Just as you can dial your sister's number and talk to her in California without knowing anything about transmission technology or switching systems, you can gather information through the Internet by simply typing an address or clicking on a hypertext link. You can find everything you need to connect your PC to the Internet in this book.

With the introduction of Internet Explorer 3, Microsoft has produced a World Wide Web browser that offers serious competition to the *de facto* market leader, Netscape Navigator. It's not yet clear which product will ultimately win this particular race, but Microsoft is putting a huge amount of money and energy behind Internet Explorer. In the meantime, the program is free; there's no good reason not to try it.

Finally, I must offer a word of warning: the Internet can be as much of a time-waster as television or video games. Don't let it take over your life; "virtual reality" is a lot more virtual than real. Visiting a Web page for gardeners is not the same as growing your own tomatoes or roses.

That said, if you plan to use Internet Explorer for business, I hope you're a wild success. If you're using it for entertainment, do enjoy yourself. And if we pass on that well-known "information highway," don't forget to wave.

Chapter 1

HOW THE
INTERNET WORKS

- **Understanding how the Internet connects computers**
- **Connecting to another computer as a distant terminal with telnet**
- **Downloading and uploading files with FTP**
- **Participating in Internet newsgroups**
- **Exchanging e-mail through the Internet**
- **Finding information with gopher**
- **Accessing the World Wide Web**

In order to get the most out of Microsoft Internet Explorer, you should begin with a general understanding of the Internet itself. This chapter contains an explanation of the Internet's basic structure and descriptions of the major Internet services that you can reach through Internet Explorer.

The Structure of the Internet

When you connect a pair of computers together through a communications link, the two machines can exchange commands, messages, data files, and programs. If you connect a third computer, you have the beginnings of a network. Using a computer connected to a network, you can run programs and read files on other computers connected to the same network.

In the simplest possible terms, the Internet is a worldwide "network of networks" that connects computers around the world together. All of these computers use the same timing and data formats, known as *networking protocols.* Since 1969, the Internet has expanded from its origins as an experimental network that included computers operated by a handful of American universities and government contractors. By 1973, the network reached Europe, and it now extends to millions of computers in just about every country of the world.

Strictly speaking, you don't connect your computer directly to the Internet, but to a network that connects to other networks through a network *backbone.* Interconnections (called *gateways*) between these backbones make it possible for a computer on one network to exchange messages and data with another computer connected to any other network. In the United States and Canada, most network backbones are operated by private telecommunications businesses like AT&T and MCI, and by network service companies like UUnet, PSInet, and Netcom. In the rest of the world, backbones are provided by government telecommunications authorities, private companies, or both. Figure 1.1 is a simplified diagram of the Internet's interconnected backbones.

The set of networking protocols that controls the Internet is known as TCP/IP (Transmission Control Protocol/Internet Protocol). The specifications for TCP/IP include the addressing schemes that identify each computer on the Internet and rules for several kinds of programs, such as file transfer and remote command entry.

One of the most important features of the Internet is that it isn't limited to a specific type of computer or operating system. Versions of TCP/IP can run on just about any kind of computer built in the last 20 years. Therefore, you can connect your desktop PC through the Internet to a room-filling mainframe computer just as easily as you can connect it to another PC. TCP/IP programs always present the same appearance to the network, regardless of the type of computer on which they're operating.

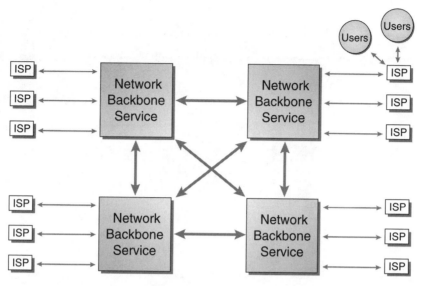

ISP=Internet Service Provider

FIGURE 1.1:   The Internet is a worldwide system of interconnected networks.

It might be helpful to think about the Internet as a system similar to the utility that provides the electric power you use in your house and your office. On one side, there are a variety of devices that generate electric power—hydroelectric dams, coal-fired generators, nuclear reactors, and windmills, among others. All of these sources provide electricity to the same distribution grid in a form that meets a commonly accepted specification (alternating current at 50 or 60 cycles per second). At the receiving end, toasters, refrigerators, computers, and vacuum cleaners all can use power that comes from the grid.

As Figure 1.2 shows, the Internet is a huge distribution grid for data. Connecting one computer to the Internet doesn't accomplish anything useful; but when you connect it *through* the Internet to another computer, you can reasonably expect that each machine will recognize and understand the commands and data that it receives from the other.

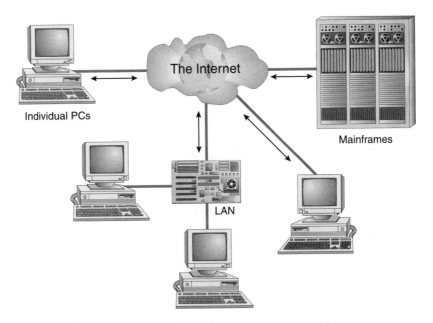

FIGURE 1.2:   The Internet is the framework that connects computers together.

Clients and Servers

Before we start to talk about specific features and functions that you can use through the Internet, there's one more general concept that you should understand. With very few exceptions, the programs and services that operate through the Internet use a *client/server* design in which a client program on the user's computer sends commands or information requests to a server, which may respond by creating a live connection or by sending data back to the client.

For example, to download a copy of a file located on another computer, you must use a program called an FTP (File Transfer Protocol) client, which sends a file request to an FTP server program on a computer that contains a file archive. When the server program receives the request, it locates the file and sends a copy back to the client.

Electronic mail (e-mail) is more complicated, because there's more than one server in the path between origin and destination, but it still uses a client/server model. Here are the steps involved in delivering an e-mail message:

1. The person who sends the message uses an e-mail client program to send the message to a post office server.
2. The post office server examines the header of the message and identifies the address of each recipient.
3. The post office server sends the message through the Internet to the mail server that handles mail for each recipient's address.
4. The mail server stores the message in the recipient's mailbox.
5. The recipient uses an e-mail client program to request new messages from the mail server.
6. The mail server sends the messages in the recipient's mailbox back to the client.

In all cases, a client sends a request to a server, and the server responds by sending a file or other data back to the client. This is even true in a *telnet* connection, where it appears that you have a live connection to the server. In fact, the client sends commands to the server, which interprets and processes each command and sends the result back to the client.

Microsoft Internet Explorer is a particularly flexible type of client program called a *Web browser*, which can obtain files and other data from several different kinds of servers. In the rest of this chapter, we'll explain how each of these servers works.

Telnet

Before the days of desktop personal computers, people exchanged commands with computers through terminals that sent commands to the computer and received and displayed the computer's responses on a printer or a video monitor screen. Telnet is the Internet tool that connects one computer to a second computer as a distant terminal. In other words, the telnet server (also called a *host*) treats incoming commands from the Internet as if they came from a terminal connected directly to the host. Entering commands through a telnet client program produces exactly the same results as typing them on a local terminal.

Telnet has several common uses. If you have an account on a distant computer (the "distant" machine might be across the hall or halfway around the world), you can use any other computer with an Internet connection to send commands and retrieve data from the first machine. For example, Figure 1.3 shows a telnet connection to The Well, an online conference service based in California.

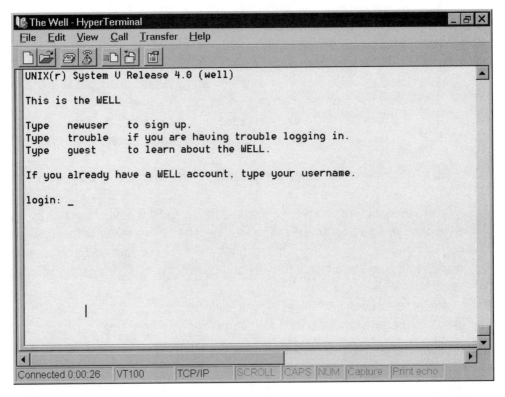

FIGURE 1.3: A telnet connection to The Well, a Unix host

Other computers are configured as public telnet hosts. Even if you don't have an account on one of these systems, you can still use some of the host's programs. Many libraries make their catalogs accessible through the Internet on public telnet hosts.

Internet Explorer is not a telnet client, but there's a separate telnet program included in Windows 95. Internet Explorer can use this telnet program to establish links to telnet hosts. Chapter 13 contains more detailed information about using a telnet client program.

FTP File Transfer

FTP (File Transfer Protocol) is an Internet tool for uploading and downloading files between computers. A file transfer must take place between a client and a server, but the files can move in either direction (either from the server to the client or from the client to the server).

FTP servers are fairly straightforward; when a server receives a file request from an FTP client, it sends a copy of that file back to the client. Other commands instruct the server to send the client a directory of files or to accept an upload from the client.

Most often, you will use FTP to download files from public file archives on FTP servers. There are thousands of these archives, with hundreds of thousands of files, located all over the Internet. For example, many software companies maintain FTP archives that contain upgrades, drivers, and patches for their products. Other archives contain huge collections of shareware and freeware programs. If you can establish a connection to one of these servers through the Internet, the owners are happy to let you download copies of these files at no charge. Other FTP archives contain copies of scholarly papers and reports, graphic images, and recipes, among many other things.

These archives are sometimes known as "anonymous FTP" archives, because they accept the word "anonymous" as a login name, with the user's e-mail address as a password. When Internet Explorer connects to an FTP server, it automatically handles the anonymous login unless you instruct it to send a different name and password.

Not all FTP servers accept anonymous logins, and those that do frequently limit access to files in specific directories. If you have your own account on an FTP server, you may be able to download programs and data files that are not available to members of the general public, and to upload files to the server.

TIP

There's a separate FTP client program included with Windows 95, but it's really awful. Windows FTP is a text-based utility that operates within a DOS window. Don't waste your time with it. If you need an FTP tool separate from the one in Internet Explorer, you can find several in FTP archives (use Explorer to download them). One of the best is WS-FTP, available from ftp.usma.edu in the directory /pub/msdos/winsock.files. The file name is ws_ftp32.zip.

You can find more information about using Internet Explorer to download files from FTP archives in Chapter 8, along with a description of Archie, a tool for searching through many archives to locate specific files. There are descriptions of some third-party FTP programs in Chapter 13.

News

Many Internet users participate in ongoing conversations in *newsgroups*, devoted to almost every imaginable topic, from cellular biology and general semantics to home winemaking and restoring antique phonographs. There are more than 15,000 of these groups floating around the Internet, with new ones added all the time. In each newsgroup, participants post individual *articles* that may either be replies to earlier articles or completely new postings.

Some newsgroups are not much more than question-and-answer sessions for technical or hobby topics ("Can anybody tell me how to align my 1937 Whoopee-Flow diathermy machine?"), but many others have evolved into online communities with their own traditions and personalities. The relationships that develop in some newsgroups have been described as an alternative reality based on typing.

WARNING Newsgroups can be an extremely fast and efficient channel for distributing information, but that's both their strength and their weakness. Anybody with an Internet connection can post an article to a newsgroup, whether they really know anything about the subject or not. Except for replies attacking the original message, there's little or no quality control over the information that appears in net news. There's no assurance that the person posting something that sounds like an authoritative description of the latest weapons systems didn't get the information out of a Tom Clancy novel.

The set of standards for distributing news through the Internet is called Network News Transfer Protocol, so you might also see news servers called NNTP servers.

A news client program (also called a *newsreader*) performs several tasks:

- It downloads and displays a list of newsgroups currently available on the news server.
- It allows a user to "subscribe" to individual newsgroups.
- It downloads and displays a list of articles in the currently selected newsgroup, sorted by subject, originator, time, or sorted into threads, with replies and other comments following questions.
- It allows users to select and read individual articles.
- It provides a method for posting new articles and replies to existing articles.

When you post an article to a newsgroup, your news client program transfers the article to your Internet access provider's news server, which distributes copies to all the other news servers that support the newsgroup in which you posted the article (the operators of some news servers have chosen not to include every newsgroup).

There's a newsreader program included with Internet Explorer. Chapter 11 contains a description of Explorer's news functions.

Electronic Mail

Electronic mail (also known as e-mail) is the process of sending and receiving messages and files between individual addresses. Unlike news, in which the same messages are accessible to anybody who wants to read them, the Internet's e-mail system delivers messages (and files) to specific recipients.

E-mail is not a substitute for either telephone calls or postal mail. It's a new communications medium that has its own set of advantages and disadvantages. It's faster and less expensive than writing letters, and it's not as intrusive as a ringing telephone. And since you're not on a live connection to the recipient of your message, you can take all the time you need to reflect on what you have to say before you send it. But it doesn't permit the kind of live interaction that takes place during a telephone call, and it may not be as secure or private as a written letter.

The rules for Internet e-mail are defined in a specification called Simple Mail Transfer Protocol, or SMTP. An e-mail message passes through these steps on its way from originator to recipient:

1. The person originating the message uses a mail client program to compose the text and, if necessary, to attach a file to the message.

2. The mail client program sends the message to the post office server where the user has an account.
3. The post office server connects to the mail server where the recipient's mailbox is located, and transfers a copy of the message.
4. The recipient's mail client program connects to the mail server to check for new mail, either on a regular schedule or on in response to a command.
5. If there are messages in the recipient's mailbox, the mail server downloads them to the client.

Internet Explorer is not an e-mail client program, but it has links to external programs, such as the Microsoft Exchange client e-mail program that's included in Windows 95 or with the Internet Mail program that's available with the newsreader. You can find detailed information about using e-mail with Internet Explorer in Chapter 12.

Gopher

The amount of information available through the Internet can be mind-boggling. There are literally millions of separate files, databases, and other online resources ready and waiting for you to download. But they won't do you much good unless you know how to find them.

The Internet Gopher was the first large-scale attempt to organize the Internet's resources into logical menus. It was created at the University of Minnesota (home of the Golden Gophers) in 1991 as a guide to information services on the university campus, but it quickly spread to the Internet.

A gopher server contains one or more menus with pointers to items that may be located anywhere on the Internet. Some menus are lists of items related to a specific topic or of items supplied by the owner of the server. Others are arranged by location; still others are more-or-less random links to items that the person who created the menu considered interesting or amusing. For example, Figure 1.4 shows part of a list of gopher resources located in the state of Oregon.

Most gopher menus also include pointers to other menus, so the overall effect is a vast, interconnected list of lists. The top-level menu, on a server at the University of Minnesota (the "Mother Gopher") has links to every gopher server in the world. Most menus have links to higher-level menus, so it's almost always possible to move from one menu to any other menu with a small number of jumps.

Reduced to basics, just about everything that moves through the Internet is a downloadable file, a live telnet connection, a public news article, or a private e-mail

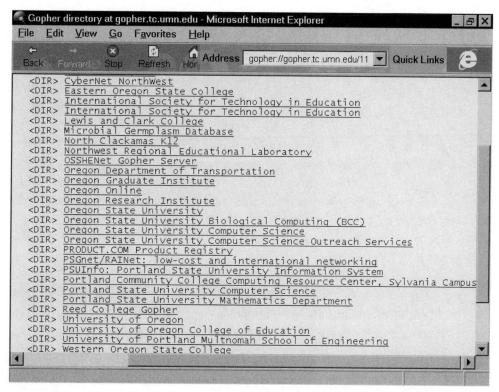

FIGURE 1.4: A top-level gopher menu

message. When you select an item from a gopher menu, your gopher client identifies the resource type and connects your computer to the server that contains that item. If the resource is a file, the client program downloads a copy to your own computer and uses a local file viewer to display its contents. If it's a telnet server, the client displays instructions for logging on to the host. If the server is a database, the gopher client asks for the specific information you're looking for.

As an Internet browsing tool, gopher has been overshadowed by the World Wide Web, but it's still an efficient and effective way to locate files and services online. It's also an excellent way to discover unexpected goodies in servers that you didn't know about before you started wandering around in gopherspace. Either as part of a Web browser like Internet Explorer or as a separate client program, gopher should be part of your Internet toolkit.

The World Wide Web

The World Wide Web blends text, images, and access to files and other Internet resources into a seamless display. Unlike gopher menus, which have a formal hierarchical structure, Web pages can have *hot links* anywhere within their design. Clicking on a link may take a user to another location within the same page, to another Web page, or to any other type of Internet resource, including gopher menus, FTP archives or individual files, telnet hosts, and newsgroups. The destination of a link may be on the same server as the current Web page or anywhere else on the Internet. It's also possible to jump to an e-mail editor that automatically addresses a message to a specific recipient.

The rules that define the World Wide Web are called Hypertext Transfer Protocol (HTTP). HTTP was originally designed at the European Particle Physics Laboratory in Geneva as a way to move technical information across the Internet; footnotes and cross-references in reports and other documents could be formatted as links, so readers could easily obtain additional data without losing their place in the original document.

HTTP identifies every file on every computer connected to the Internet with a unique Uniform Resource Locator (URL) code, which specifies the type of file and its exact location. All URLs use this format:

```
type://address/path/file.ext
```

The *type* portion of the address shows the type of server that contains the file. The most common types are:

Web pages	http://
FTP servers	file:// or ftp://
Gopher	gopher://
Telnet	telnet://

If you don't include a *path* and *file.ext* in a URL, your HTTP client program will jump to the page or directory that the server's owner has chosen as the default, or "home page".

It's not universally observed, but many commercial Web sites have named their servers www.*name*.com. Therefore, if you're looking for a company's Web site, you can try a link to http://www.*name*.com. For example, the URL for the top-level Microsoft home page is http://www.microsoft.com, and the URL for British Airways is http://www.british-airways.com.

Today, HTTP and Web browser programs like Internet Explorer have become much more complex and sophisticated than they were two or three years ago. They can combine graphic elements, audio and video, along with text, still pictures, and interactive access to databases and other services to create an almost unlimited variety of interesting variations. And since a Web page can contain links to just about anything, anywhere on the Internet, a Web browser combines the functions of many different kinds of client programs. A program like Internet Explorer can be all you need to take advantage of most of the things the Internet has to offer.

Figure 1.5 shows a typical Web page. This page contains information about Andorra, a tiny country in Europe. The underlined words on this page are links to other parts of the same page and to other pages with related information. The variety of typefaces, the flag and other images, and the decorative background make a Web page like this one a great deal more interesting than a simple gopher menu.

Browsing the Web looks more complicated than using one of the other Internet tools, but the underlying structure is about the same: a client program (the browser) sends commands to a server, which sends files, messages, and other data back to the

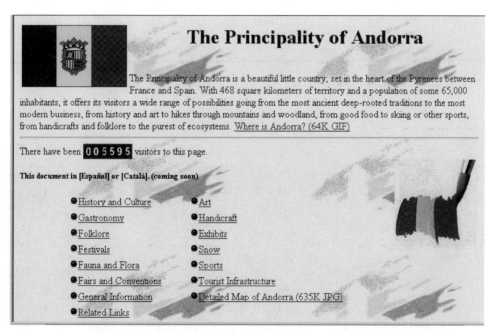

FIGURE 1.5: A World Wide Web page includes links to other Internet resources.

client. The Web is more flexible than other Internet services because it can move text, images, and different kinds of files and other data through the same client program. It's more attractive than many other tools because it can integrate text, pictures, and other images into a single screen.

Welcome to the Internet

To summarize, the Internet is a "network of networks" that can allow your desktop computer to exchange data, messages, and files with any of the millions of other computers with an Internet connection. And since there are servers all over the world that contain text, pictures, sounds, moving images, and discussions of every imaginable topic, you can use the Internet to import a huge amount and variety of information for business, entertainment, and education. If something can be reduced to digital form—and includes music, video, and text—it can be transported through the Internet.

In the remaining chapters of this book, you'll learn how to obtain and install Microsoft's Web browser client program, Internet Explorer, and how to use the program's features.

Chapter 2

WHERE TO FIND INTERNET EXPLORER

- **Finding the correct version of Internet Explorer**
- **Downloading Internet Explorer through the World Wide Web**
- **Downloading Internet Explorer from Microsoft's FTP archive**
- **Downloading Internet Explorer through MSN's Internet Center**
- **Obtaining Internet Explorer from The Microsoft Download Service**

Unlike most of its other products, Microsoft gives away Internet Explorer. It's free—no charge—and worth every penny. As a giveaway, Explorer does not include a fancy package, but at the price, it's hard to complain.

Microsoft was forced into this uncharacteristic generosity because the most popular competing browsers, most notably Netscape Navigator and NCSA Mosaic, are also freely distributed, at least for "evaluation." The long-term effect of this contest to see who can give away the most browsers remains to be seen, but as consumers, we should enjoy it while it lasts.

A version of Internet Explorer is included in the Microsoft Plus! package of add-ons to Windows 95 and the Microsoft Internet Starter Kit, and it's supplied with MCI's Internet access service. And both America Online and CompuServe have signed agreements with Microsoft to distribute Internet Explorer. However, it's not necessary to buy any of these products (or any of the others that Microsoft is likely to bundle with Internet Explorer) to obtain the program; there are plenty of other ways to get it.

No matter how you obtained your original copy of Internet Explorer, you should check Microsoft's Product Update Web site (http://www.microsoft.com/ie), shown in Figure 2.1, to make sure that you have the latest release. Upgrades are free, so there's no good reason not to keep up to date.

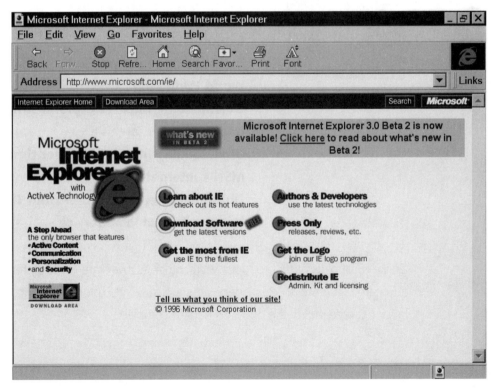

FIGURE 2.1:   Check Microsoft's Internet Explorer site to obtain the latest version of the program.

Which Version?

Internet Explorer exists in separate versions for Windows 95 and Windows 3. *x*. On the surface, choosing the right one seems like a no-brainer; but there are some cases where you should use the Windows 3. *x* version, even if you have installed Windows 95. (There are also versions of Internet Explorer for Macintosh and Unix users, but they don't cause the same problems; if you have a Mac, use the Mac version of Internet Explorer; if you have a Power Mac, use the Power Mac version.) The problem occurs because Internet Explorer, like all other Internet application programs for Windows, requires a separate interface program called a Winsock (short for Windows Sockets) to make the actual connection to the network.

Because the TCP/IP protocol stack and telephone line dialer (or LAN interface) are in the Winsock program, it's possible to use client programs from more than one software developer through the same Internet connection; you can use the same connection for many Internet tools.

Microsoft has included a quite adequate Winsock program with Windows 95, so most of the other companies who offer Internet applications for Windows 95 don't bother to include their own Winsocks. There are a couple dozen Winsock programs available for Windows 3.1; the Windows 3.1 version of Internet Explorer should work with any of them. If you don't already have a Winsock program in place, you can download one from Microsoft along with Internet Explorer for Windows 3.1

32-Bit or 16-Bit Winsock?

Internet Explorer for Windows 95 requires a 32-bit Winsock, but many Internet access products and services come with 16-bit Winsocks, so they'll be compatible with both Windows 3.1 and Windows 95. If your Internet access is through a 16-bit Winsock program, the 32-bit Windows 95 Internet Explorer (and the other 32-bit Internet application programs supplied with Windows 95) won't work properly.

Among others, some or all versions of these Internet access products use 16-bit Winsocks:

- America Online (AOL)
- CompuServe
- GNNnet
- IBM Internet Connection
- Internet Chameleon
- Internet in a Box

- NetCom NetCruiser
- Pipeline USA
- Spry Mosaic
- SuperHighway Access
- Trumpet Winsock

The companies responsible for many of these products are developing new 32-bit versions of their programs, but older, 16-bit versions are still out there. As a rule of thumb, if your Internet access uses Windows 95 Dial-Up Networking, or some other Winsock designed specifically for Windows 95, it will work with the Windows 95 version of Internet Explorer. If you're using a Winsock that claims to work with both Windows 95 and Windows 3.1, you'll need the Windows 3.1 Internet Explorer. In practice, the best way to find out if you have a 32-bit Winsock is to ask the developer's tech support group.

Internet access through America Online and Prodigy are special cases. You can use Internet Explorer for Windows 3.1 with version 2.5 of AOL for Windows, but you must download and install the AOL Winsock first (keyword: Winsock). If you've upgraded to AOL's version 3.0 software, you don't need to download the Winsock, because it's included in the 3.0 package. Prodigy's software did not support external Winsock applications at the time this was written, but they're is likely to add this feature sometime in the near future (unless the whole Prodigy system gets absorbed by some other online service first).

If you're still using Windows 3.1 or Windows for Workgroups, Winsock compatibility is not a problem for you; you should use Internet Explorer for Windows 3.1, regardless of the type of Internet access you have. If you don't already have an account with an Internet service provider, you can use the TCP/IP protocol stack and dialer programs in the Windows 3.1 Internet Explorer package to set up a new account with Microsoft (although you can find less costly service from other suppliers that will work equally well). If you have an existing SLIP (Serial Line Internet Protocol), PPP (Point to Point Protocol), or LAN (local-area network) access to the Internet, you can use Internet Explorer with the Winsock already installed on your PC.

Even though it's designed for a 16-bit version of Windows, Internet Explorer for Windows 3.1 is actually a 32-bit program. In order to use it with Windows 3.x, you need a set of interface programs called Win32s. Fortunately, Win32s is another freebie, available for download from Microsoft at all the same places as Internet Explorer. Even if you've already installed Win32s to use another 32-bit program, such as NCSA Mosaic, you might need to replace it with a later version before you can use it with Internet Explorer.

Finding Internet Explorer on the Internet

Downloading a Web browser through the Internet is a chicken-and-egg problem: before you can get a copy of the program from a Web site, you must already have a browser or other file transfer client. If you don't have any access to the Internet, a World Wide Web address doesn't do much good. Your best bet is to get your first copy of Internet Explorer through an online service or one of the other sources described later in this chapter.

But if you already have an Internet account, or an account with an online service that offers access to the Internet, you can download Internet Explorer from either the Microsoft FTP archive or the Web site.

Downloading through the World Wide Web

If you already have a working Web browser, such as Netscape Navigator, or if you have an account with America Online, CompuServe, or Prodigy, you can obtain a copy of Internet Explorer from one of Microsoft's Web sites. You can find pointers to all of them at http://www.microsoft.com/ie/. If you're using Windows in a language other than American English, click on Localized Versions or International Versions to select the one you want to use.

Downloading from Microsoft's FTP Archive

If you don't have a working Web browser, but you can use an FTP client (such as a shell account on a Unix host), you can download Internet Explorer from Microsoft's FTP archive. This archive is located at ftp.microsoft.com in the directory /msdownload/ie3.

Downloading Internet Explorer from Microsoft Network

Microsoft Network (MSN) is Microsoft's entry in the online information service market that is dominated by CompuServe and America Online. After MSN had been in operation for about four months, Microsoft announced plans to convert MSN's emphasis from proprietary services to Internet access and make the MSN content areas accessible through the Internet. The Windows 95 package includes access software for MSN and a free trial account.

If you have an MSN account, you can download Internet Explorer through MSN's Internet Center.

Installing MSN

Even if you don't plan to use MSN as your Internet access provider, the free trial offer makes it a good way to get your hands on a copy of Internet Explorer. If you didn't install MSN when you installed Windows 95, follow these steps to add it now:

1. Open the Windows 95 Control Panel from the Start menu.
2. Double-click on the Add/Remove Programs icon.
3. Select the Windows Setup tab to display the dialog box shown in Figure 2.2.

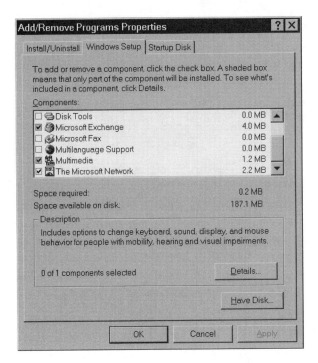

FIGURE 2.2:
Place a checkmark next to The Microsoft Network to install the software.

4. Click on the box next to The Microsoft Network to place a checkmark in the box.
5. If it's not already installed, select Microsoft Exchange and click on the Details button.
6. When the Microsoft Exchange dialog box appears, place a checkmark next to the Microsoft Exchange component, and then click on the OK button.
7. Click on the OK button at the bottom of the Add/Remove Properties dialog box.
8. Follow the instructions that appear on your screen to insert your Windows 95 diskettes or CD-ROM.

After you have loaded the MSN software, you will see an MSN icon on your desktop. Turn on your modem and double-click on the icon to call MSN and set up a new trial account.

After you log on to MSN, you can find Internet Explorer in the Internet Center area, as shown in Figure 2.3. To download the software, find the icon for the version in the language you want to use and double-click on it. MSN will transfer the program to your computer and automatically install it.

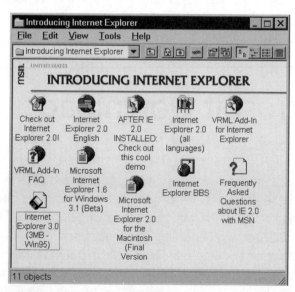

FIGURE 2.3: You can download Internet Explorer from the Internet Center area of MSN.

Obtaining Internet Explorer through Other Online Services

Microsoft has forums or conferences on all the other major online information services, including America Online, CompuServe, Prodigy, and GEnie. However, they have chosen not to place Internet Explorer in the various download libraries, so you'll need to use the built-in Web browser or FTP file transfer client supplied with your service to download the program from http://www.microsoft.com or the Microsoft FTP archive (ftp.microsoft.com).

If you already have an account with one of these services, or if you received a free trial diskette or CD with your computer or modem (or if one fell out of a magazine), and if there's a local telephone number that you can use to connect, this is probably the easiest and least expensive way to get your hands on a copy of Internet Explorer.

To be fair about it, you really should spend some time exploring the other resources an online service has to offer during the free trial period, and if you find it interesting, entertaining, or useful, maybe even keep the subscription going after they start charging for it. But as long as the service is offering free trial access, you might as well take advantage of it.

Using the Microsoft Download Service

There's one more online source for downloading Internet Explorer, but unless you're located in or near Seattle or Cooksville, Ontario, it's an expensive option, because your telephone company will charge you more for a long-distance call than you would pay to connect to MSN or another online information service or Internet access point. The Microsoft Download Service is a dial-in bulletin board that contains many of the same files as the Microsoft FTP archive. Microsoft does not expect users from outside North America to use the Download Service, so foreign-language versions of Internet Explorer are not available through this channel. The Download Service does not offer beta test versions of new software that may be available from the Microsoft Web site.

The Microsoft Download Service's telephone numbers are 206-936-6735 (Seattle) and 905-568-3503 (Cooksville). The Seattle number is supposed to be for callers in the United States, and the Cooksville number for Canadian callers, but if you're on the East Coast, long-distance rates to Ontario may be less expensive than those to Seattle. From British Columbia, Alberta, or the Yukon, the Seattle number is probably the better choice.

When you log in to the Download Service, you will see a main nenu like the one shown in Figure 2.4. Choose the File Index option and then type **F** for File Search. Use Internet Explorer as the search key to find the exact file name for the latest version of the program. Make a note of the file name, and then return to the main menu to download it.

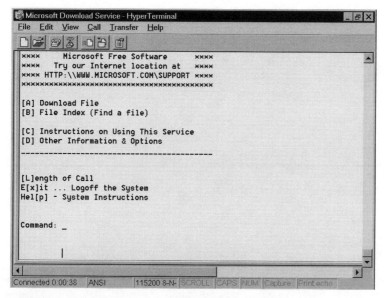

FIGURE 2.4: The Microsoft Download Service main menu

Using internetMCI

MCI offers Internet access services for businesses and individual users through local dial-up numbers, toll-free 800 service, and high-speed dedicated access connections. As part of this service, MCI supplies internetMCI software that includes Microsoft's Internet Explorer. If you obtain your Internet access through MCI, the company will provide a copy of Internet Explorer along with the other software necessary to connect your computer to the Internet. You can request software or obtain more information about MCI's Internet access products by calling 1-800-550-0927.

No matter which method you use to obtain the Internet Explorer software, you will also need a connection to the Internet in order to use it. Chapter 3 contains detailed instructions for making that connection.

Chapter 3

CONNECTING TO THE INTERNET

- **Setting up your modem**
- **Choosing an Internet service provider**
- **Making connections with more than one online service**
- **Configuring a Dial-Up Networking connection profile**
- **Adding Internet access to an MSN account**
- **Connecting with Windows 3.1**
- **Using high-speed data and network connections**

Before you can use Internet Explorer (or any other Internet application program), you must connect your own computer to the Internet. In this chapter, you will find information about choosing an Internet service provider; making the connection through a modem, a LAN, or other link; and installing and configuring your system for a TCP/IP connection.

If you already have an Internet connection that supports other TCP/IP Internet client programs, you may be able to use it with Internet Explorer. If that's the case, you can skip this chapter.

What Kind of Connection?

Choosing a way to connect your computer to the Internet is a trade-off between performance and cost; more money gets you a faster link between your own system and the backbone. While the difference between file transfers through a modem and a high-speed link can be dramatic, the cost of improved performance may not always be justified. For most home users and many small businesses, a dial-up telephone line and a 28.8 kbps modem is still the most cost-effective choice.

If it's available in your area, you might want to consider ISDN (Integrated Services Digital Network) as an alternative to conventional POTS (Plain Old Telephone Service) lines. ISDN is more expensive and complicated to install and configure, but once it's in place, it offers substantially faster network connections. Your Internet service provider can tell you if ISDN service is available and explain how to order the lines and obtain the necessary interface equipment.

In a larger business, where many users can share the same link to the Internet, a connection with more bandwidth is probably a better approach. Many users can share a single high-speed connection through a LAN, so the cost per user may not be significantly greater than that of a second telephone line.

If your PC is already connected to a LAN, you should ask your network administrator or help desk about setting up an Internet account; it's likely that there's already some kind of connection in place.

As with most decisions related to data communications, the simple answer to "What kind of connection should I use?" is "The fastest that you can afford."

Installing and Configuring a Modem

For most individuals and small businesses, the most practical way to connect is through a dial-up telephone line and a modem. *Modem* is a made-up word constructed out of *mod*ulator-*dem*odulator. A modem converts digital data from a computer into sounds that can travel through telephone lines designed for voice communication (that's the *modulator* part), and it also converts sounds that it receives from a telephone line to digital data (that's the *demodulator* part).

Choosing a Modem

For reasons of economy, convenience, or simplicity, you've decided to go with an inexpensive connection to the Internet through a modem and a telephone line. What now? If you don't already have a modem, go find one. There are three things to consider when you choose a modem: speed, form, and compatibility.

Modem Speed

The speed of a modem is the maximum number of data bits that can pass through the modem in one second. You might find some extremely inexpensive 9600 bps (bits per second) modems, but that's really too slow for programs like Internet Explorer. Don't waste your time or your money. Anything slower than 9600 bps is most useful as a paper weight or a boat anchor.

Today, almost all new modems have maximum speeds of either 14,400 bps or 28,800 bps. As a general rule, buy the fastest modem you can afford. Modem connections, even at 28,800 bps, are a lot slower than dedicated data circuits. But a fast modem is good enough for many users, especially because most households and offices already have at least one telephone line, so there's no added expense for installing a new circuit.

Modem Form

Modems come in three forms: internal, external, and on a credit-card size PCMCIA card (also known as a PC Card). Each type has specific advantages and disadvantages.

- Internal modems are expansion cards that fit inside your PC. They're the least expensive type of modem, and they don't require special data cables or power supplies. However, they're a nuisance to install, and they don't include the status lights that show the progress of your calls.
- External modems are separate, self-contained units that are easy to install and move between computers. They cost more than internal modems, and they need a separate AC power outlet. In order to use an external modem, your computer must have an unused serial (COM) connector.
- PC Cards are small, lightweight devices that fit into the PCMCIA slots on many laptop computers. They're the most convenient modems for people who travel with their PCs, but they're also the most expensive.

Modem Compatibility

The third thing to consider when you choose a modem is compatibility with standards. In order to connect your computer to a distant system, the modems at both ends of the link must use the same methods for encoding and compressing data. Therefore, you should use a modem that follows the international standards for data communication. The important standard for 28,800 bps modems is called V.34; the standard for slower modems is V.32bis. Don't even consider a modem that doesn't follow one of these standards.

After you physically connect the modem to your computer, you must also notify the operating system that there's a new modem in place. The modem configuration procedures are different in Windows 95 and Windows 3.1.

Installing a Modem in Windows 95

In Windows 95, communications control functions are located in a central application programming interface (API) which moves data between your modem and individual communications programs. One of the benefits of this design is that you can configure Windows 95 to work with your modem just once, rather than repeating the process for each application program that uses a modem.

If your modem follows the Plug and Play specification, Windows 95 should automatically detect it when you turn on your computer. If you're using an older modem ("older" means anything made before late 1995), you may need to add it to the configuration manually.

Follow these steps to add a modem to your Windows 95 configuration:

1. Click on the Start menu to open the Start menu.
2. Move the cursor to Settings and click on the Control Panel command in the Settings submenu.
3. When the Control Panel window opens, double-click on the Modems icon. The Modems Properties dialog box, shown in Figure 3.1, will appear.
4. If Windows 95 has already detected your modem, its name will appear in the Modems Properties dialog box.
    - If the correct modem is already listed, you can close the dialog box now—skip to step 7.
    - If there is no modem listed, or if the name on the list does not match the modem you want to use, click on the Add button to run the Install New Modem wizard.

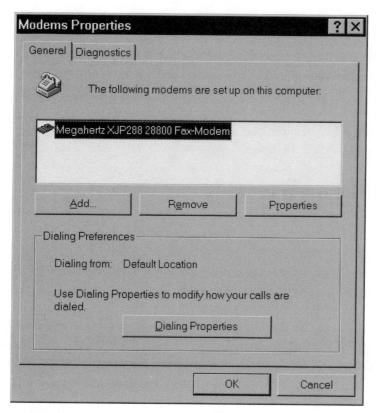

FIGURE 3.1: The Modems Properties dialog box identifies the modem
currently installed in your system.

5. The wizard will look for a modem on each of your COM ports. If it fails to
find a modem, it will ask you to specify the make and model and the port to
which the modem is connected. If it finds a modem, but it does not
recognize the make and model, it will use one of the (Standard Modem
Types) options.

- If your modem came with a Windows 95 installation diskette, put the diskette in your
computer's drive and click on the Have Disk button to load the configuration software for
your modem.
- If you don't have a disk, don't worry about it; the (Standard Modem Types) settings will
almost certainly work just fine.

6. When the wizard completes the installation, it will return you to the Modems Properties dialog box, which should now include the modem you just installed in the list of modems. If the list shows more than one modem, you can select the ones you're not using and click on the Remove button, but it's not really necessary; Windows 95 will identify the active modem every time you turn on your computer.

7. Click on the Close button and close the Control Panel to complete the installation.

Installing a Modem in Windows 3.1

In Windows 3.1, the communications driver program, comm.drv, is the interface between individual communications programs and the COM port connected to your modem. Unlike Windows 95, where modem control is centralized in the Communications API, each communications program in Windows 3.1 provides its own separate set of modem commands and controls. As a result, you must provide information about your modem every time you install a new communications program.

Therefore, installing a modem is fairly simple: connect it to a COM port or insert it in an expansion slot or a PCMCIA slot. If you're using an internal modem, follow the instructions provided to assign a port number and interrupt request line (IRQ) number.

Choosing a Service Provider

As you know, the Internet is the result of connecting many networks to one another. Therefore, you can connect your own computer to the Internet by obtaining an account on one of those interconnected networks.

Several different kinds of businesses offer Internet connections, including large companies with access points in many cities, smaller local or regional Internet service providers, and online information services that provide TCP/IP connections to the Internet along with their own proprietary information sources. You can use Internet Explorer with a connection through any of these services.

When you order your account, you should request a PPP connection to the Internet. PPP is a standard type of TCP/IP connection, which any ISP (Internet service provider) should be able to supply.

Using a National ISP

The greatest advantage of using a national or international ISP is that you can probably find a local dial-in telephone number in most major cities. If you want to send and receive e-mail or use other Internet services while you travel, this can be extremely important.

The disadvantage of working with a large company is that it may not be able to provide the same kind of personal service that you can get from a smaller, local business. If you must call halfway across the continent and wait 20 minutes on hold for technical support (especially if it's not a toll-free number), you should look for a different service provider.

Many large ISPs can give you free software that automatically configures your computer and sets up a new account. Even if they don't include Internet Explorer in their packages, you should be able to use some version of the program along with the application programs they do supply. However, most of these proprietary Winsock programs are designed to work with both Windows 3.1 and Windows 95, so you won't be able to use the 32-bit version of Internet Explorer unless you use Microsoft's Dial-Up Networking program instead of the ISP's proprietary Winsock.

You can obtain information about Internet access accounts from these national service providers:

AT&T WorldNet	1-800-WORLDNET (1-800-967-5363)
internetMCI	1-800-955-6505 (Business)
	1-800-550-0927 (Home)
SPRYnet	1-800-SPRYNET (1-800-777-9638)
GNNnet	1-800-819-6112
IBM Global Network	1-800-455-5056
PSInet	1-800-774-0852
Netcom	1-800-353-6600

Many local telephone companies and more than a few cable TV companies are also planning to offer Internet access to their subscribers. If it's available in your area, you should be able to obtain information about these services from the business office that handles your telephone or television service.

Using a Local ISP

The big national and regional services aren't your only choice. In most metropolitan areas and in a growing number of other places, smaller local service providers also offer access to the Internet.

If you can find a good local ISP, it might be your best choice. A local company may be more responsive to your particular needs and more willing to help you get through the inevitable configuration problems than a larger national operation. Equally important, reaching the tech support center is more likely to be a local telephone call.

But unfortunately, the Internet access business has attracted a tremendous number of entrepreneurs who are in it for the quick dollar—some local ISPs are really terrible. If they don't have enough modems to handle the demand, or if they don't have a high-capacity connection to an Internet backbone, or if they don't know how to keep their equipment and servers working properly, you'll get frequent busy signals, slow downloads, dropped carriers, and unexpected downtime rather than consistently reliable service. And there's no excuse for unhelpful technical support people or endless time on hold. If a deal seems too good to be true, there's probably a good reason.

To learn about the reputations of local ISPs, ask friends and colleagues who have been using the Internet for a while. If there's a local "Computer User" magazine, look for schedules of user group meetings where you can find people with experience using the local service providers. If you can't get a recommendation from any of those sources, look in the list of ISPs at http://thelist.com.

TIP

No matter which service you choose, wait a month or two before you print your e-mail address on business cards and letterhead. If the first ISP you try doesn't give you the service you expect, take your business someplace else.

Connecting through an Online Service

If you already have an account with an online information service, you can use the same account for access to the Internet. Three of the four major services—America Online (AOL), CompuServe, and Prodigy—have built-in Web browsers, but it's also possible to use Internet Explorer as an external add-on program though AOL and CompuServe. The fourth major service, Microsoft Network, uses Internet Explorer as its default browser. In most cases, Internet Explorer (or Netscape Navigator, for that matter) is faster and easier to use than the browsers that are supplied by the online services.

Like the software supplied by nationwide Internet-only services, the programs provided by AOL, CompuServe, and Prodigy are all 16-bit packages designed to work with both Windows 3.1 and Windows 95. Therefore, you must use them with Internet Explorer for Windows 3.1, even if you are running Windows 95.

Using America Online

To use Internet Explorer through AOL, you must either upgrade to AOL's Version 3.0 software or download a winsock.dll file from AOL's Winsock Central area (keyword: Winsock). Because the AOL Winsock is a 16-bit program, you'll need the Windows 3.1 version of Internet Explorer, even if you have installed Windows 95. When AOL introduces software for Windows 95, it will be compatible with the 32-bit version of Internet Explorer.

Installing AOL's Winsock

Follow these steps to install AOL's Winsock:
1. Download the winsock.dll file from AOL.
2. Look in your \windows directory for a winsock.dll file. If you find one, rename it to winsock.old.
3. Copy winsock.dll from c:\aol25\download to your \windows directory.

Using Internet Explorer with AOL

To use Internet Explorer (or any other Winsock-compliant client program) through AOL, follow these steps:
1. Start AOL and connect as you would to use AOL's own services.
2. Minimize the AOL window.
3. Double-click on the Internet Explorer icon.

Using CompuServe

CompuServe's Winsock is very much like AOL's, but it's included in the WinCIM 2.01 package, so you don't need to download it separately.

Copying the CompuServe Winsock

In order to use the CompuServe Winsock with Internet Explorer, you must have a copy of the winsock.dll program in your \windows directory or some other directory in your DOS path. Follow these steps to copy the program:

1. Look in your \windows directory for a winsock.dll file. If you find one, rename it to winsock.old.
2. Copy the winsock.dll file from your c:\cserve\mosaic directory to the \windows directory.

Using Internet Explorer with CompuServe

To use Internet Explorer (or any other Winsock-compliant client program) through CompuServe, follow these steps:

1. Start WinCIM and connect as you would to use CompuServe's own services.
2. Minimize the WinCIM window.
3. Double-click on the Internet Explorer icon.

Using Prodigy

At the time this book was written, Prodigy had not yet released a Winsock-compatible Internet access service. When it does appear, it will almost certainly use a winsock.dll file like the ones used by CompuServe and AOL.

Using More Than One Online Service

If you want to use Internet Explorer and other TCP/IP programs through more than one online service, or if you have accounts with both an online service and a separate ISP, things will be more difficult, because you will have conflicts between the winsock.dll files that connect you to each service. Even though the files have the same name, they are not cross-compatible.

When you start a client program, it looks for winsock.dll in this order:

1. In the same directory as the client program
2. In your \windows directory
3. In the directories in your DOS path

The application tries to use the first Winsock file it finds, even if some other Winsock is currently connected. Therefore, you must make sure that the one you want to use is the one the application finds.

There are several ways to work around this problem, but none are particularly attractive:

- Copy a new winsock.dll file into the \windows directory each time you want to connect through a different service.
- Maintain multiple copies of Internet Explorer and other programs in separate directories, with a different Winsock file in each directory.
- Use Internet Explorer with just one ISP or online service.
- Use an ISP to connect to the Internet, and then use the TCP/IP option to reach the online services.

These are all more or less unsatisfactory solutions to the problem. If you have the space on your hard drive, the best choice is probably to create several directories and place a Winsock file and a copy of Internet Explorer in each one. Create separate icons in your Windows 3.1 File Manager or shortcuts on the Windows 95 desktop or Start menu called *Internet Explorer via AOL* and *Internet Explorer via SPRYnet* (or whatever Internet access providers you're actually using).

If you use Windows 95 and you have accounts with more than one ISP (rather than online information services), you don't need to worry about this problem; you can find instructions for creating and using multiple Dial-Up Networking connection profiles in the following sections.

Setting Up Windows 95 Dial-Up Networking

If you've chosen an ISP other than Microsoft Network, and you're using Windows 95, you must set up a Dial-Up Networking profile that will dial your ISP's closest telephone number whenever you start Internet Explorer or some other Winsock-compliant application program.

Creating a new profile is not difficult, but it's a little more complicated than simply clicking on an option in the Setup wizard. To configure a Dial-Up Networking connection profile, you must complete two separate procedures: load the software and create a connection profile.

Loading the Software

If you didn't load Dial-Up Networking when you installed Windows 95, you must add it before you can connect to the Internet. Follow these steps to add the software:

1. Open the Control Panel.
2. Double-click on the Add/Remove Programs icon.
3. Click on the Windows Setup tab to display the Windows Setup dialog box.
4. Select the Communications item from the Components list and click on the Details button.
5. Make sure there's a checkmark next to the Dial-Up Networking component and click on the OK button.
6. When you see a message instructing you to insert software disks, follow the instructions as they appear.
7. When the software has been loaded, restart the computer.
8. The Control Panel should still be open. Double-click on the Network icon.
9. Click on the Add button to display the Select Network Component Type dialog box, shown in Figure 3.2.

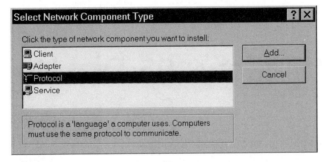

FIGURE 3.2: Use the Select Network Component Type dialog box to set up Dial-Up Networking.

10. Select Protocol in the list of component types and click on the Add button.
11. Select Microsoft from the list of manufacturers and TCP/IP in the list of network protocols. Click on the OK button.
12. You should see TCP/IP in the list of network components. Click on the OK button to close the dialog box.

Creating a Connection Profile

Once you've added support for TCP/IP networking, you're ready to set up one or more connection profiles. Follow these steps to create a profile:

1. Start Dial-Up Networking from either the My Computer window on the desktop or the Programs ➤ Accessories menu.

2. Double-click on the Make New Connection icon.

3. The Make New Connection wizard will start. The name of the computer you will dial is also the name that will identify the icon for this connection profile in the Dial-Up Networking folder. Therefore, you should use the name of your service provider as the name for this profile. If you have separate profiles for telephone numbers in different cities, include the city name as well. For example, if you use SPRYnet as your access provider, you might want to create profiles called SPRYnet Chicago and SPRYnet Boston.

4. Click on the Next button to move to the next screen, and type the telephone number for your ISP's PPP access.

5. Click on the Finish button to complete your work with the wizard.

6. You will see a new icon in the Dial-Up Networking window. Right-click on this icon and select the Properties command.

7. When the Connections Properties dialog box, shown in Figure 3.3, appears, click on the Server Type button.

8. When the Server Types dialog box, shown in Figure 3.4, appears, choose the PPP option in the drop-down list of dial-up server types.

9. Make sure there are checkmarks next to these options:

    Log on to network

    Enable software compression

    TCP/IP

10. Click on the TCP/IP Settings button.

11. Ask your ISP how to fill in this dialog box. You will probably use a Server Assigned IP Address and specific DNS addresses, but your ISP can give you the exact information you need.

12. Click on the OK buttons to close all the open dialog boxes.

To confirm that you have set up the connection profile properly, turn on your modem and double-click on the new icon. When the Connect To dialog box, shown in Figure 3.5, appears, type your user ID and password and click on the Connect button. Your computer should place a call to the ISP and connect your system to the Internet.

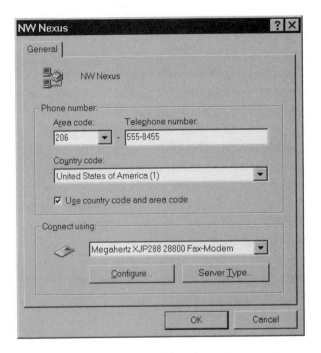

FIGURE 3.3:
Use the Connections Properties dialog box to configure Dial-Up Networking.

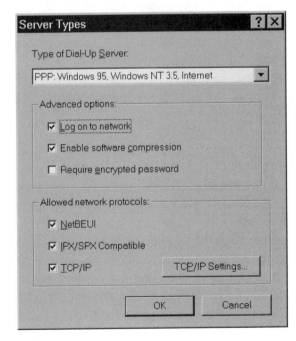

FIGURE 3.4:
Use the Server Types dialog box to set up a PPP connection.

If you have accounts with more than one ISP, or if you carry the same computer to different cities, you can create separate connection profiles for each ISP or each telephone number. By choosing a connection profile before you start any Winsock application, you can make your connection through a profile other than the default.

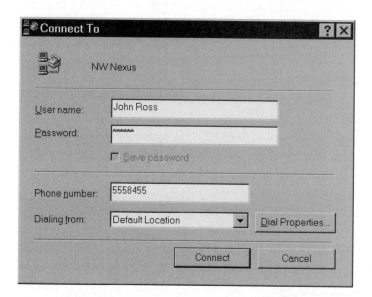

FIGURE 3.5:
The Connect To dialog box shows the name and telephone number of your ISP.

Connecting to the Internet through Microsoft Network

Along with all those other service providers, Microsoft has an Internet access product of their own. The Microsoft Network (MSN) was established as an online information service that would compete with AOL and CompuServe. But a few months after it was launched, Miscrosoft announced that MSN would be converted to an Internet-based service with content areas that would be available to any Internet user.

Microsoft wants you to use their Internet access service (and send them more money every month for the privilege), so they've made it extremely easy to load and configure a Windows 95 Dial-Up Networking connection to MSN. If you already have an account with MSN, or if there's an MSN telephone number that supports Internet access within local calling range of your office or home, the Microsoft service may be the easiest (but probably not the least expensive) way to set up a Windows 95 Internet connection.

When you install Internet Explorer, the Setup wizard will ask if you want to connect through Microsoft Network or through some other service provider, as explained in Chapter 4. If you choose MSN and state that you don't already have an MSN account, the wizard will step you through the process of finding a local telephone number and establishing a new account. If you already have an MSN account, you can easily add Internet access:

1. Double-click on the MSN icon.
2. When the Sign In window appears, click on the Settings button.
3. Click on the Access Numbers button.
4. In the Microsoft Network dialog box, choose Internet and The Microsoft Network as your service type.
5. Click on the Change buttons to select the closest Primary and Backup telephone numbers.
6. Click on the OK buttons to close all the dialog boxes and save your selections.

When setup is complete, you will have a Dial-Up Networking connection profile for Microsoft Network, and if you specified a backup telephone number, a separate backup connection profile.

Changing the Default Connection

When setup is complete, you will have a Dial-Up Networking connection profile for each of your ISPs. Internet Explorer and other Winsock-compliant programs will use the current default to connect your computer to the Internet whenever you start the programs.

To change the default, follow these steps:

1. Right-click on the The Internet icon on your desktop and select the Properties command from the menu.
2. When the Internet Properties dialog box appears, click on the Connection tab to display the dialog box shown in Figure 3.6.
3. Choose the name of the Dial-Up Networking connection profile you want to use from the drop-down list.
4. Click on the OK button to close the dialog box.

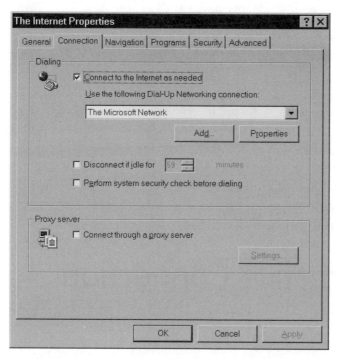

FIGURE 3.6:   Use the Connection tab to change the default connection profile.

Windows 3.1 Connections

Unlike Windows 95, there's no built-in Winsock program supplied with Windows 3.1, so you must install a separate Winsock program in order to use Internet Explorer. If you don't already have a Winsock stack, you can download one from Microsoft along with your copy of Internet Explorer for Windows 3.1.

Other Winsocks that work well with Internet Explorer are included with many third-party Internet programs, including Internet in a Box, Internet Chameleon, Eudora Pro, and Netscape Navigator. You should be able to find most of these programs in retail computer stores and mail-order software catalogs.

The IBM Internet Connection package is another good collection of Internet tools. It includes a full set of application client programs along with a Winsock interface. It's available from IBM Direct at 1-800-342-6672, priority code SE001.

There's also at least one good shareware program called Trumpet Winsock that you can download from many online services and software archives. If you already have access to the Internet, you can find Trumpet Winsock at http://www.coast.net/ simtel/vendors/trumpet/ or via FTP from ftp.synapse.net/.mirrors/simtelnet/ trumpet/winsock.

You might also obtain a Winsock program from your ISP. As explained earlier in this chapter, all of the large national service providers offer either their own proprietary software or a customized version of one of the commercial programs. Smaller, local and regional ISPs may not have their own software, but they should be able to recommend one or more programs that work well with their network host and give you a script file that automates your login. If an ISP's salesperson doesn't know what a Winsock program is, thank them politely and find a different access provider.

Using Alternative Connection Methods

A telephone connection is the most common and least expensive way for individuals to reach the Internet, but it's not your only option. If they're not available now, high-speed data services will probably become available from your telephone company, cable TV service, and other new information utilities within the next few years. You can also use Internet Explorer with high-speed network connections through a corporate LAN or a campus-wide network.

Each of these services requires a special network interface device that allows your computer to send and receive data more quickly than the COM port can handle it. The specific hardware and software requirements are different for each type of connection; your network service provider will tell you exactly what you need.

As far as Internet Explorer is concerned, the only difference between a dial-in connection to the Internet and a faster network link is the amount of time it will take to download and display Web pages and other files. All of the features and functions described in the rest of this book will work with any kind of Internet connection.

Chapter 4

INSTALLING AND CONFIGURING THE PROGRAM

FEATURING

- **Installing and setting up Internet Explorer**
- **Using the Internet icon's right-button menu**
- **Customizing the appearance of pages in Internet Explorer**
- **Reducing the amount of time needed to download pages**
- **Creating and changing file associations**

Before you start to use Internet Explorer, you must install the program onto your PC. The installation process is fairly painless, but it does ask you to make a handful of decisions while the program loads. After installation is complete, there are some other possible tweaks that can make Internet Explorer easier to use.

In this chapter, you can find explanations of all the installation options and instructions for configuring the program after installation is complete. While it's entirely possible to simply install the program and start using it, the suggestions in this chapter will help you make the most of some of Internet Explorer's less obvious features.

Installing Internet Explorer in Windows 95

Microsoft has designed Internet Explorer to be easy to install. For the most part, they've succeeded. When you run the msie*nn*.exe program, it automatically extracts the compressed files from the distribution file and places them in the appropriate folders or directories.

Some download methods automatically offer to install the program after they copy the distribution file to your hard drive. If it's not automatic, follow these steps to install Internet Explorer:

1. Copy the distribution file to a temporary folder.

2. Open the folder that contains the distribution file and double-click on the icon for that file. If you're installing Internet Explorer as part of the Plus! package, or upgrading from an earlier version of the program, the installation routine will automatically decide where to place the program files. If you're loading the program for the first time, you must specify a location. It doesn't really matter where you put the files, but there are a couple of logical choices:

   • **The hard drive (C:) root folder:** Subfolders and files in the root folder are easy to find, but they contribute to a cluttered window, and there's always a chance that you might have a conflict among files with the same name that belong to different programs. Since you may never actually open the Microsoft Internet folder (because you will use a shortcut from the desktop or Start menu to start the program), there's no really good reason to make it a top-level folder.

   • **The Program Files folder:** In Windows 95, many well-behaved application programs place their files in subfolders within the Program Files folder. This seems like an entirely logical place for Internet Explorer.

   • **A new top-level folder or directory called Internet Tools:** If you decide to use other Internet tools along with Internet Explorer, such as the ones described in Chapters 11, 12 and 13, it makes a lot of sense to store them in subfolders within the same top-level folder. If you prefer, you might want to consider placing the Internet Tools folder within the Program Files folder.

In practice, if Internet Explorer recommends a destination folder during installation, it's probably a good idea to accept that suggestion.

The first time you click on the Internet icon or select the Internet Explorer command from the Start menu after you load the software, Internet Explorer will step you through the Setup Wizard. The wizard will ask if you want to use The Microsoft Network or some other service provider to connect to the Internet, as shown in Figure 4.1.

If you choose MSN as your connection to the Internet, the wizard will find the closest telephone number for dial-in access, and help you set up a new account if you don't already have one. If you choose a different service provider, the wizard will ask for additional information that Internet Explorer will use to process mail and directory services. If you haven't already configured a Dial-Up Networking connection profile for your ISP (as described in Chapter 3), the wizard will use this information to create one for you.

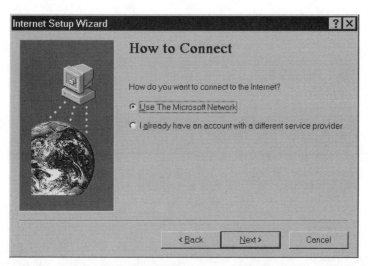

FIGURE 4.1:   The Internet Setup Wizard offers you the choice of connecting through MSN or another Internet access provider.

The Desktop Internet Icon

When installation and setup are complete, you will see a "The Internet" icon on your Windows 95 desktop, as shown in Figure 4.2, and an Internet Explorer command in the Start menu's Programs submenu. When you double-click on the icon (or choose the menu command), Internet Explorer will automatically connect your computer to the Internet and display the Start Page. You can find information in Chapter 5 about customizing the default Microsoft Start Page or substituting a different page.

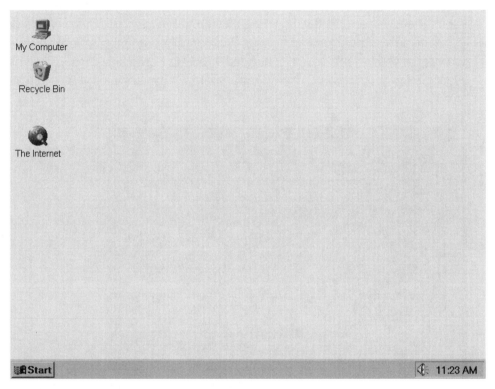

FIGURE 4.2: Internet Explorer adds an Internet icon to the Windows 95 desktop.

Using the Internet Properties Dialog Box

Like all other Windows 95 icons, The Internet has a Properties command in the menu that appears when you click on the Internet icon with your right mouse button. You can also open the Properties dialog boxes with the Options command in the View menu within Internet Explorer.

Figure 4.3 shows the Connection tab in the Internet Properties dialog box. If you're using Dial-Up Networking to connect to the Internet, make sure there's a checkmark next to the Connect to the Internet as Needed option, and choose your default connection in the drop-down list. If you're connected to the Internet through a LAN or a direct high-speed link, you can remove the checkmark from the Connect as Needed option.

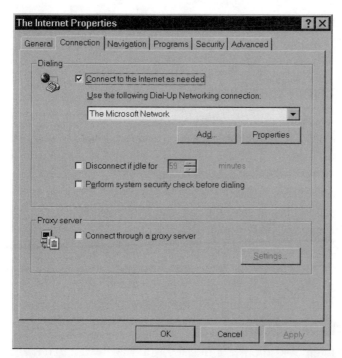

FIGURE 4.3: Use the Internet Properties dialog box to control automatic connection to the Internet.

You can use the Properties button to change an existing connection profile, or the Add button to create a new profile. The Disconnect If Idle option breaks your connection to the Internet and hangs up the telephone line if there's no activity for the specified number of minutes. Unfortunately, the program does not monitor third-party application programs like Netscape Navigator or Winsock FTP, so you might see a "Disconnecting in 30 Seconds" message in the middle of an active session. This is a nuisance, because it means that you can't go away from your computer and do something else during a long file transfer, so you may want to disable this option if you expect to use other Internet programs along with Internet Explorer.

The Perform System Security Check Before Dialing option limits access to shared printers and files through the Internet. If your PC is not on a LAN, you can safely turn off this option.

The Proxy option turns access to a proxy server on or off. If you're using Dial-Up Networking, this option should be off. If you connect through a LAN that has a "firewall" to protect against unauthorized outside access to your local network, you may need to use a proxy server. Your LAN administrator or help desk can supply the information you need to use Internet Explorer through a firewall.

All of the other tabs in the Internet Properties dialog box control Internet Explorer options. There are explanations of these options later in this chapter.

Removing the Icon from Your Desktop

Unlike shortcuts to programs and data files, you can't remove the Internet icon from your desktop by dragging it to the Recycle Bin. If you don't want to use the icon, there are two ways to eliminate it:

- Use the Delete command in the right-click menu.
- Use a free program called Tweak UI (available as part of the Windows 95 Power Toys collection from Microsoft's Web site at http:// www.microsoft .com/ windows/software/powertoy.htm).

Tweak UI is the better choice, because it allows you to restore the icon to the desktop if you change your mind about removing it, and because it also controls other desktop icons, as shown in Figure 4.4.

Changing the Name of the Icon

If you keep the The Internet icon on your desktop, you might want to rename it to Internet Explorer, especially if you also use other Internet application programs. There's a Rename command in the menu that appears when you move the cursor over the icon and press the right mouse button.

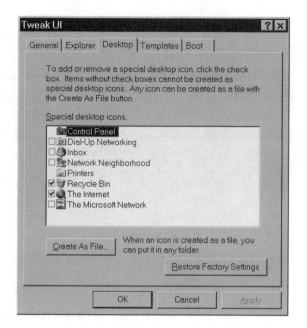

FIGURE 4.4:
Use Microsoft's free Tweak UI program to hide or display special desktop icons, including the one for The Internet.

Changing Internet Explorer's Appearance and Performance

As you work with Internet Explorer (or any other Web browser), it's useful to understand that a Web page or other HTML document does not always include information about the specific colors and type fonts that appear on your screen. The Web browser program receives the page as text with embedded formatting commands, and it performs the formatting when it displays the page.

Therefore, you can change the way Internet Explorer formats a page by choosing different colors and typefaces. The wrong choices can make a page completely unreadable, but other options might actually improve the way a page looks.

It's also possible to reduce the amount of time needed to download a page by skipping artwork, sounds, and animation. This is especially useful if you're using a slow modem

> **NOTE**
>
> For many users, Internet Explorer's default configuration will do everything they want or need. "If it's not broke, don't fix it" is a completely acceptable working philosophy for installing and using the program. If you're happy with the typeface and other appearance options, and if you don't mind waiting for graphic images and sound files to download, you don't have to make any changes.

Options in the General Tab

To control the appearance of pages in Internet Explorer, follow these steps:

1. If it's not already running, start Internet Explorer.
2. Open the View menu and select the Options command.
3. If it's not visible, click on the General tab to display the dialog box shown in Figure 4.5.

Working with Multimedia Elements in Web Pages

The Multimedia section of the General tab includes these options:

- **Show Pictures:** When Show Pictures is not checked, Internet Explorer does not automatically download pictures and other graphic elements embedded in Web pages. Hiding the pictures can reduce the amount of time needed to download a page, but it may also eliminate much of the information contained in a Web site. If you don't show pictures when you download Web pages, you can click on an image icon to download an individual picture later. If the page includes graphic links or an image map, you won't be able to use any of the links until you download the picture. Figure 4.6 shows the same Web page with and without pictures.

- **Play Sounds:** Some Web pages are accompanied by audio recordings of background music, sound effects, or voice narration. If your computer has a sound board, Internet Explorer will automatically play these sounds when you download a page, but like everything else in a Web page, sounds take time to download. If you don't have a sound board, or if you're not interested in hearing anything, turn off the Play Sounds option.

- **Play Videos:** Animated images and other moving pictures require extremely large files. To avoid waiting for them to load, remove the checkmark from the Play Videos option.

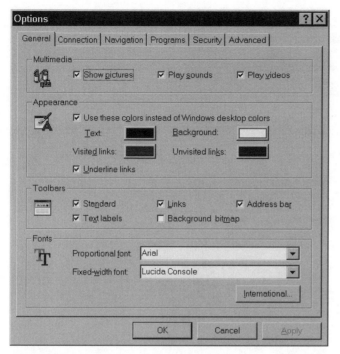

FIGURE 4.5: Use the General tab of the Options dialog box to change the fonts and colors of Web pages.

- **Play Videos:** Animated images and other moving pictures require extremely large files. To avoid waiting for them to load, remove the checkmark from the Play Videos option.

Controlling the Colors of Web Pages

The Use These Colors Instead of Windows Desktop Colors options specify the colors that Internet Explorer uses to display text, background, and links in Web pages. When there is no checkmark next to Use these Colors, Internet Explorer will use the color settings defined in the Windows Display Properties dialog box, unless a Web page specifies a text or background color. To change the default colors, place a checkmark in the box next to Use these Colors and click on the Text or Background buttons to select a new color. As a general rule, you should use a dark color for text and a light color for background to make your pages as easy to read as possible.

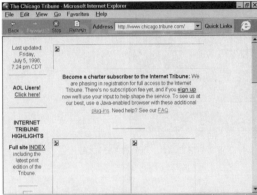

FIGURE 4.6:
A Web page with and without pictures.

Changing the Appearence of Text links

Internet Explorer maintains a history file that contains a list of URLs that you have recently downloaded. When a Web page contains a shortcut to one of the URLs in your history file, it will display the shortcut in the color shown on the Viewed Links button. Click on the button to choose a different color. When a Web page contains a shortcut to a URL that is not in your history file, Internet Explorer will display the shortcut in the color shown on the Unvisited button. Click on the button to choose a different color.

NOTE   When you click on a link, Internet Explorer downloads the file identified in that link. If the target is another Web page or other URL. Internet Explorer loads and displays it; if it's another type of file, it uses the association for the file name extension to decide how to handle the file.

When Underline Links is active, Internet Explorer displays links in Web pages with a single underline. When this option is not active, you will see links in the colors specified by the Visited Links and Unvisted Links options.

Configuring the Internet Explorer Toolbars

The Toolbars section of the General tab hides or displays portions of the toolbars that appear just above the main window, as shown in Figure 4.7. It includes these options:

- **Standard:** The Standard toolbar contains command buttons that duplicate important menu commands.
- **Text Labels:** When the Text Labels option is active, the Standard toolbar includes a caption under each command icon that identifies the function of that command.
- **Links:** The Links toolbar is a set of five quick links to Web pages that you visit frequently. Use the Navigation tab to specify the destinations of your quick links.
- **Address Bar:** The Address Bar shows the URL of the current Web page.
- **Background Bitmap:** When the Background Bitmap option is active, there's a pattern under the icons and text in all visible toolbars. When this option is not active, the background is a light solid color.

Changing Type Fonts

The HTML code for most Web pages does not include an instruction to use a specific typeface for headlines or body text. Instead, the Web page designer leaves the choice of a font to the browser. In Internet Explorer, the options that specify your default font are in the General tab of the Options dialog box.

To change a font, click on the arrow at the left of the option field and choose the font you want to use form the drop-down list.

Use the Proportional Font field to change the typeface that Internet Explorer will use to display headlines and body text in Web pages. It's called "proportional" because some letters are wider than others—for example, compare an I with an M. The default proportional font is Times New Roman, which was originally designed for ink on paper. Some other fonts, such as Arial, are better choices for on-screen reading. To select a different font, open the drop-down list and select the one you want to use.

FIGURE 4.7: You can hide or display one or more toolbars from the General tab.

Use the Fixed-width Font field to change the typeface used for tables and other text elements that must maintain a constant width. The default fixed-width font is Courier New, which looks like the print from an old-fashioned typewriter. Lucida Console is a better choice, because it's easier to read and it looks more like real print.

Using a Foreign Character Set

Different languages may use different character sets, so you can configure Internet Explorer to recognize the one you use most often by clicking on the International button. In most cases, the International dialog box shown in Figure 4.8 will list the home language for the version of Internet Explorer that you're using. If your version of the program supports more than one character set, or if you've added support for another language after installation, you can set different default fonts for each language.

To change to a different character set, follow these steps:

1. In Internet Explorer, open the View menu and select the Options command.
2. Click on the General tab.
3. Click on the International button to open the International dialog box.
4. Select the character set that you want to use.

Changing the Address Format in the Status Bar

The Show Friendly URLs option in the Advanced Options tab controls the format that Internet Explorer uses to display addresses in the status bar. When Show Friendly URLs is active, the status bar shows the address without the extra URL information, like this:

www.destination.com

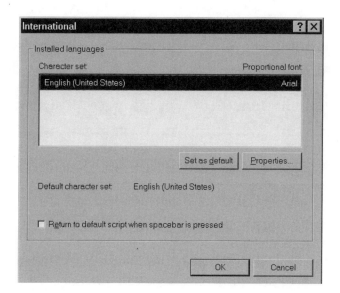

FIGURE 4.8:
Use the International dialog box to use a different character set.

When the option is not active, the status bar shows the address with all the URL coding, like this:

http://www.destination.com/

Associating File Types to Programs

When you open a file from the Windows 3.1 File Manager or the Windows 95 desktop or Explorer, Windows uses the file name extension to identify an application or utility that can read the file. For example, if you select a text file called report.doc, Windows might load the file into Microsoft Word. If you choose an HTML file called picture.htm, Windows might use Internet Explorer to display the contents of the file. The installation routines for Windows and many application programs automatically assign file associations to the particular file name extensions that are normally used with those programs.

Internet Explorer adds MIMEs (Multipurpose Internet Mail Extensions) to the list of file associations used with other Windows programs. Therefore, when you select a file for download through the Internet, Internet Explorer looks for the file name extension in the list of registered file types, and takes the action specified for that type. Depending on the file type, Internet Explorer might open and display the file within its own window, start another program to display or run the file, or store the file in a directory or folder.

> **NOTE** There's a very good chance that you will never have to worry about associating a MIME with a program, because the default associations will do everything you ever need.

When you download a new file type, Internet Explorer will offer you several choices:

- Open this file, but don't permanently associate the file name extension with an application program or utility.
- Associate the file name extension with a MIME, so all future files of this type will automatically open.
- Store the file in a folder or directory.

If you prefer, you can create a new MIME type or change an existing MIME before you download a file. Follow these steps to add or change a file type:

1. In Internet Explorer, open the View menu and select the Options command.
2. Click on the Programs tab.
3. Click on the File Types tab to display the dialog box in Figure 4.9.
4. To create a new file association, click on the New Type button. To change an existing association, select a description from the list of Registered File Types and click on the Edit button. You'll see the New File Type or Edit File Type dialog box, which have similar fields.
5. To assign an application to a MIME, choose an existing item from the Actions field (for example, you might want to choose Open as an action) and click on the Edit button, or click on the New button to create a new action. You'll see the dialog box shown in Figure 4.10 (which may be headed "Editing Action for Type" or "New Action").
6. Use the Browse button in the dialog box to select the program that you want to use with this file type. Then click on the Open button to close the browser, and the OK button in the dialog box.
7. If you want Internet Explorer to offer you a choice of either opening a file as soon as it has downloaded that file or storing the file without opening it, place a checkmark next to the Confirm Open After Download option in the New File Type or Edit File Type dialog box. As a general rule, this option should be active for executable files and for data files that you may not want to run or examine until after you have broken your connection to the Internet.
8. Click on the OK buttons in the dialog boxes.

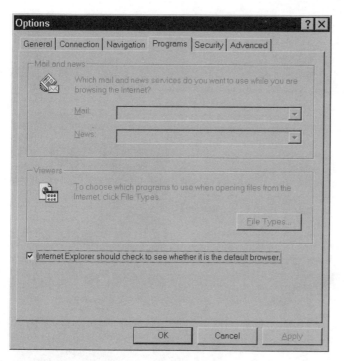

FIGURE 4.9: Click the File Types button to assign programs to file name extensions.

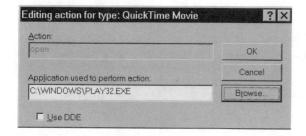

FIGURE 4.10:
Use one of the Action dialog boxes to attach an application program to a file type.

Once your installation and configuration is complete, you're ready to start using Internet Explorer. In the next chapter, you can find information about the program's basic tools for moving between Web sites and finding information and other resources.

Chapter 5

BROWSING THE WORLD WIDE WEB

- **Using the features of the Internet Explorer screen**
- **Jumping to Web pages**
- **Choosing, changing, and customizing Start Pages**
- **Working with Internet search tools**

Installing and configuring Internet Explorer, and connecting your computer to the Internet are essential steps that you must complete before you can explore the World Wide Web. Once you make your connection, you're ready to start looking around.

In this chapter, you'll find the information you need to use Internet Explorer to display Web pages and other Internet resources. After you spend a little time working with the program, you will quickly stop noticing the details of Internet Explorer and devote your attention to the Web pages themselves.

Starting Internet Explorer

In Windows 95, you can start Internet Explorer by double-clicking on the Internet icon on your desktop, or by selecting the Internet Explorer command in the Start menu's Programs submenu. In Windows 3.1, double-click on the Internet Explorer icon in a Program Manager window.

When Internet Explorer starts, it will look for an active connection to the Internet through your Winsock stack. If you use a modem and telephone line to make your connection, and there isn't an active connection, the Winsock program will automatically use Dial-Up Networking to take your telephone line off-hook, dial your ISP, and set up a new TCP/IP link.

One of the benefits of a Winsock connection is that you can use it with more than one application program at the same time. If you have other Internet tools, such as a telnet client or IBM's News Ticker program, you can run them along with Internet Explorer through the same network connection. This can be especially convenient when you're using one program to download a large file while you're using another program to read your e-mail or participate in an online conference.

The Internet Explorer Screen

Figure 5.1 shows the main Internet Explorer screen. If you've been using Windows 95 for more than a couple of hours, you will probably recognize many parts of the Internet Explorer layout.

The Internet Explorer screen includes these features and functions:

- **Title bar:** The title bar contains the name of the current Web page or other file on display in the Internet Explorer window, along with the familiar sizing buttons and Close button.
- **Menu bar:** The menu bar contains a set of menus that each includes individual commands that you can use to control the way Internet Explorer works. You can find a complete command summary in Chapter 9.
- **Toolbar:** The Internet Explorer toolbar has three parts: a set of command buttons that duplicate many of the most frequently used menu commands, an address field, and a group of Quick Links that you can assign to your most frequently used Web sites. When you move your cursor over a button or a

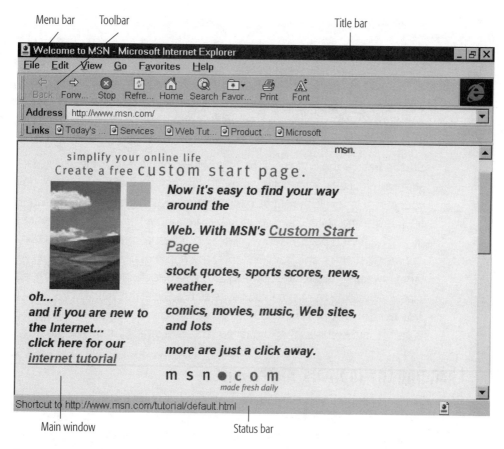

Menu bar   Toolbar   Title bar

Main window   Status bar

FIGURE 5.1: The Internet Explorer screen uses many standard Windows 95 conventions.

Quick Link, the icon changes from black and white to color. To enter a command from the toolbar or jump to a Quick Link site, click on a button. Using the address field and Quick Links to go to Web pages is explained later in the chapter.

- **Activity indicator:** The Internet Explorer symbol to the right of the toolbar is animated when Internet Explorer sends and receives data from the network.
- **Main window:** The main portion of the Internet Explorer screen displays the text, images, and other graphic elements of the most recent Web page or other file.

NOTE It's important to understand that the Web pages and other data you see in Internet Explorer are located on your own computer or LAN. Internet Explorer downloads copies of files from distant servers, but it does not maintain a live connection to the server after the download is complete.

- **Status bar:** At the bottom of the Internet Explorer window, the status bar supplies additional information about the current Web site. When you move your cursor to a link, the status bar shows the destination of that link. During a file transfer, the status bar displays a bar graph that shows the progress of the transfer. If a Web page includes multiple pictures, graphic elements, audio clips, or other files, the status bar will display the name of the specific file that is currently being transferred. Some Web pages also include a special script that places a scrolling message that moves across the status bar.
- **International Globe:** If you have more than one installed language, a globe is visible in the status bar. To change character sets, click on the globe.

Changing the Toolbars' Appearance

Earlier in this chapter, you learned that you can use the General Options dialog box to hide one or more of the three toolbars (the Standard toolbar, the Address Bar and the Quick Links toolbar). It's also possible to combine two or more of the toolbars on a single line by dragging and dropping. When more than one toolbar occupies the same line, you can view the hidden toolbar by dragging left or right.

To move the toolbar, follow these steps:

1. Place your cursor over the name of the section you want to move. Notice that the cursor changes to a pointing finger.
2. Hold down your right mouse button and drag the portion of the toolbar up or down.

To move a toolbar within the same line, place your cursor over the double bar at the left side of the toolbar you want to move, and drag left or right.

Creating Your Own Quick Links

The Links toolbar contains five quick links to specific Web sites. When you install Internet Explorer, all five quick links are assigned to Microsoft sites, but you can assign each link to any other URL that you visit frequently.

The default Quick Links are:

- **Today's Links:** Click on Today's Links to jump to MSN's Link Central page, which contains links to a selection of new and timely Web sites, including pages devoted to current sports and news events, interesting new Web services and recent movies and television shows.
- **Services:** Click on Services to jump to a page with links to a variety of online information sources, including financial services, telephone and address directories, home and garden information, and online reference books.
- **Web Tutorial:** Click on Web Tutorial to jump to a series of Web pages that provide an introduction and guide to using and understanding the Internet.
- **Product Updates:** Click on Product Updates to jump to a Microsoft page that contains information about the latest versions of Internet Explorer and links to file downloads.
- **Microsoft:** Click on Microsoft to jump to a page with links to information about Windows and other Microsoft products and free downloads of programs, patches, and add-on software for Microsoft programs.

Follow these steps to change your quick links:

1. Jump to the Web page or other site that you want to define as the destination of a quick link.
2. Open the View menu and select the Options command.
3. Click on the Navigation tab to display the dialog box shown in Figure 5.2.
4. Click on the arrowhead at the right side of the Page field to open the drop-down menu.
5. Click on the Quick Link number that you want to change.
6. Click on the Use Current button to assign a quick link to the current Web page.
7. In the Name field, type the name for the site that you want to appear in the Links toolbar. Try to limit the name to about nine characters, so the entire name can fit on the link button.

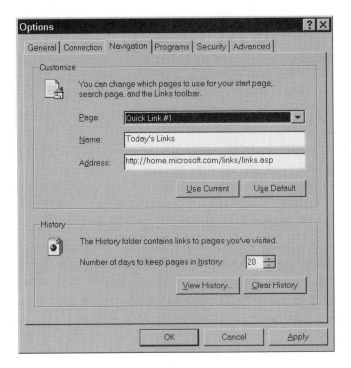

FIGURE 5.2:
Use the Navigation tab in the Options dialog box to create new quick links.

Moving around the Web

The whole World Wide Web is built around seamless links from one place on the Internet to another. Any Web page can include links to other files that may be physically stored on the same computer or on any other computer connected to the Internet. At its center, Internet Explorer is a tool for retrieving Web pages and following those links.

There are several ways to tell Internet Explorer which Web page or file you want to see next:

- Click on a link in the currently visible page.
- Type the URL of a new site in the address field.
- Choose a URL from a list of favorites.
- Choose a URL from a list of sites you've visited before.
- Use the Back and Forward buttons in the toolbar to return to a site you've recently seen.
- Click on one of the Quick Links.
- Double-click on a shortcut to a Web site from the Windows desktop or Start menu.

Typing an Address

When you discover a Web site address in a magazine article, on a TV show, in an online mention in e-mail or a newsgroup, or from some other source, you can visit that site by typing its URL into Internet Explorer. Simply type the URL of the Web site or other Internet file or service you want to see into the address bar, and then press the Enter key.

If you don't include the URL type, Internet Explorer assumes that you're trying to reach a Web page or other HTML document, and it will automatically add *http://* to the beginning of the URL. Therefore, you will reach exactly the same Web site if you type either **www.well.com** or **http://www.well.com**.

If you're trying to reach some other type of server, such as an FTP archive, a telnet host, or a gopher server, you must type the full address, including the type designator. For example, the URL for an FTP site might be ftp://ftp.archive.edu. If you leave out the type, Internet Explorer will try to reach the wrong kind of server.

TIP	If you don't know the address for a company's home page, try http://www.*name-of-company*.com. That format doesn't always work, but it's the most common URL for a business home page.

You can also use the address field to open up a file located on your own computer's hard drive, on a floppy disk, a CD-ROM, or on another computer connected to yours through a LAN. For example, to see a file called schedule.txt in your c:\calendar folder, type **c:\calendar\schedule.txt** in the address field. You don't need to worry about a URL type identifier when you load a local file into Internet Explorer, but you should remember that DOS and Windows use the backslash (\) to separate folders in a path, instead of the forward slash (/) used by most Internet servers.

Using Hot Links

Except for a handful of Web sites like www.incrediblelink.com and www.leonardo.net/ BennysBBQ that specialize in spicy sausages, "hot links" on the Internet are places on a Web page that contain jumps to other Web pages, files, and online services. A link may be a word or phrase in a block of text, a graphic image such as a picture of a push-button, or an image map that contains links to several different URLs, depending on the exact location within the image map. Figure 5.3 shows a Web page with several links.

When you move your cursor over a link, the cursor changes to a pointing finger, and the destination of the link appears in the status bar at the bottom of the Internet Explorer window, as shown in Figure 5.4. To jump to that URL, click on the link.

Internet Explorer displays text links in a different color from other text. If an entire picture or other image is a link to another Web site, you may see a colored border around the image.

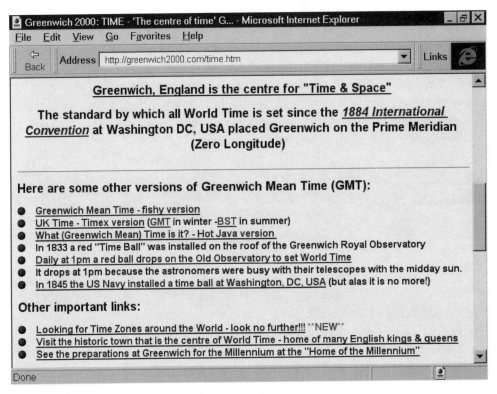

FIGURE 5.3: Click on a link to jump to another Web page.

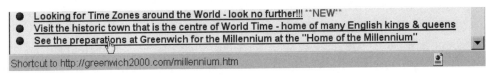

FIGURE 5.4: When you move the cursor over a link, the destination appears in the status bar.

Returning to Sites You've Recently Visited

After you have viewed a Web page, Internet Explorer stores a copy in a temporary folder, so you can return to that page without needing to wait for another download. This is very convenient, because Internet Explorer can load and display a file from your hard drive a lot more quickly than it can transfer it from a distant server. However, there are two possible drawbacks to this technique: if the original Web page has changed since the original download, you won't see the changes, and you're filling up your hard drive with Web pages.

Fortunately, there are ways to work around both of these problems. The Advanced Options dialog box includes a Temporary Internet Files settings button that opens the dialog box shown in Figure 5.5.

The Settings dialog box includes these options:

- **Check for Newer Versions of Stored Pages:** When the Once Per Session option is active, Internet Explorer will obtain a new (and possibly updated) copy of a Web page the first time you request it during an operating session, even if there's a copy of that page in the Temporary folder. When the Never option is active, Internet Explorer will always use the file in the Temporary folder. To check for a new version of a Web page you've already seen, click on the Refresh button in the command toolbar or the View menu.

- **Amount of Disk Space to Use:** Move the slider to the left to reduce the maximum size of the Temporary Internet Files folder, or to the right to increase the maximum size of the folder.

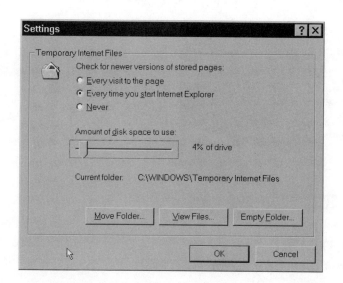

FIGURE 5.5:
Use the Settings dialog box to control the way Internet Explorer uses temporary Internet files.

- **Move Folder:** Click on the Move Folder button to change the path of the folder that contains your temporary files.
- **View Files:** Click on the View Files button to open your Temporary Internet Files folder. To view a file in a new Internet Explorer window, double click on the name of that file.
- **Empty Folder:** Click on the Empty Folder button to delete all the files in your Temporary Internet Files folder.

Using the History Folder

Whenever you view a Web site, Internet Explorer adds a shortcut to that site to the History folder. You can use these shortcuts to return to Web sites you've recently visited. There are two ways to display the contents of the History folder:

- Click on the down-arrow at the right side of the address field in the toolbar. Select the URL you want to revisit to jump to that site.
- Open the Go menu and select the Open History Folder command. Select a shortcut to jump to that site.

Moving Forward and Backward

Internet Explorer uses the History list to identify backward and forward links. Use the Back Command in the toolbar or in the Go menu to return to the Web page from which you jumped to the current page. Use the Forward command in the toolbar or the Go menu to repeat the last jump you made from the current site.

TIP	The Back command is particularly useful when you try to follow a series of links, but you discover that you've reached a dead end—either a link to a site that's no longer available or a site that doesn't have any links that you want to follow. You can retrace your steps to return to a page with other links that you want to follow.

Using More Than One Window at a Time

Normally, when you click on a link or enter a URL in the address bar, Internet Explorer loads the new page into the same window. But sometimes it's convenient to keep the current page visible while you open a new page in a separate Internet Explorer window.

For example, you might want to read the text in one window while you wait for the next one to load, or you might want to keep one eye on a page that automatically updates the score for the big game, while you conduct other online business in a second window.

To open another copy of the current Web page in a new window, select the New Window command in the File menu.

To jump to a new Web page and load it into a new window, follow these steps:

1. Move your cursor over the link to the Web site you want to visit.

2. Press your right mouse button to display the right-click menu.

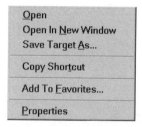

3. Select the Open in New Window command.

The new window works exactly the same as the existing one. Once it's open, you can use the address field, the Favorites list, the History list, and other navigation tools to move around the Web, while keeping an earlier page visible in the other window.

NOTE If you have more than one Web browser program installed on your computer, the Open in New Window command will start your default browser, even if it's not Internet Explorer.

Start Pages and Home Pages

Every time you start Internet Explorer, the program will automatically load and display the page that you have specified as your Start Page. Almost every other Web browser calls this the home page, and that's probably what you'll see it called online. The icon on the Open Start Page command button in the Internet Explorer toolbar is a little house marked "Home," so it would appear that Microsoft's designers also think of the Start Page that way.

Unfortunately, *home page* also has another meaning: it's a page that an individual or organization uses to provide pointers to other related pages or files. For example, many people have created home pages that contain links to information about their hobbies, favorite entertainers, and other interests. Businesses frequently have home pages with links to separate pages about each of their products or divisions.

Choosing a Start Page

Your Start Page is the first Web site you will see every time you start Internet Explorer, so it's a good idea to choose a page that contains information you can actually use, rather than one that has nothing but advertisements for products and services that you may not ever want to use. You should replace the Internet Explorer default Start Page with one of these options:

- Microsoft's Custom MSN Start Page option.
- A home page from another online information provider, such as GNN's Whole Internet Catalog (http:www.gnn.com/wic/index.html) or PC/Computing's Web Map (http:www.zdnet.com/pccomp/java/webmap/).
- One of the online search tools described later in this chapter, such as Yahoo, Lycos, AltaVista, or search.com.
- Your own home page with links to your favorite sites, using an HTML editor, such as the free Internet Assistant add-ons, Excel, and other application programs to Microsoft Word. You can download Internet Assistant from the Microsoft Office Web site at http://www.microsoft.com/msword/fs_wd.htm.

Changing Your Start Page

To change the Start Page, follow these steps:

1. Jump to the page you want to use as your Start Page.
2. Open the View menu and select the Options command.
3. Click on the Navigation tab to display the dialog box shown in Figure 5.6.
4. Choose the Start Page option in the Page field.
5. Click on the Use Current button in the Change Address box to define the current page as your Start Page.

Creating a Custom MSN Start Page

Internet Explorer's default Start Page is http://www.msn.com, as shown in Figure 5.7. Microsoft offers a free service that can add your choice of links to up to half a dozen of your favorite Web sites, and links to news, weather, sports, ski conditions, a daily cartoon,

FIGURE 5.6:
Use the Navigation tab of the Options dialog box to change your Start Page.

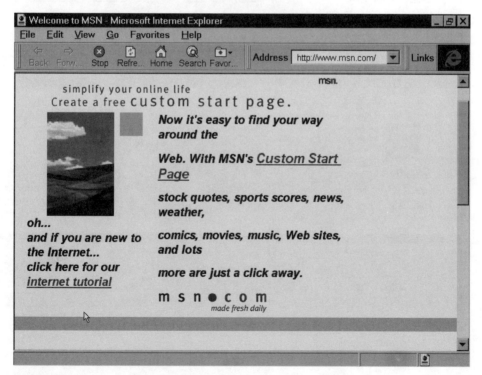

FIGURE 5.7: The default Internet Explorer Start Page is www.msn.com.

and other possibly useful or entertaining information, plus input fields to one or more online search engines.

To customize your Start Page, follow these steps:

1. Start Internet Explorer.

2. If it's not your home page, jump to http://www.msn.com. The MSN home page will appear.

3. Click on the Start Page link. The Custom Options page will appear.

4. You can use the Custom Options page to add the features and functions listed in the following table to your version of the MSN Start Page.

5. When you have selected all of the items you want to see in your Start Page, click on the Set Up Page button at the bottom of the Custom Options page. Figure 5.8 shows part of a customized Start Page.

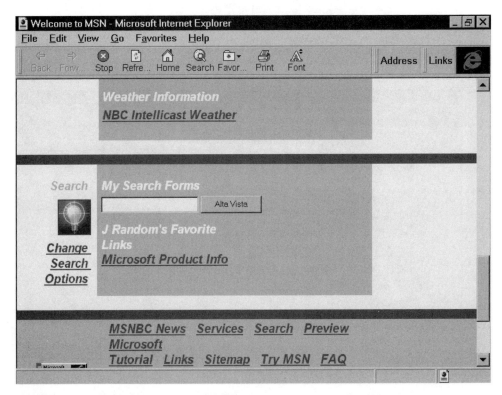

FIGURE 5.8: Customized Start Pages contain links to Web sites chosen by each user.

Feature or Function	Description
Favorite Links	Use the Favorite Links fields to add jumps to up to half a dozen URLs that you expect to visit frequently. For each entry, choose the type of URL (http, ftp, or whatever) from the drop-down list in the left-hand column. Type the site's address in the middle column, and a brief description in the right column. Your Start Page will use the text of the description in the list of links.
Search Forms	Search Forms are online databases that you can use to find Web sites and other Internet resources. It's a good idea to include search fields for one or two of these services in your Start Page. You can find more detailed information about search tools later in this chapter.
Stock Quotes	If you want to use the Internet to keep track of your stocks or other investments, type the ticker symbols of the stocks you want to follow in one or more of the Stock Quotes fields. Your Start Page will include links to a page that contains recent prices for these stocks.
Sports Scores	Click on the box next to the name of a league to add links to recent scores to your Start Page.
News	Choose one or more categories of news to include links to the latest stories from Reuters or Ziff-Davis.
TV	Click on your time zone to add a link to a schedule of television programs to your Start Page.
Comic Strips	Click on the name of one or more comic strips to include links to recent episodes on your Start Page.
Weather Information	You have the choice of either placing a link to a weather map on your Start Page or displaying the map itself. If you prefer, you can choose a local forecast.
Ski Reports	If you select one or more states, provinces, or countries from the drop-down lists, your Start Page will include links to reports of current ski conditions within that locale. Along with well-known ski resorts in Vermont, Utah, and Colorado, you can include some unlikely places like North Dakota, Kansas, Indiana, and Rhode Island. Apparently, there really are ski resorts in all those places.
Web Picks	Web Picks are links to interesting or unusual Web sites, or those whose owners have paid to be listed. Microsoft changes their Web Picks every few days.
MSN Today	Click on the MSN Today box to include links to special events on Microsoft's online information service.
Movie Link	Select Movie Link to include a link to a list of movies that are playing in theaters near you.
Music Clip	If you have a sound card and speakers in your PC, you can play a musical selection when you open your Start Page.

Feature or Function	Description
Graphics	If you have a high-speed connection to the Internet, you can choose High Graphics to display your Start Page with complex graphics and animated images. If you're using a modem and dial-up telephone line, Medium or Low graphics are better choices.
Background Color	Choose the color you want to use as a background for the customized links in your Start Page. As a rule, light background colors are your best choice.
Text Color	Choose a contrasting color for the text on your Start Page. Dark letters on a light background are easiest to read.
Viewed Link Color	A viewed link is a link to a site that you have recently visited. Choose the color you want your Start Page to use for viewed links.
Unviewed Links Color	An unviewed link is a link to a site that you haven't recently visited. Choose the color you want your Start Page to use for unviewed links.
Welcome	Select the Welcome option to include a message in your Start Page that greets you by name. (This seems like a complete waste of space, but if it amuses you, go ahead and use it.)
Personal Info	The Start Page uses the name and address that you type in the Personal Info fields to retrieve your local weather forecasts, movie information, and so forth. If you want Microsoft to send you announcements of new services and other electronic junk mail, fill in your e-mail address and place a checkmark in the Add Me to Your Mailing List box.

Tips on Customizing Your Start Page

There's no particular reason to create a list of Favorite Links in your Start Page rather than using the Favorites menu. Since you can open the Favorites menu at any time, even if your Start Page is not visible, it might be faster and easier to choose an item from the menu instead of returning to your Start Page.

If you're really serious about tracking your investments, you might want to try a program that updates and displays stock quotations in a separate window rather than adding a stock quotes link to your Start Page. You can find pointers to about half a dozen stock quote programs through TUCOWS (www.tucows.com).

If your computer has a sound card and speakers, you might be tempted to include a short piece of music that will play whenever you open your Start Page. This may seem like a clever idea at first, but you will probably want to turn it off after about the third or fourth time you've heard the same tune. If you're using the program in an office, you probably won't want to broadcast to everybody within earshot every time you start browsing the Word Wide Web (and it's a safe bet that they won't want you to do so).

Using Internet Search Tools

The World Wide Web resembles a huge library where all the books are arranged by size and color. You may stumble across a lot of interesting things by accident, but without a catalog to tell you exactly where to look for a specific item, specific information is extremely difficult to find. In the library, you can search for a book by looking up the title or subject in a catalog or by asking a librarian for help. Internet search tools serve a similar purpose.

When you look for, say, a Hebrew dictionary in a library catalog, you will discover that the Dewey Decimal number is 492.43. Since the librarian places books on the shelves in numerical order, you'll find Hebrew books (492.4) between books about Balto-Slavic languages (491.8) and those about the Arabic language (492.7). Once you know where to look, that dictionary is easy to locate.

On the Internet, URLs serve the same purpose as the library's shelf numbers. And like the library catalog, the Internet's search tools can point you to the item you want to find.

Most Web search tools work in a similar manner: you type the words you want to search for and click on a Search button. The search engine looks for those words in a database and displays a list of URLs that match your request, with links to each one. To examine a possible match, click on the link. If that's not what you want, click on the Back button to return to the list and try another item.

There are about two dozen major general-purpose Internet search tools, and a couple hundred more specialized ones. Each uses a somewhat different set of rules to conduct its search, and each will give you a different list of URLs in response to a request. Some tools search for individual pages, others will take you to entire sites, and still others search through the text of each page rather than limiting their searches to titles or keywords. Some include subjective reviews or ratings of individual sites, while others list everything they find.

As a result, the same search through several different services can produce radically different results. For example, a search for the keywords *"Joseph Conrad"* produced 244 hits with Yahoo, 4351 with Lycos, and about 30,000 with AltaVista. A search for *"Andrew*

Jackson" produced 55 hits using Lycos, 231 with Open Text, and "about 2000" matches with AltaVista.

WARNING The links that a search tool identifies are not always useful, especially when you enter more than one keyword, because some search engines include partial matches that include just one word in the search phrase. For example, a search for "Andrew Jackson" using the Magellan search engine produced 85 matching links. However, only one of the first ten had anything to do with the seventh President; the other nine were pointers to a Web page about the Jackson State University Computer Science Department, Steve Jackson Games, and singers named Alan Jackson, Michael Jackson, and Joe Jackson.

If you're looking for a popular Web site, you can probably find it with almost any search engine. But if you want everything related to a specific subject, you should perform the same search through several different services.

Jumping to a Search Tool

Internet Explorer makes it easy to jump to the search tool of your choice, or to a Web page that contains links to several different search tools. When you select the Search the Internet command in the Go menu, or click on the Search button in the toolbar, the program opens the URL specified as your Search Page in the Start and Search Pages Options dialog box.

The default Internet Explorer Search Page is located at Microsoft's msn.com Web site. As Figure 5.9 shows, this page contains links to five popular Internet-wide search engines, and another that limits its searches to Microsoft Web pages.

The default page is about as good a starting point as any, although it doesn't include one of the largest and best of the current batch of search tools, Digital's AltaVista (www.altavista.digital.com), which conducts full-text searches in more than 21 million pages. One excellent alternative to the MSN page is c|net's search.com (http://www.search.com), shown in Figure 5.10, which contains links to more than 250 separate search engines.

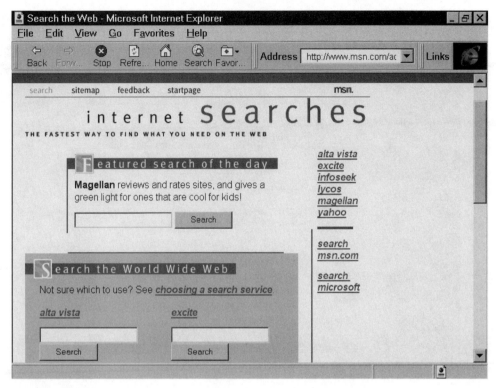

FIGURE 5.9: The default Search Page has links to half a dozen separate services.

Changing Your Search Page

To change your designated Search Page, follow these steps:

1. Jump to the page you want to use as your Search Page.
2. Open the View menu and select the Options command.
3. Click on the Navigation tab.
4. Open the drop-down menu shown in Figure 5.11.
5. Click on Search Page.
6. Click on the Use Current button.

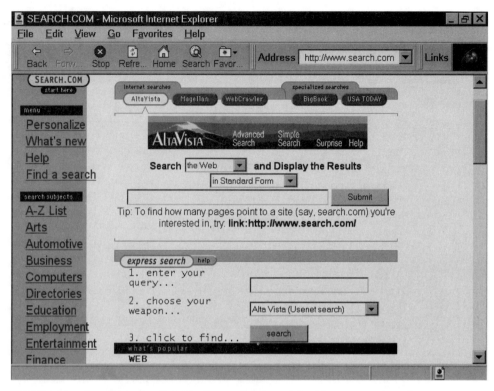

FIGURE 5.10: Search.com is a directory of general and specialized Internet search engines.

FIGURE 5.11:
Select Search Page
from the drop-down list.

Jumping to Favorite Pages

Favorite pages are Web sites that you have included in your own list of URLs that you want to visit again. Netscape and most other Web browsers call these lists "bookmarks." To return to a page, open the Favorites menu and select the listing for the page you want to see.

You can also create shortcuts to Web sites on your Windows desktop or Start menu. When you click on a shortcut, Internet Explorer opens and automatically loads the page you requested. You can find information about working with favorite pages and shortcuts in Chapter 7.

After you learn how to use the navigation tools in this chapter, you should be able to find just about anything on the Internet. But there's more to the World Wide Web than just jumping between URLs. In the next chapter, you will find out how to use more complex Web pages with interactive elements, and how to send information back to a Web server.

Chapter 6

WORKING WITH INTERACTIVE WEB PAGES

- **Filling in text fields**
- **Choosing checkboxes**
- **Selecting from radio button options**
- **Choosing from drop-down menus and scrollbar lists**
- **Using Submit and Reset buttons**
- **Playing interactive games**

The simplest Web pages contain text, maybe a picture or two, and links to other Internet sites. But many Web designers have built additional features into their designs that allow you, as a visitor to their site, to send information back to the Web server. Some Web sites use these features to obtain information from visitors, such as their names and e-mail addresses; others provide remote access to other programs that run on the same computer as the server, or on other computers connected to the server through a LAN. As a category, these interactive Web tools are called *forms*.

Forms make it possible to do a lot more through the Web than just reading text, looking at pictures, and jumping to other pages through hot links. Among other things, you can search for other Internet files and services; obtain airline schedules and make flight reservations; order books, flowers, and computer equipment from online retailers; and play games with a computer or with other human players. One of the most common uses of fill-in-the-blank forms in Web pages is a space where you can send the server your credit card number or password, so the people who run the Web site can charge you for the information or services they supply.

In Internet Explorer, most forms on Web pages look like the options and commands you see in Windows dialog boxes. In this chapter, you will learn how to work with the most common types of forms that appear in Web pages.

Text Fields

A text field is a space where a user can type a string of characters that the browser will send back to the server. You will see many Web pages that instruct you to enter your name or password, or the keywords for a database search, into a short text field to obtain access to additional information. Other pages have larger text fields where you can type a brief message to the people who maintain the Web site.

For example, Figure 6.1 shows part of the United Parcel Service (UPS) Package Tracking page. You can use this Web page to find the current location of a shipment by typing the UPS tracking number in the text field. When you click on the Track This Package button, Internet Explorer will send the tracking number to UPS, where the server will pass it along to another computer that contains records of every package in the UPS system. That computer returns a customized report to the server with the specific information you requested, and the server sends it back to you.

World Wide Web search tools are another place where Web designers use text fields. In the search page, shown in Figure 6.2, each of the text fields is a link to a different destination. When you type a keyword into one of the text fields and click on a Search button. Internet Explorer sends your request to the specific search engine you requested; the destination doesn't have to be on the same server that sent you the Web page that contains the form.

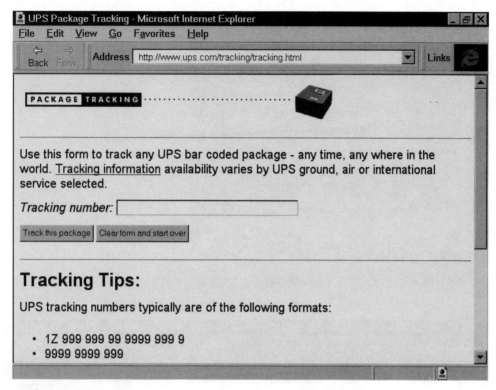

FIGURE 6.1: To send data back to a Web server, type it into a text-entry field.

Checkboxes

Checkboxes are multiple-choice options; you can select as many as you want. When you click on a checkbox, Internet Explorer will place a checkmark in the box. Click again to remove the checkmark.

For example, Figure 6.3 shows part of the online *Time-Life Garden Encyclopedia*. The Virtual Garden uses the checkbox options to recommend specific flowers and plants that meet the criteria you requested.

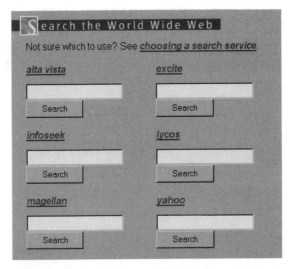

FIGURE 6.2: Each of the search text fields sends a search request to a different destination.

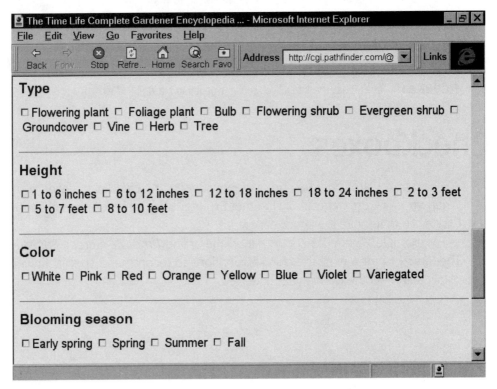

FIGURE 6.3: Click on a checkbox to make an option in a Web page active.

Radio Buttons

Radio buttons are like the buttons on your car radio: you can select only one option at a time. In any group of radio buttons, there's always one, and only one, active option. When you click on a radio button, you automatically turn off the previously selected option.

Unlike checkboxes, which are square, Internet Explorer shows radio buttons as circles. The currently active button has a dot inside the circle.

For example, Figure 6.4 is part of MSN's Custom Options configuration page. Because you can select only one item from each group of options, the radio buttons limit your choice to just one selection in each group.

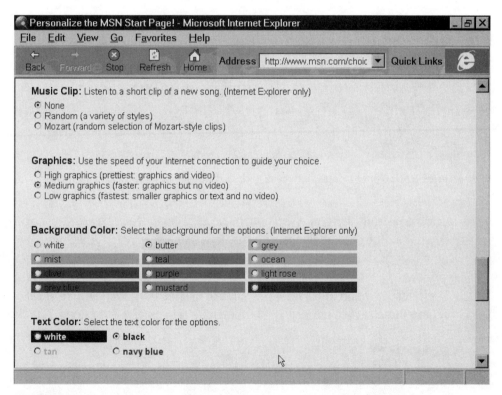

FIGURE 6.4:   One radio button in every group of buttons is always active.

Drop-Down Menus and Scrollbar Lists

Sometimes a Web page designer may want to offer a long list of options without taking up the space on the page that a radio button for each option would fill. There are two kinds of list forms that can squeeze many choices into a tight space: drop-down menus and scrollbar lists.

A drop-down list displays the currently selected option in a box, like the example in Figure 6.5, which is taken from an online airline reservation service. When you click on the arrow button next to the box, a menu of other options appears. To change the active option, click on the one you want.

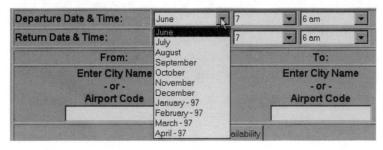

FIGURE 6.5: To open a drop-down menu, click on the button at the right of the menu field.

Scrollbar lists display only a few options on the Web page but allow you to move up or down the list to see additional choices. To make a selection, highlight the item you want; if it's not visible, click on the up- and down-arrow buttons, or drag the scrollbar up or down.

The scrollbar menu in Figure 6.6 is a list of airlines from the same reservation service. Only three airlines are visible, but the entire list contains more than 200 choices.

FIGURE 6.6:
Use the arrow buttons or the scrollbar to move up and down a scrollbar list.

Submit and Reset Buttons

When you click on an option or choose an item in a menu, you're working with the copy of the current Web page that you downloaded from a server to your own computer. In other words, the server doesn't receive any of your input until you instruct your computer to transmit the data. Therefore, every Web page that uses interactive forms includes at least one Submit button (it doesn't always say "Submit" on the button, but that's the default name). Until you click on that button, the information in the forms doesn't go anywhere. Figure 6.7 shows the Submit buttons in several interactive Web pages.

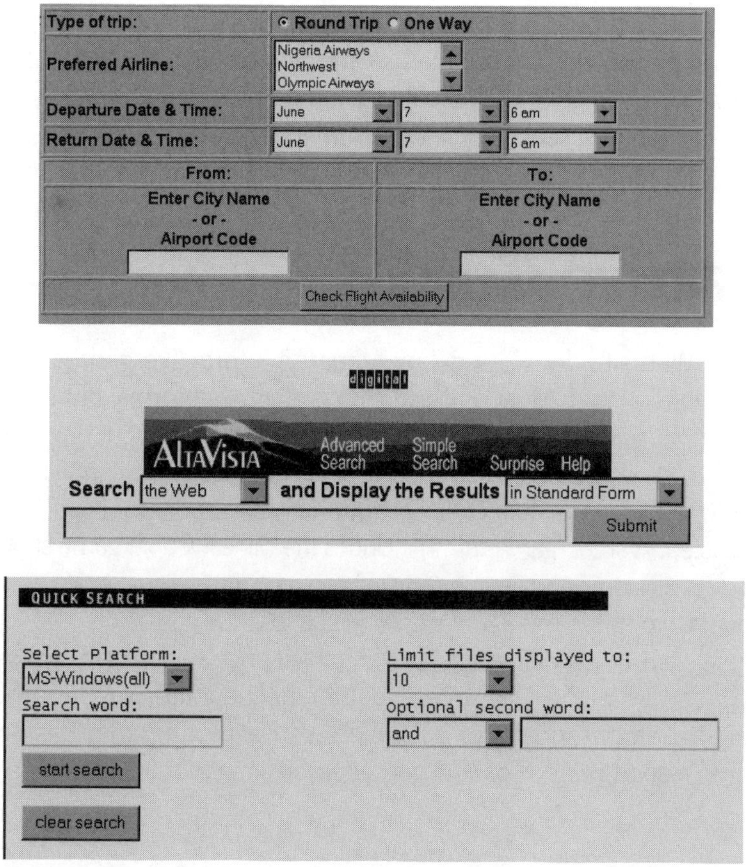

FIGURE 6.7: Click on the Submit button to send your filled-in form back to the server.

Some Web pages have more than one Submit button, especially if they contain forms that send information to different servers. That's how a Web site like search.com is able to let users send requests to several search engines from the same page. Assuming the page is organized reasonably well, it should be obvious which button is associated with a particular set of forms.

Until you click on the Submit button, you can edit text fields and mess around with other types of form fields to your heart's content. But sometimes, especially in a long and complicated questionnaire, you might want to cancel everything and start over again. That's what the Reset button is for. Most considerate Web page designers include a Reset button (which, like the Submit button, may have a label other than "Reset") in all their forms. When you click on a Reset button, Internet Explorer deletes everything in the form that contains the button, so you've got a clean slate to start over again. It does not send anything back to the server.

You might also want to use the Reset button when you use the Back command to return to a Web page after you have sent a request for information to the server. For example, if your first search for information from a database doesn't give you the information you want, you can return to the search page to try another set of keywords.

Interactive Games

Many Web site developers have created interactive games that you can play through the Internet. Most of these games don't use forms, but they're "interactive" because the server responds to your actions by uploading a new screen when you "move" by clicking on the game board, or entering characters into a blank field.

For example, the collection of interactive Web games at Boston University (www.bu.edu/games/games.html) includes the Minesweeper game shown in Figure 6.8. When you click on a square, the server shows you if there's an explosive mine under it. If you guess wrong, the mine blows up, and you lose the game.

There's not much difference between this Minesweeper game and the version on the Windows 95 CD-ROM, except that the online Minesweeper sends your moves hundreds or thousands of miles (unless you're playing from Boston), and it takes longer to respond. Even so, it's a good demonstration of an interactive game.

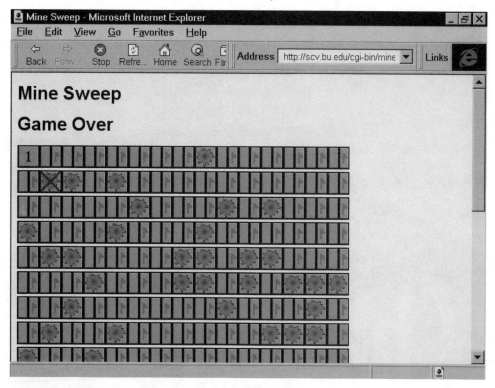

FIGURE 6.8: The World Wide Web version of Minesweeper

Over time, more complicated and sophisticated games and other interactive services are certain to appear on Web sites. As ActiveX extensions and Java programs become more common, Web site developers will create animated action games and interactive application programs that allow you to run programs across the Web as if they were located on a local computer.

Moving between Web sites and returning data to a server through forms and other interactive pages, using the techniques described in this and the previous chapter, are the two most basic functions you need to understand in order to navigate the World Wide Web with Internet Explorer. In the next chapter, you can learn how to create a list of your favorite Web sites and set up shortcuts from the Windows desktop directly to Web pages.

Chapter 7

RETURNING TO FAVORITE WEB PAGES

FEATURING

- **Adding Web pages to the Favorites list**
- **Managing your Favorites list**
- **Creating your own hot list page**
- **Creating shortcuts to Web pages**

As you wander around the World Wide Web and other parts of the Internet, you will discover sites that you want to revisit later. You could write down the URL of each site on a notepad, and then retype it into Internet Explorer's address field every time you want to return to that site, but that approach is both tedious and messy. There's an easier way—you can use shortcuts to interesting Web sites.

In fact, there are two easier ways. You can create a list of links to your favorite pages that you can open from within Internet Explorer, or you can place shortcuts to Web sites on your desktop or Start menu, just like shortcuts to programs and files located on your own hard drive. In this chapter, we'll talk about using both of these techniques.

Working with the Favorites List

When you come across an interesting Web page, you can save a link to that page by adding it to your list of Favorites. Later, you can return to that page by opening the list and clicking on the name of the page.

For example, the Web page at www.unitedmedia.com/comics/alleyoop contains a daily installment of Alley Oop, the comic strip about a caveman, as shown in Figure 7.1. The syndicate posts a new strip to the Web every day, one week after it appears in newspapers. If you want to follow the story, you'll probably return to the Oop site every few days, so this page is a prime candidate for your Favorites list.

FIGURE 7.1: The Alley Oop Web site contains a new episode every day.

> **NOTE**
>
> In Netscape and other Web browsers, this list of sites that you want to revisit is called a *bookmark list*. A Web page that suggests that you "bookmark this site" is encouraging you to add it to your Favorites list.

Adding Items to the Favorites List

To add the current Web page to your Favorites list, follow these steps:

1. Open the Favorites menu.

Add To Favorites...
Organize Favorites...

2. Select the Add To Favorites command.

If you prefer, you can use the menu that appears when you click with your right mouse button. When you use the right-click menu to add an item to your Favorites list, the exact location determines whether you will add the current page or a link on the current page to the Favorites list:

- If your cursor is over a link when you right-click, you will add the destination of that link to your list, rather than the current page.
- If you right-click on a picture or other graphic, you will add that image to the list without the rest of the current Web page.
- If the cursor is over any other part of a page, you will add the current page to your list.

Opening the List

Now that you have added some Web sites to your Favorites list, how do you return to those sites? You can open the list from the menu bar or the toolbar. Either way, you will see a menu like the one in Figure 7.2. To return to one of the sites on your list, click on the name of that site.

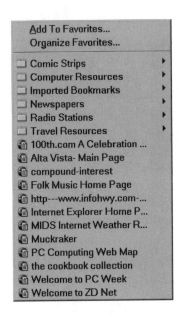

FIGURE 7.2:
Select an item from your
Favorites list to jump to
that site.

If your list has too many entries, the bottom of the list might run off the screen. When that happens, you can display the whole list by clicking on the Organize Favorites command at the top of the menu. Rather than keeping everything in one list, you should break it into smaller groups, organized by category. The next section explains how to do that.

Organizing Items in Your Favorites List

Internet Explorer stores shortcuts to each item on your list of favorite Web sites in a Windows 95 folder called Favorites. Like other Windows 95 folders, the Favorites folder can contain an unlimited number of items, which you can display in The Organize Favorites dialog box as either a list of titles or a detailed list.

> **TIP**
>
> Internet Explorer can open and display local files (including Windows 95 folders) just as easily as it downloads files from the Internet. In fact, all of the pages you see in Internet Explorer are really copies that you have downloaded to your own system. Therefore, the program treats the Favorites folder (which is a subfolder located within the top-level Windows folder, although the exact location doesn't matter) just like any other Web page. You can open this folder (or any other folder on your hard drive or LAN) by typing the path in the Internet Explorer address field.

After you use the Organize Favorites command to display the contents of this folder, you can do most of the same things that you can do from any other Windows 95 folder:

- Open files (which may be shortcuts to Web pages)
- Change the way the program displays the files in the folder
- Add and delete files and subfolders
- Import files or shortcuts to files
- Move files to subfolders
- Change the names of files
- Change the icon assigned to a file

Changing the Appearance of the List

The Organize Favorites dialog box, shown in Figure 7.3, offers two view options: List and Details. To change views, use the buttons at the top of the dialog box.

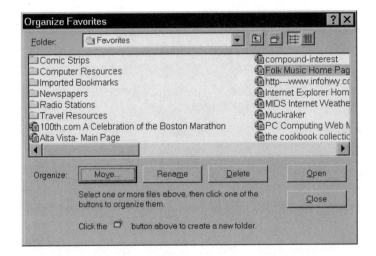

FIGURE 7.3:
The Favorites list can appear as either a list or a set of icons.

TIP
If you use List view, or if you just like messing around with your screen layout, you may want to assign a distinctive icon to each item on the list. See the section "Changing a Web Shortcut Icon" for more information.

Adding Other Items to Your Favorites List

The Favorites list is not limited to Web sites. It can also include shortcuts to any other program, data file, or folder on your own computer or on a computer connected to yours through a LAN. This feature can make Internet Explorer even more flexible.

Here are some of the things you might want to add to your Favorites list:

- Copies of HTML documents or text files stored on your hard drive.
- A shortcut to the Notepad program. When you want to extract text from a Web page, you can select and copy the text, open Notepad, paste the selected text, and save it as a text file.

- A shortcut to the Windows desktop folder (c:\windows\desktop). If you keep shortcuts to frequently used files and programs on your desktop, you can use the Favorites list to open them from within Internet Explorer. If you do create a shortcut to your desktop, you should also use the Shortcut tab in the Properties dialog box to change the shortcut icon to the one shown below.
- A shortcut to your e-mail program, or some other Internet client program.

Creating New Subfolders

Once your list of Favorites reaches about a dozen entries, you should start to think about moving some of them into subfolders. If there are a few Web sites that you expect to revisit more often than others, you can leave shortcuts to those pages in the main Favorites list (or you could create quick links to those sites), and move less frequently used items to subfolders. You can organize your shortcuts whatever way best suits your needs For exampleyou can sort them:

- By topic
- In alphabetical groups (A through D, E through H, and so forth)
- In separate folders for particular types of Web sites, such as FTP archives or news summaries

The Favorites list places folders at the top, with an arrow at the right side of the list window. When you move your cursor over the name of a folder, the submenu appears, as shown in Figure 7.4.

To create a new folder, follow these steps:

1. Open the Favorites list from the Internet Explorer menu bar.
2. Click on the Organize Favorites command.
3. When the Organize Favorites dailog box appears, click on the Create New Folder button.
4. A new folder will appear at the bottom of the list, as shown in Figure 7.5.
5. Type the name you want to assign to this folder, and press the Enter key.

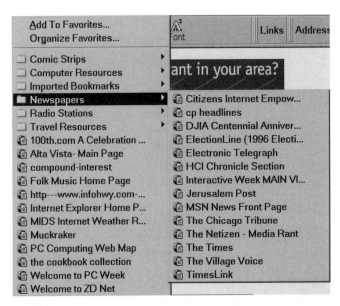

FIGURE 7.4: A submenu appears when you move your cursor over a folder.

The next time you open the Favorites list, the name of the new folder will move to the top of the list, in alphabetical order relative to other folder names. To move an item from the main list to a subfolder, follow these steps:

1. Select the name of the Web page or folder you want to move.
2. Click on the Move button.
3. When the Browse for Folder dialog box appears, select the destination folder and click on the OK button.

When your list gets even larger and more complicated, you might want to consider placing subfolders within subfolders. For example, you might want to create a folder called Travel, with separate subfolders called Airlines, Trains, and Hotels. Or you may want separate Subfolders for each letter within an alphabetical list.

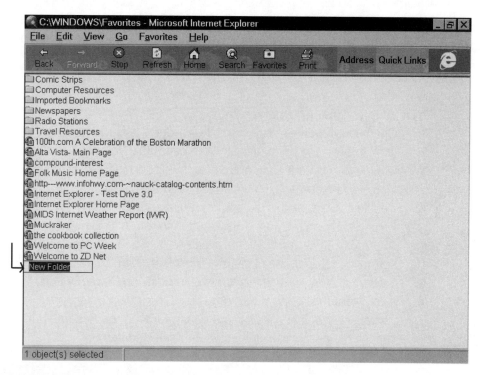

FIGURE 7.5:   The new folder appears at the bottom of the list of Favorite pages.

Cleaning Out the List

So there you are, surfing your way around the World Wide Web, finding all kinds of amusing and interesting Web sites. "Add to Favorites." Click. "Add to Favorites." Click. Click. Click.

The next time you open your list of Favorites, it has dozens of items, most of whose names you don't recognize. And when you select a site, you cannot imagine why you thought it was worth saving in the first place. Did you really think that you would ever want to return to the History of Corn Flakes home page?

It's time to do some serious weeding. If you're never going to use a link, there's no good reason to keep it on your list at all. On the other hand, it's entirely reasonable to maintain a "not-so-hot list" separate from the main folder. You might want to keep this list in a subfolder or in a separate folder with a shortcut from the Favorites list. This secondary list will be just a couple of mouse clicks away, but its contents will be out of the way when you're looking for your daily news updates.

To clean up your list, follow these steps:

1. Open your Favorites folder from the Favorites menu or toolbar.
2. Look through the list for links to Web pages that you don't recognize.
3. Double-click on the entry or icon for the first doubtful item to take one more look at this Web page.
4. Decide if you think this page is important enough to save on your list of Favorites. Then click on the Back button to return to the list.
5. To remove an item from your Favorites list, use the Organize Favorites command to open the Organize Favorites dialog box.
6. Select the item you want to remove and click on Delete button.
7. If you want to keep this item on your list, consider changing the name to something that identifies it more clearly. Click on the Rename button to change the description of the currently selected item.

> **TIP**
>
> As a rule of thumb, your top-level Favorites list should have no more than about 16 or 18 items in it—maybe a few more if you have a larger screen. When the list gets bigger than that, it's time to start moving things to submenus.

Importing a Netscape Bookmark List

In Netscape Navigator, bookmarks serve the same purpose as favorites in Internet Explorer. If you're using Netscape Navigator as well as Internet Explorer, or if you've decided to replace Navigator with the Microsoft program, there's an easy way to transfer your Netscape bookmarks to Internet Explorer. Microsoft has a free utility that will find your Netscape bookmark file and copy its contents to your Internet Explorer Favorites folder.

To find this conversion program, use Internet Explorer to jump to http://www.microsoft.com/ie/download/winbm2fv.exe. After the program downloads, it will start automatically. When conversion is complete, your Favorites list will include your Netscape bookmarks, along with the items that were already in your Favorites folder.

Making Your Own Hot List

The Favorites list is easy to use, but it doesn't tell you much about the Web sites that are listed. If you want to give yourself more information about each link, you might want to create a local Web page with a one- or two-sentence description of your favorite sites. If you place a link to your hot list page in the top level of your Favorites list, you can jump to the hot list with two mouse clicks.

Creating a Hot List Page

The easiest way to create a quick-and-dirty HTML page (and quick and dirty is all you need for your own hot list, since you're the only person who will see it) is to use one of the freeware or shareware HTML editor programs that you can download through the Web. You can find a guide to currently available HTML editors at TUCOWS (The Ultimate Collection of Winsock Software) at http://www.tucows.com and mirror sites around the world. Look for collections of HTML editors for Windows 3.1 and Windows 95 in the Utilities sections.

When you save your HTML hot list, name the file **hotlist.htm**. Figure 7.6 shows a sample hot list set up as a Web page. Each item on the list includes a link to another site and a description of the information or service that's offered at that site. To jump to a site, click on the link, just as you would on any other Web page.

Adding the Hot Link Page to Your Favorites List

When the page is ready to use, follow these steps to add it to your Favorites list:

1. Open the folder that contains the hotlist.htm HTML document.
2. Double-click on the hotlist.htm icon. Internet Explorer will open and load hotlist.htm.
3. Open the Favorites menu and select the Add to Favorites command.
4. When the Add to Favorites dialog box appears, change the name to **A Better Hot List**.

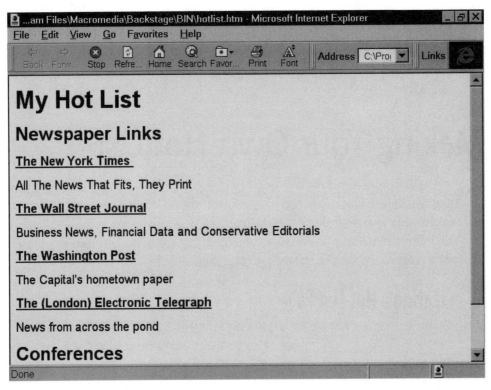

FIGURE 7.6: Use a local HTML document as a hot list with more information than the Favorites folder.

The next time you open your Favorites list, you should see a link to this page at or near the top of the alphabetical list of Web sites, but after all the folders. Click on the link to open the page.

Creating and Using Web Shortcuts

Internet Explorer extends Windows 95's file-management features to files that it downloads through the Internet. Therefore, you can set up shortcuts to Web pages in exactly the same way that you use shortcuts to programs, documents, and data files located on your own hard drive. In fact, the Favorites list and the History list in Internet Explorer are really just Windows 95 folders full of shortcuts to Web sites.

Like other shortcuts, a Web shortcut may be located on your desktop, in any folder, or in your Start menu. When you click on a shortcut to a Web site, three things happen:

- Internet Explorer starts.
- Dial-Up Networking connects your computer to the Internet.
- Internet Explorer downloads a copy of the Web page specified in the shortcut.

The benefit of using a shortcut is obvious: you can go directly to a Web page with just a couple of mouse clicks.

You can create a shortcut to the current Web page, to a graphic file embedded in the current Web page, or to a link on the current page.

Creating a Shortcut to the Current Web Page

To create a shortcut to the current Web page, load the target page in Internet Explorer, and either select the Create Shortcut command in the File menu or move your cursor over a place on the page that is *not* a link or an image, and select the Create Shortcut command from the right-click menu.

When you create a shortcut, Internet Explorer places the shortcut icon on your Windows desktop, as shown in Figure 7.7. You can drag-and-drop the icon from the desktop to any folder or to a diskette, network drive, or other destination, just like any other shortcut.

Changing a Web Shortcut Icon

Internet Explorer uses the same icon for all Web shortcuts, but it's easy to change the icon to something that's related to the contents of the target Web site.

> **TIP**
>
> You can download more extra icons than any rational person could ever want from the file archives at ftp://mjablecki.extern. ucsd.edu/archive/cica/win3/icons/ or ftp://ftp.cdrom.com/pub/ cica/win3/icons/ (these are mirror sites that contain the same files). The index file contains descriptions of each of the files in this archive.

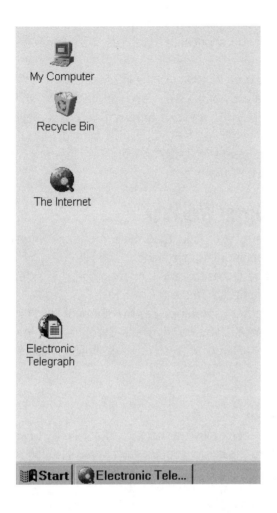

FIGURE 7.7:
Internet Explorer places new shortcuts on the Windows desktop.

Here's the way to change icons:

1. Right-click on the item whose icon you want to change.
2. Select Properties from the right-click menu.
3. Click on the Internet Shortcut tab.
4. Click on the Change Icon button at the bottom of the dialog box.
5. When the Change Icon dialog box, shown in Figure 7.8, appears, choose an alternative from the Current Icon field, or click on the Browse button to find an icon in another file or folder.

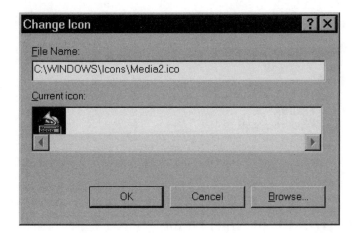

FIGURE 7.8:
Use the Change Icon dialog box to assign a new icon to an item in your list of Favorites.

6. Click on the specific icon you want from the Current Icon field in the Change Icon dialog box. If necessary, use the slider bar at the bottom of the icon display to see additional choices.
7. To use the currently selected icon, click on the OK button.
8. In the Properties dialog box, click on the OK button.

Creating a Web Shortcuts Folder

If you have more than three or four Web shortcuts on your desktop, you might want to place them in a separate Web Shortcuts folder, with a shortcut to the folder on the desktop. Follow these steps to create a new folder:

1. Move your cursor to a blank spot on your desktop.
2. Click the right mouse button and select the New ➤ Folder command. A folder icon like the one in Figure 7.9 will appear.
3. Type **Web Shortcuts** as the new name for this folder.
4. Drag the icons for each of the Web shortcuts you want to place in this folder from the desktop to the folder icon.

Unfortunately, Windows won't let you change a folder icon to something more interesting, so you're stuck with the boring old file folder.

FIGURE 7.9:
Windows assigns an icon
like this one to new folders.

Adding a Web Shortcut to the Start Menu

As you know, you can use the Windows Start menu to open programs, folders, and files. If you don't want to see a bunch of shortcuts on your desktop every time you turn on the computer, the Start menu is another convenient place to hide them.

Start menu commands may be in the main menu that appears when you click on the Start button or in submenus that open when you select a folder in the main menu. In the example here, I've added shortcuts to the main Start menu for the Folk Music Home Page and The Well, along with a folder of shortcuts to Internet client programs.

NOTE	The Well is an online conferencing service based near San Francisco. I changed the icon that connects me to The Well to a picture of the Golden Gate Bridge, because it resembles the view from the place where Well regulars conduct their periodic face-to-face parties.

To add a Web shortcut (or other command) to the top-level Start menu, drag the icon for that command to the Start button.

Adding a Web Shortcut to a Start Submenu

To create a new submenu or to add a command to an existing submenu, follow these steps:

1. Open the Start menu and select Settings ➤ Taskbar.
2. Click on the Start Menu Programs tab to display the dialog box shown in Figure 7.10.
3. Click on the Add button to add new shortcuts to a menu, or on the Advanced button to move existing shortcuts to a different place in the Start menu structure.

Opening Shortcuts from the Keyboard

There's still another way to use a shortcut to start Internet Explorer and jump to a Web site. You can define a set of keystrokes as a keyboard shortcut. Keyboard shortcuts are especially convenient when you're using a word processor, spreadsheet, or other application, because you don't need to take your hands away from the keyboard.

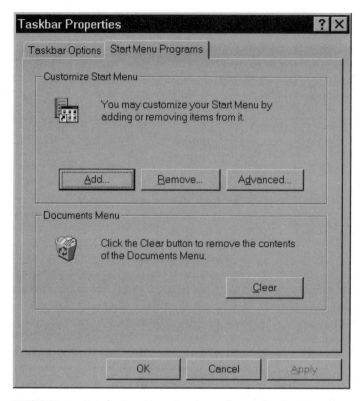

FIGURE 7.10: Use the Start Menu Programs tab to make changes to your Start menu.

Keyboard shortcuts are combinations of the Ctrl key, the Alt key, and almost any other key. When you press all three keys at the same time, Windows will automatically start Internet Explorer and open the Web page assigned to that combination.

To create a keyboard shortcut, follow these steps:

1. Right-click on the Web shortcut icon for which you want to create a keyboard shortcut.

2. Select Properties from the right-click menu.

3. When the Properties window opens, click on the Internet Shortcut tab to display the dialog box shown in Figure 7.11.

4. Move your cursor to the Shortcut Key field.

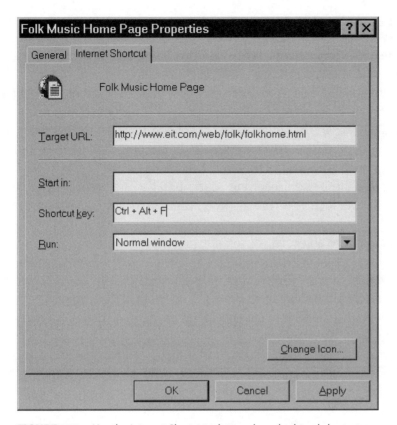

FIGURE 7.11: Use the Internet Shortcut tab to assign a keyboard shortcut.

5. Hold down the Ctrl or Alt key and the letter or other key you want to assign to this shortcut. Even though you don't press both Ctrl and Alt, the keyboard shortcut will require both of those keys. If you plan to use this shortcut with Microsoft Word, don't use Ctrl + Alt + a number key, because those combinations are already assigned in Word.

6. While you have the Internet Shortcut dialog box open, make sure the Run field is set to Normal Window rather than Maximized. When you use the keyboard shortcut from a maximized application program, Internet Explorer will open in a less-than-full-screen window, so you will be able to switch back to the application more easily when you're finished with the Web browser.

7. Click on the OK button.

Sending a Shortcut to Another User

Unlike shortcuts to programs and data files located on your own system, the target addresses of Web shortcuts are universal; you can point to a URL from anywhere on the Internet. Therefore, you can embed a Web shortcut into a document or copy it to a floppy disk and send it to another user. For example, you might want to send a daily or weekly "best of the Web" bulletin to friends and customers, with shortcuts to new or otherwise important Web sites that you want them to see. The recipients can jump to the sites you describe by clicking on the shortcuts within the bulletin. If you and the person receiving your messages are both using an e-mail client that can handle Rich Text Format (RTF), you can include your shortcuts in a message.

To attach a shortcut to an existing document, follow this procedure:

1. Open the document in a word processor such as WordPad or Word for Windows 95.
2. Drag and drop the shortcut icon into the open application window.
3. Use the formatting tools in the application program to control the placement of the icon in the document.

In general, you can treat a Web shortcut just like any other embedded object in a Windows 95 application program. If you haven't worked with embedded objects before, consult the manual and online help for your application.

Creating Shortcuts in Windows 3.1

Technically, there are no shortcuts in Windows 3.1 like the ones in Windows 95. However, you can add a URL to the command that starts Internet Explorer, so it is possible to create an icon in Program Manager that takes you directly to a particular Web page.

Here's the procedure:

1. Create a new Windows program group for your Web shortcuts, or open the existing group where you want to place them.
2. Open the File menu and select the New Command.
3. When the New Program Object dialog box appears, select the Program Item option and click on the OK button.
4. In the Program Item Properties dialog box, shown in Figure 7.12, type the name of the target Web page in the Description field.
5. Click on the Browse button and select the iexplore.exe program file, probably in the iexplore directory.
6. Click on the browser's OK button.

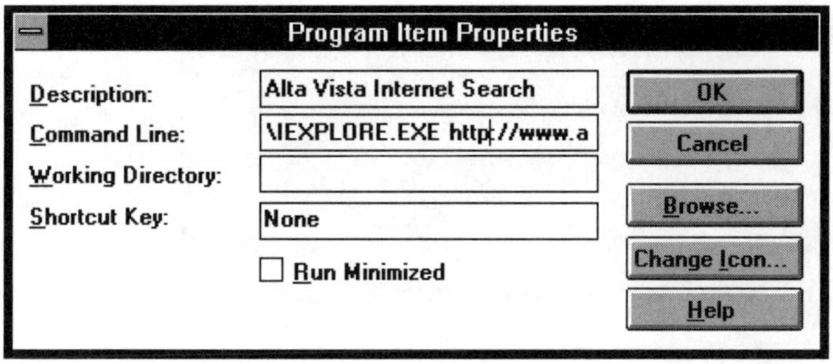

FIGURE 7.12: In Windows 3.1, you can set up a Web shortcut as a program group item.

7. In the Program Item Properties dialog box, move your cursor to the end of the Command line field, which now contains the IEXPLORE.EXE command. Type the full URL of the Web page (or other Internet resource) you want to open with this command.

8. If you don't want to use the default Internet Explorer icon, click on the Change Icon button and select a different icon.

9. Click on the OK button to close the Properties dialog box.

Shortcuts and favorites are convenient methods for returning to Web sites that you visit frequently. You won't use these techniques for every site you ever visit; but when you go back to the same site more than once or twice, adding a favorite or creating a shortcut will save you a bunch of time and trouble.

Changing the Default Browser: A Warning

If Internet Explorer is your only Web browser, you can skip this section. But if you have both Internet Explorer and Netscape Navigator or some other browser loaded on your computer, only one program at a time can be your default browser.

When you open a browser that is not your current default, it will display a message like the ones in Figure 7.13, asking if you want to change the default. As you read the rest of this section, you will understand why you should always make the current browser the default.

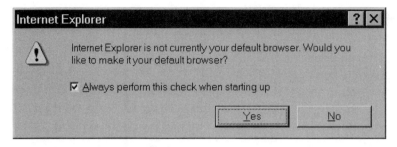

FIGURE 7.13: When you start a browser that is not your default, it will ask if you want to change the default.

The default browser is the program that Windows associates with HTM and HTML files. In other words, the default program is the one that starts when you use a shortcut to a Web page. Just because you used Internet Explorer to create a short-cut, you won't automatically start Internet Explorer rather than some other browser when you select that shortcut. To make things even more confusing, Windows uses the default browser to open Web sites in the Internet Explorer Favorites and History folders.

If the current browser is not the default when you start it, things can get extremely messy. If Internet Explorer is not the default, it will open the default browser when you try to jump to a new Web site. If you open the Favorites folder, you will see an icon for the current default browser next to each item. And in general, things won't always work the way you expect them to work.

The only way to avoid this confusion is to answer "Yes" whenever a browser asks if you want to make that program the default. Just because that browser is not your favorite, you should still make it the default, at least for the moment. This is really not a big deal, because it's so easy to change defaults. Using a non-default browser is just not worth the trouble.

In the next chapter, you can find information about using Internet Explorer to transfer programs, documents, pictures, sound recordings, and other data files across the Internet.

Chapter 8

DOWNLOADING FILES

- **Changing and adding MIME file associations**
- **Saving Web pages to view offline**
- **Downloading files from Web pages**
- **Getting files from FTP archives**
- **Downloading files from gopher servers**

There's more to using Internet Explorer than just visiting Web pages. You can also use the program to transfer programs, documents, and data files from Web sites and other servers to your own computer. Some of these files are accessible through links from Web pages, but many more are in file servers all over the world. In this chapter, you can learn how to find files and download them through Internet Explorer.

Every time you jump to a new Web page, Internet Explorer downloads a copy of a text file encoded in Hypertext Markup Language (HTML). As the Web page arrives at your computer, Internet Explorer uses the HTML codes to figure out how to display the page on your monitor. If the page incorporates pictures or other graphic elements, Internet Explorer downloads them as separate files and places them in the location specified in the HTML document. If the page includes sounds, video clips, or other special files, Internet Explorer plays or displays them along with the text and graphics.

But Web pages are only one of the many types of files that exist on computers connected to the Internet. When you download a file that isn't part of a Web page, Internet Explorer can either store that file on your hard drive or immediately open the file in another application program. For example, if you download a document in Microsoft Word format, you can read it in Word as soon as the download is complete or store it now to use later. When you download an executable program file, Internet Explorer offers you the choice of running the program immediately or storing it.

Associating MIME Types with Application Programs

Internet Explorer uses the same list of registered file types (in Windows 95) or file associations (in Windows 3.1) that Windows uses to handle local files. It combines the MIME (Multipurpose Internet Mail Extensions) method used by most Web browsers with the file-handling system that Windows uses for local files.

As you know, when you open a file, Windows uses the file name extension to identify the program that it will run to open the contents of that file. For example, if you open a .txt file, Windows will run a text editor such as Write or WordPad; if you open an .xls file, it will load that file into Microsoft Excel.

The MIME protocol extends that same approach to the Internet. When you download a file, the server identifies the MIME type to Internet Explorer. As with file name extensions for local files, each MIME type has an application program associated with it. If you download a file that does not have a MIME type attached to it, Internet Explorer will use the application associated with the file's file name extension.

When you download a program or a data file from the Internet, Internet Explorer offers you several choices:

- You can save the file on your hard drive or a floppy disk.
- You can load the contents of the file into the application program associated with its MIME type or file name extension.

- If the file is an executable program (with a .exe or .com file name extension), you can run the program now.
- If no application is attached to this MIME type or file name extension, you can select an application now, either for this download only or for all files with the same MIME type or file name extension.

When you install Internet Explorer, you also add a long list of MIME types to your Windows file associations. The defaults are a good start, but if you add new file viewer applications (such as audio or video players) to your system, you may want to attach those applications to specific MIME types or file name extensions.

For example, you might install a graphic file viewer program such as PaintShop Pro or LView to display and print pictures in formats that Microsoft Paint can't recognize. To automatically open the file viewer when you download an image, you should associate the standard file name extensions for those formats with the viewer program.

Many Windows 95 application programs automatically set up file associations when you install them. Unfortunately, many program developers operate on the assumption that theirs is the latest and greatest, and *of course* you will always want to use their shiny new program rather than one from their competition. If the program is working with a unique format (such as a specialized type of multimedia), this is not a problem; but if it overwrites an existing file association, you may want to manually reset the file association to use the program it used before you installed the new program or instruct Windows to let you choose a viewer each time you download a new file.

Changing an Existing File Association

If you have a favorite file viewer, that's the one you should associate with the appropriate MIME types, even if it's not the original default.

To change a file association, follow these steps:

1. Select the Options command from the Internet Explorer View menu, or the menu that appears when you right-click on the Internet icon on your desktop.
2. When the Options window appears, select the Programs tab and click on the File Types button to display the dialog box shown in Figure 8.1.
3. Select the file type whose association you want to change and click on the Edit button. File types are listed in alphabetical order by description rather than by file name extension.
4. When the Edit File Type dialog box, shown in Figure 8.2, appears, select Open from the list of actions, and then click on the Edit button. You'll see the Editing Action for Type dialog box.
5. Use the Browse button to open a file browser where you can select the

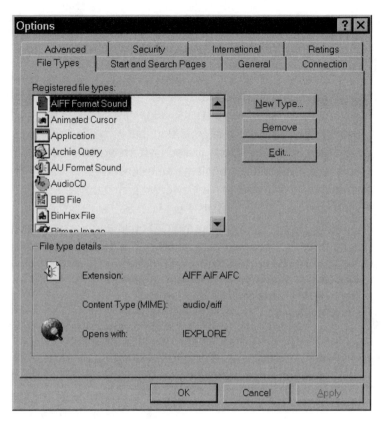

FIGURE 8.1: Use the File Types tab to link applications to files.

program you want to use to open this type of file. Then click on the Open button to close the browser.

6. Confirm that the program you just selected is named in the Application Used to Perform Action field, and then click on the OK button.

7. If you want to change the description that appears in the list of file types, enter the new text in the Description of Type field in the Edit File Type dialog box.

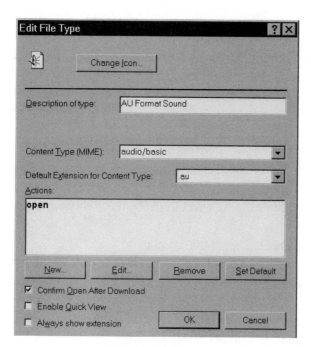

FIGURE 8.2:
Use the Edit File Type dialog box to attach an application to a file type.

8. If there's already a MIME type associated with this file type, the MIME will be named in the Content Type (MIME) field. Don't change it. If no type is specified, look for that MIME type in the drop-down list in the Content Type (MIME) field. If you can't find the MIME type you want in the list, type it directly into the field. Make sure you have the name of the MIME type exactly as it will come from the server. The manual or readme file that came with the program should include information about the MIME type the program expects.

9. If you want Internet Explorer to automatically open every file of this type immediately after it downloads the file, remove the checkmark next to Confirm Open After Download. If you want Internet Explorer to offer a choice of either opening the file right away or saving it to disk, place a check in the box. Don't worry about the other two checkbox options; they don't apply to downloaded files.

10. Click on the OK buttons in the Edit File Type dialog box and the Options dialog box.

Adding a New File Association

In general, it's easier to wait until you download a new file type before you create a file association for that type. When Internet Explorer doesn't recognize the MIME type of a file, it will offer you a choice of either saving the file to a disk or opening the file now. If you instruct Internet Explorer to open the file, you'll need to specify an application program.

Follow this procedure to attach a new file association to a downloaded file:

1. When you download a file for which there's no association, Internet Explorer will first ask if you want to open the file or save it to disk, as shown in Figure 8.3.

2. Click on the Open It button. The Open With dialog box, shown in Figure 8.4, will appear.

3. Type a description of the file type in the Description field.

4. If you want to open this file type with the same application you use for other files, select that program from the list. If the application is not on the list, click on the Other button and choose the program from the file browser.

5. To use the same application program for all files of this type, make the Always Use This Program option active.

6. Click on the OK button to close the dialog box.

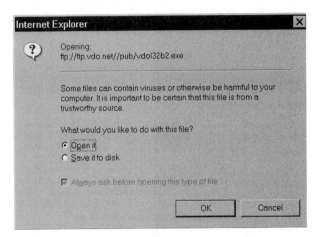

FIGURE 8.3:
Click on the Open It radio button to see the contents of a downloaded file.

When the download is complete, Internet Explorer will load the file into the viewer program you specified. If you know the MIME type used for files with this extension, open the View menu, select Options, and then choose the File Types tab. Click on the

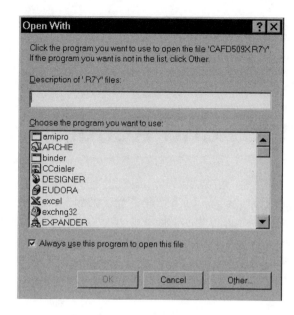

FIGURE 8.4:
Use the Open With dialog
box to attach an application
to a file type.

Edit button, and type the MIME type in the Content Type (MIME) field. If you don't know the MIME type, look in the documentation (such as the user's guide or readme file) supplied with the program.

Finding New File Viewers

When you encounter a file in a new format, you may not discover that you don't have a tool for reading that format until after you have downloaded it. When that happens, you should save the data file and then find a program that recognizes the format.

The first place to look for a program that can read a strange format is on the Web page where you found the file. If there's a link or a graphic that says "click here to download the WhoopieMatic player," go ahead and do it. It will probably take you to the application developer's home page, where you can find instructions for obtaining and installing the program. If you don't see any obvious link to a source for an application program, use one of the Web search services described in Chapter 5 to find what you need.

Pictures and other graphic images are a special case. Internet Explorer includes a built-in viewer for some of the most commonly used graphic formats, but if you find a picture in a more obscure format, you will need an external viewer. Two of the best general-purpose shareware image viewers are Paint Shop Pro, available for download from ftp.jasc.com, and LView, which you can find through the shareware search service at shareware.com (http://www.shareware.com). Both Paint Shop Pro and LView exist in separate versions for Windows 3.1 and Windows 95.

Saving Web Pages and Reading Them Offline

If your Internet service provider charges you for the time you spend online, downloading and saving files and Web pages rather than taking the time to read them while you're connected can help reduce your monthly bill. Reading Web pages offline may be a little awkward when you want to follow a series of links, but it's ideal for reading articles from magazines, newspapers, and other online information sources.

Saving a Web Page

Follow these steps to save a Web page:

1. Jump to the Web page you want to save.
2. Open the File menu and select the Save As File command.
3. Find the folder in which you want to place a copy of this page, or click on the Create New Folder button to place the page in a new subfolder within the current folder.
4. If you created a new folder, change the name of the folder to something that describes the pages you plan to save.
5. Type a file name for this page. Use the file name extension **.htm**.
6. Click on the Save button.
7. Repeat the process for each additional page you want to save.
8. Disconnect your computer from the Internet.

Viewing a Saved Web Page

To read a Web page that you saved earlier, follow these steps:

1. Open the folder where you saved the Web page.
2. Double-click on the icon for the first page you want to see.

Internet Explorer will open and load the local Web page you requested. If you click on a link in the local Web page, Internet Explorer will reconnect to the Internet through your Winsock stack and jump to the destination you requested, just as it would jump from a "live" Web page.

To jump to another local page, type the path and file name in Internet Explorer's address field.

Downloading Files from Web Pages

A link to a downloadable file in a Web page can look exactly like a link to another Web page. Of course, this should not be surprising, because a Web page is really just a specialized type of file.

When you click on a link in a Web page, Internet Explorer uses the MIME type or other file association to determine the action that it will take when the download is complete. Therefore, when you transfer a Web page (which is a text file with a .htm or .html extension), the page opens in Internet Explorer. When you download an audio or video file, Internet Explorer will use an add-on program that may either embed the audio player within the Internet Explorer window or open a separate window with specific controls for this type of file.

But when you want to transfer a file that you don't want to use right away, you must instruct Internet Explorer to save the file someplace on your hard drive rather than loading it into a program. In most cases, these files will be things like documents, pictures, and executable program files. These are the file types that should have the Confirm Open After Download option active.

For example, this is what happens when you download a program file:

1. During the file transfer, you will see the same kind of window that appears when you copy a local file in Windows 95.

2. While the transfer is in progress, Internet Explorer displays the Confirm File Open window shown in Figure 8.5. Click on the Open It radio button to open the file now, or the Save It to Disk button to save the file for later use.

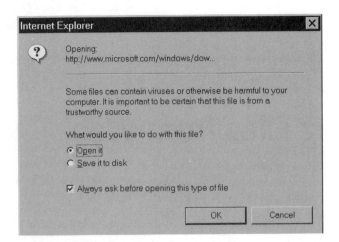

FIGURE 8.5:
The Confirm File Open window provides the choice of either opening or saving a downloaded file.

Downloading Files from FTP Archives

Web pages aren't the only online resources that Internet Explorer can recognize. Among other things, you can also use the program to obtain files from FTP servers. Some Web pages contain links to FTP servers, but you can also reach them directly by typing the server's URL into Internet Explorer's address field. The standard URL format for FTP servers is ftp://*address*.

To move to a different directory or download a file, click on the link to that directory or file, just as you would click on a link in a Web page.

> **TIP**
>
> If you download a lot of files from FTP archives, you should consider using a dedicated FTP client program instead of Internet Explorer, because FTP clients can be faster and easier to use. Chapter 13 contains more information about FTP clients.

Moving around an FTP Archive

Internet Explorer displays the contents of an FTP archive as a list of links to sub-directories and individual files, as shown in Figure 8.6. FTP archives are organized very much like the files-and-folders structure of your own hard drive. If you start at the top-level directory, you will probably see a list of subdirectories, and possibly a file called readme, readme.txt, or something similar. It's always a good idea to download and open a readme file, especially in the top-level directory, because it probably contains a guide to the way the archive is organized, along with descriptions of the other files in the same directory.

Another useful file that shows up in many directories is called index or maybe index.txt. The index file is usually a list of all the files in the current directory, with a brief description of each one. If the title of a file doesn't give you enough information about its contents, you might find more information in the index.

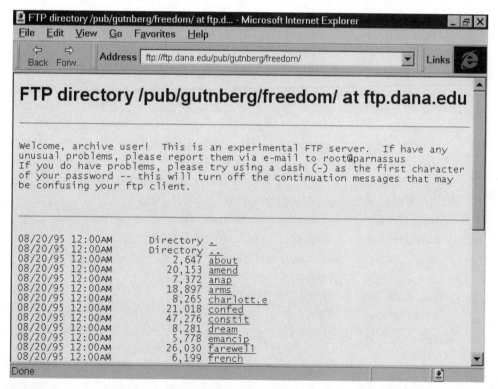

FIGURE 8.6: FTP archives contain files available for download.

Although it's not as common as a readme file or index file, some FTP servers also contain a file called ls-lR in their top-level directories. An ls-lR file contains a complete list of all the directories and files on the server.

Some FTP servers are dedicated computers that do nothing else, but many others are also used by their owners for other purposes, so they refuse access to some files and directories. It's common practice to place the files that are available for public access in the /pub/ directory. If you don't see a directory name that describes the type of files you're looking for, /pub/ is always a good place to start your search.

When you display the contents of a subdirectory, you will see a link at the top of the list with two periods (..) instead of a name. Click on that link to move up one level in the directory structure. If there's no .. in the directory, you're already at the top-level directory.

Finding Files with Archie

There are almost two and a half million files in more than 1500 FTP servers around the world. In other words, there's a huge amount of stuff out there, and you'll need help from a trained native guide in order to find a specific file. If you know the name of the file you want, you can use Archie to locate it.

Archie is a database that contains directories for almost every public FTP archive in the world. Once a month, the master Archie server in Montreal contacts each FTP server and downloads a copy of that server's directory. As it updates the file directory, the master server sends copies to each of the other Archie servers around the world.

To locate a file, you can enter a complete or partial name or keyword into a client program, which will send your request to an Archie server. When the server finds matching file names or descriptions in its database, it returns a list of archives that contain files that match your search terms.

Stand-alone Archie client programs are available for both Windows 3.1 and Windows 95, but it's just as easy to use an Archie gateway service through the World Wide Web. You can find Archie web pages at http://www-ns.rutgers.edu/htbin/archie, and at http://hoohoo.ncsa.uiuc.edu/archie.html. There's a list of other Archie gateways at http://web.nexor.co.uk/archie.html.

As an example, let's try a search through a site that uses ArchiePlex, the most common Web-based Archie search engine, as shown in Figure 8.7. Other Archie forms may look a bit different, but they all ask for the same information.

The ArchiePlex form includes these fields:

- **Search for:** You can use Archie to search for a specific file name, for a partial name, or for a string of characters within a name. You can also use Unix

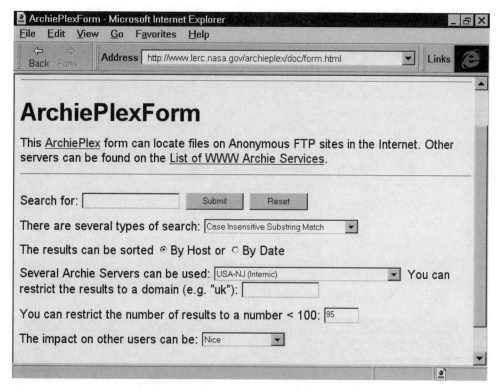

FIGURE 8.7: Use the ArchiePlex request form to search for files in FTP archives.

regular expressions to search for matching patterns (such as *name.** for a file called *name* with any file name extension).

- **Type of search:** Choose the search type from the drop-down list. If you don't know the exact name of the file you want, choose Case Insensitive Substring Match.

- **Sort by:** Choose Sort by Date if you're looking for the most recent version of a file that might be available from more than one site; otherwise, choose Sort by Host so you can download the file from the nearest host.

- **Choose an Archie server:** Use the drop-down list of servers to select the one you want to search.

- **Restrict the results to a domain:** In most cases, you should leave this field blank. It's hard to think of any good reason to limit a search to FTP servers with specific domains.

- **Restrict the number of results:** If you're looking for a specific file, you will probably find it within the first 50 to 100 items. If you're looking for everything that includes a keyword in the file name, leave this field blank.
- **Impact on other users:** This is a goofy way of setting the search priority. Other Archie search forms use a Priority field with Urgent, Standard, Medium, and Low options. Use the Nice or Standard option.

After you have filled in all the fields in the search form, click on the Submit button to send the search request to an Archie server. After a few minutes, you should receive a list of matching files like the one in Figure 8.8. In this case, a search for *oyster* produced pointers to a handful of recipe files located on a server at Columbia University. To download a file, click on the link.

Notice that the list also includes direct links to the directories and hosts that contain the files that match your search terms. This can make it easy to find other files that are related to the one you originally searched for. For example, if you jump to the shellfish directory, you'll find recipes for shrimp, scallops, crab, and other types of shellfish along with the oysters, as shown in Figure 8.9.

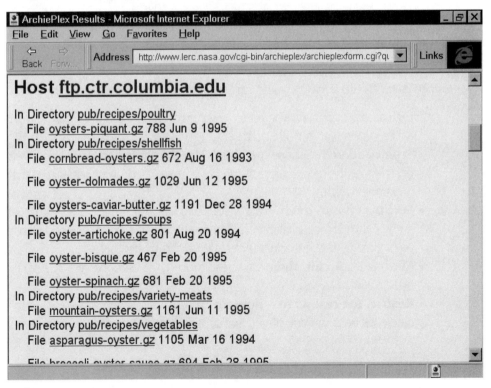

FIGURE 8.8: Archie returns a list of files that match your search terms, with a link to each file.

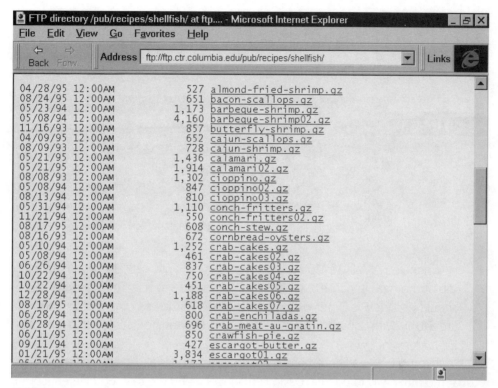

FIGURE 8.9: A directory may contain many files on topics related to the one you originally requested.

Working with Compressed Files

In order to save space on the server and reduce the amount of time needed to transfer files through the Internet, many FTP archives contain files stored in compressed form. Software developers often combine all of the files needed to install and run a program into a single compressed file.

Before you can read a compressed data file or run a compressed program file, you must "uncompress" the file. The most widely used compression format for DOS and Windows files is called zip. However, many files on FTP servers were originally created on computers that use other operating systems, so you may find many other compression formats in FTP archives. For example, the shellfish recipes in the FTP archive at Columbia shown in Figure 8.9 all have a .gz file name extension, which indicates that they use the gnu zip compression format.

To uncompress a compressed file, you must use a utility program such as Stuffit Expander or WinZip. Both of these programs can handle most common formats, including .zip, .arj, .gz, and .lzh. You can find a shareware version of WinZip at http://www.winzip.com, and Stuffit Expander (which is freeware) at http://www.aladdinsys.com.

> **TIP**
>
> **Stuffit and WinZip each has some features that the other lacks. Stuffit Expander can work with some file formats that WinZip doesn't recognize, but it's a little easier to view the contents of a compressed file with WinZip. In the end, either of these programs will probably meet most of your requirements. Your best bet is to download copies of both and see which one you prefer.**

When you install WinZip in Windows 95, it will automatically set up associations for .zip and other file name extensions. If you decide to use Stuffit as your default, you should use the File Types dialog box in either Windows or Internet Explorer to associate Stuffit with .zip and the other file name extensions listed in the About Stuffit Expander window.

If you discover a file compressed with a more obscure format, you may need to find some other way to open it. David Lemson's list of more than 60 different compression formats provides sources for programs that can decode each one. You can download the most recent version of the list from ftp://ftp.cso.uiuc.edu/pub/doc/pcnet/compression.

Downloading Files from Gopher Servers

The first gopher server was established at the University of Minnesota in 1991. Minnesota is the Gopher State, and the University's teams are known as The Golden Gophers, but that's not the only reason the folks in Minneapolis used that name. Like the small furry rodent of the same name, the Internet Gopher tunnels through the Internet to "go fer" files and services on distant computers. Gopher has been overshadowed by the World Wide Web, but it's still a useful tool for exploring the Internet and finding files and other resources related to specific topics.

Working through Gopher Menus

Each item on a gopher menu is a direct link to another menu or to a specific file, Web page, telnet host, directory, database search tool, or other server. Some gopher servers arrange menus by topic; others list all the services within a specific geographic area. Most gopher menus also include one or more links to a higher-level geographic or subject-based menu, so it's almost always possible to move from one menu to any other menu within no more than four or five steps. As with links on Web pages, you can spend hours following gopher threads and examining interesting-sounding files and services.

There are half a dozen or more separate gopher clients for Windows, but you can also use Internet Explorer (or any other Web browser) to move around gopherspace. Figure 8.10 shows a gopher menu in Internet Explorer.

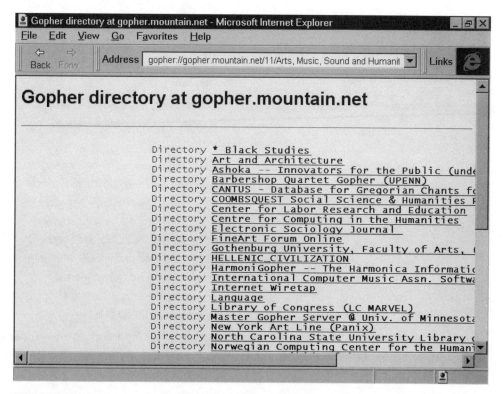

FIGURE 8.10: Gopher menus are organized by topic and geographic location.

Internet Explorer displays items in gopher menus as links. To move to a different menu, or to open a file, click on the link. Gopher servers identify files with MIME types, so Internet Explorer should automatically load data files into viewer programs for you.

Exploring Gopherspace

The original point of the gopher design was to permit anybody with a server to create pointers to resources that visitors might find interesting, entertaining, or useful, regardless of their location. Like Web pages, many gopher menus reflect the interests and prejudices of their creators. Here are some good starting places for exploring gopherspace:

gopher://gopher.tc.umn.edu gopher://gopher2.tc.umn.edu	The gopher menu at the University of Minnesota is the "Mother Gopher" that includes links to every other gopher server in the world.
gopher://gopher.mountain.net	The gopher server at MountainNet includes a large list of interesting sites, organized by topic.
gopher://cwis.usc.edu	Gopher Jewels is a catalog of more that 2000 links to specific items, arranged by subjects.
gopher://gopher.well.com	The Well is an online conferencing service based near San Francisco that attracts partici–pants from all over the English-speaking world. The regulars are about evenly split among journalists, techies, and Deadheads. Most of the items on the Wellgopher are a couple of years old, but many are still interesting. The Internet Outbound topic is an especially good list of links.

The chapters you've read so far contain just about all the information you need to use Internet Explorer. In the next chapter, you can find a complete explanation of Internet Explorer commands and a guide to using them.

Chapter 9

A QUICK GUIDE TO INTERNET EXPLORER COMMANDS

- **Menu bar commands**
- **Right-click menu commands**
- **Toolbar button commands**

This chapter contains explanations of all the Internet Explorer menu and toolbar commands. You've seen some of this information organized differently earlier in this book, but it's all here for convenient reference. You'll also find more detailed information about commands that are described only briefly or not at all in other parts of the book.

File Menu Commands

The File menu contains commands that control the way Internet Explorer works with HTML documents and other files.

New Window

Use the New Window command to open a second Internet Explorer window with the same Web page visible as in the current window. This can be convenient when you want to move quickly between two Web sites, or if you want to move to other Web sites while you download a large file.

Open

Use the Open command to load a local Web page or other file into the currently active Internet Explorer window. When the Open dialog box in Figure 9.1 appears, type the path and name of the file you want to see, or use the Browse button to find the file in a browser.

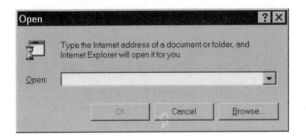

FIGURE 9.1:
The Open dialog box specifies the local file you want to load into Internet Explorer.

Save

The Save command is a standard command in many Windows applications. It instructs the program to save the changes to the current file. However, since you can't use Internet Explorer to change a Web page, the command does nothing. The fact that it's included in the program suggests that a future version of Internet Explorer may offer some kind of Web-page-editing function.

Save As File

Use the Save As File command to store a copy of a Web page or other HTML document on your own system. The Save As File command opens a file browser, which you can use to specify the location where you want to save the local file.

When you use this command, the only thing you actually save is the text and layout information in the HTML document. The pictures and other artwork, as well as any embedded audio or video, are all in separate files, so they won't show up when you open the saved file. Figure 9.2 shows a saved file as it appears in Internet Explorer.

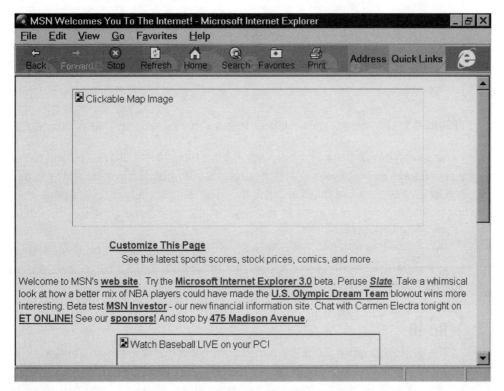

FIGURE 9.2: The Save As File command does not capture pictures along with the text.

There's one more potential problem that may occur when you try to view a saved file: if the original Web page designer used links that identify addresses relative to the current page, rather than full URLs, Internet Explorer will treat those addresses as if they were on the same computer as the saved file. When this happens, the destination address will appear in the status bar as a shortcut to a local file, as shown in Figure 9.3. Notice that the target address begins with "C:\" because Internet Explorer is reading the current page from your C: drive. Since the target file doesn't exist on your hard drive, nothing will happen when you click on one of those links.

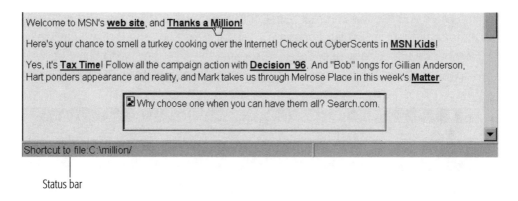

Welcome to MSN's **web site**, and **Thanks a Million!**

Here's your chance to smell a turkey cooking over the Internet! Check out CyberScents in **MSN Kids**!

Yes, it's **Tax Time**! Follow all the campaign action with **Decision '96**. And "Bob" longs for Gillian Anderson, Hart ponders appearance and reality, and Mark takes us through Melrose Place in this week's **Matter**.

Why choose one when you can have them all? Search.com.

Shortcut to file:C:\million/

Status bar

FIGURE 9.3: A relative link assumes that the target file is on the same computer as the current page.

So saving a Web page as a file doesn't store the pictures on a page, and the links in a saved page may not work. What good is this command? It's an easy way to save the text of a Web page, but that's about it. If you're using somebody else's page as a starting point for a page of your own, the Save As command is a good way to capture the HTML code in a text file.

To save a picture or other graphic element embedded in a page, you must use the Save Picture As command that appears when you move your cursor over the artwork and click with the right mouse button.

Send To

The Send To command is the same command that appears in Windows Explorer and in the right-click menu that appears when you select an icon on your desktop. To send a copy of the current Web page or other HTML file to a floppy disk, or any of the other destinations in the submenu, click on the destination.

Page Setup

Page Setup is a Windows 95 command that controls the way Internet Explorer places text or other data on a printed page. The Page Setup dialog box uses the current printer properties for page size, orientation, and paper source as defaults. In most cases, you won't want to change them. Figure 9.4 shows the Page Setup dialog box. The options in the dialog box are described in the following sections.

FIGURE 9.4:
The Page Setup dialog box controls the layout of a printed page.

Paper Size

The Paper Size field contains a drop-down list of standard sheet and envelope dimensions. In North America, the most common page size is 8 ½ x 11 inches. In most other places, the standard is A4 210 x 297 mm. If you're trying to print to a sheet size that isn't on the drop-down list, choose the User-defined Size option.

Paper Source

The Paper Source option tells your printer where to obtain blank sheets of paper. The drop-down list of options includes all possible paper sources for the current printer type.

Orientation

The Orientation option specifies the layout of text and artwork on the page. When the Portrait option is active, the narrow edges of the page are at the top and bottom. When the Landscape option is active, the narrow edges are at the sides, and the wider edges are at the top and bottom. The orientation of the picture in the dialog box shows the current setting.

Margins

The Margins settings control the amount of white space around the sides of your page.

Headers/Footers

Click on the Headers/Footers button to open the dialog box shown in Figure 9.5, which provides space for standard headers and footers that will appear on each printed page.

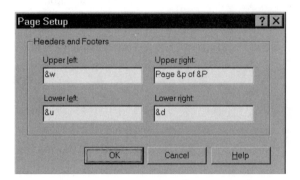

FIGURE 9.5:
Type the text you want to print on every page in the Headers and Footers dialog box fields.

In addition to plain text, you can also use variables to substitute specific information about the current page for the variable codes in the Headers and Footers fields. Internet Explorer recognizes these variable codes:

&w   Window title

&u   URL or local path of the current Web page

&d   Date in short format (*M/D/Y*–10/1/96)

&D   Date in long format (*Month D, Year*–October 1, 1996)

&t   Time of day

&T   Time in 24-hour format

&p   Page number

&P   Total number of pages

To print a single ampersand (&) in a header or footer, type two ampersands (&&).

Printer

Click on the Printer button to instruct Internet Explorer to use a different printer.

Print

Use the Print command to send a copy of the current Web page to your printer. When you enter the Print command, you will see the Windows 95 Print dialog box, with one additional option, as shown in Figure 9.6.

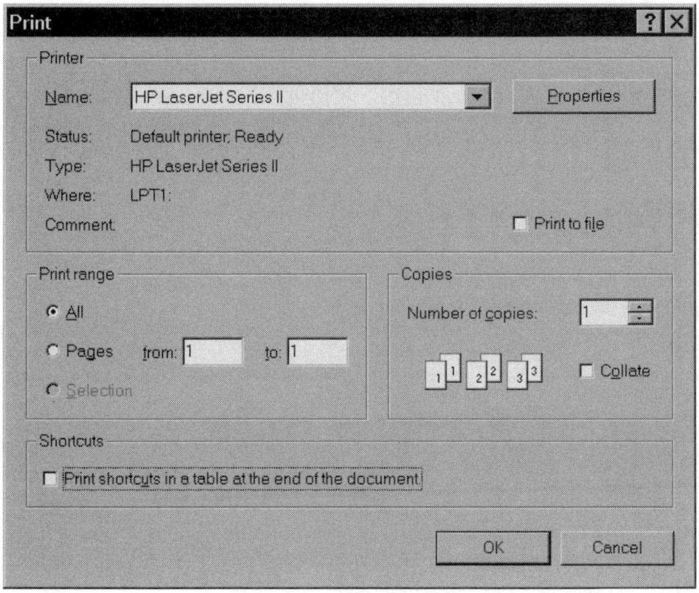

FIGURE 9.6: Use the Print dialog box to specify the range of pages and the number of copies you want to print.

Choose an option in the Print Range box to specify which parts of the Web page you want to print: all of the document, a range of pages, or just the selected text. To print more than one copy of the current Web page, change the Number of Copies setting.

The Shortcuts option adds a table to the printed page that lists the target URLs of each link in the current document. This is a nice feature when you're printing a Web page to send by fax or postal mail, or to save as a hard copy.

Create Shortcut

The Create Shortcut command produces a Windows shortcut to the current Web page and places it on your desktop. You can move the shortcut to a folder or to your Start menu by dragging and dropping the shortcut icon. To change the name of the shortcut icon, use the Rename command from the right-click menu.

Properties

Like the command in other Windows applications, the Properties command in Internet Explorer opens a Properties window, as shown in Figure 9.7.

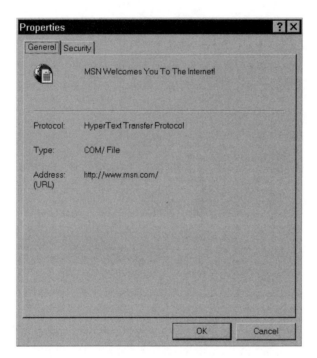

FIGURE 9.7:
The Properties window supplies additional information about the current Web page.

The only really useful information in the Properties window is the URL of the current page.

Close

The Close command shuts down Internet Explorer and returns you to the Windows desktop.

Edit Menu Commands

If you've used any other Windows programs, the commands in the Edit menu will be familiar. These commands allow you to move text or pictures to other documents through the Windows Clipboard and to search for words or other character strings in the current Web page.

To select text for the Cut or Copy command, move the cursor to the beginning of the text string you want to select, hold down the left mouse button, and drag the mouse to the end of the text you want to select. To select the entire text of the current page, use the Select All command. Internet Explorer displays selected text with reversed colors.

Cut

Use the Cut command to remove the currently selected text or other elements from a text field and place the deleted material in the Windows Clipboard. The Cut command does not work with body text in Web pages.

Copy

Use the Copy command to place a copy of the currently selected text or other items in the Windows Clipboard without removing it from the current document. From the Clipboard, you can paste the text to a text editor, word processor, or any other Windows application program.

Paste

Use the Paste command to place the contents of the Windows Clipboard into a text field.

Select All

Use the Select All command to select the whole text of the current Web page. As Figure 9.8 shows, selected text includes descriptions of embedded pictures, but it does not include the pictures themselves.

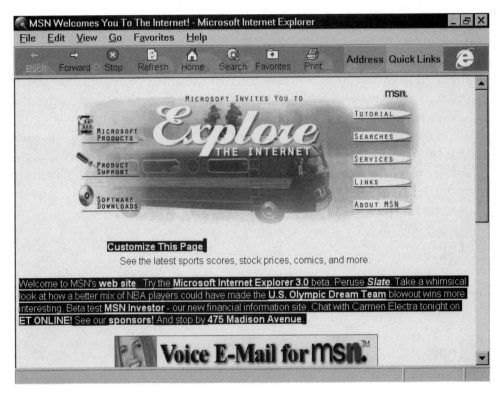

FIGURE 9.8: The Select All command selects only text, not pictures.

Find (on This Page)

Use the Find (on This Page) command to search for a word, phrase, or character string in the current Web page, including portions of the page that are not currently visible within the Internet Explorer window.

When the Find window shown in Figure 9.9 appears, type the word or phrase you want to locate in the Find field. To search through the whole document, place a checkmark next to Start From Top of Page. If there's no checkmark in the box, the search will start at the current cursor position.

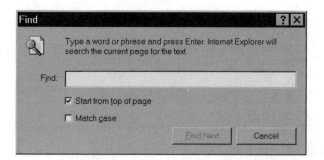

FIGURE 9.9:
To search for a text string, type the text in the Find field.

When Match Case is active, the search will be limited to an exact match with the contents of the Find field. If it's not active, the program will find any similar character string, even if it has lowercase letters instead of capitals.

View Menu Commands

The View menu contains commands that control the appearance of the Internet Explorer window.

Toolbar

Use the Toolbar command to hide or display the Internet Explorer toolbar, the address field, and the Quick Links toolbar.

Status Bar

Use the Status Bar command to display or hide the status bar at the bottom of the Internet Explorer window.

Fonts

The Fonts command controls the size of text in Web pages, if the page designer did not specify font sizes. To change the font size, select the Fonts command and choose the size you want from the submenu.

When you change font sizes, you may also change the overall size of the page and the relative position of text and some pictures. If you want to come as close as possible to the designer's original intent, use Medium fonts. Figure 9.10 shows the same Web page with both medium and large fonts.

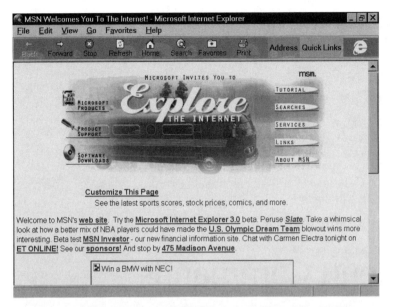

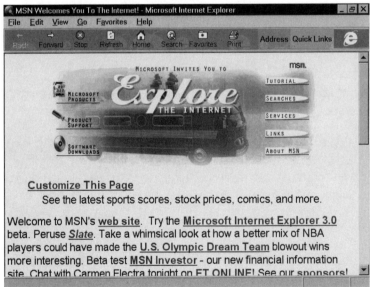

FIGURE 9.10: The Fonts command changes the size of text in Web pages.

> **NOTE** The Fonts command controls the size Internet Explorer uses to display text, but it has no effect on the typeface. To change the typeface, open the International tab with the Options command.

Stop

The Stop command interrupts a download in progress and cancels your request to open a new page or file. When a page seems to be taking too long to load, or if you click on a link by mistake, you can use the Stop command (or the Stop button in the toolbar) to cut off the current download.

Refresh

The Refresh command instructs Internet Explorer to start downloading the current Web page again from the beginning.

When you're looking at a page that updates itself frequently (such as a news bulletin or a picture from a video camera), or if Internet Explorer loads a copy of a page from the local cache on your own computer or your ISP's server, the Refresh command may get you a more recent version of the page than the one already on your screen.

Refresh may also be useful when a page seems to stop before the download is complete. A slow or interrupted download can happen when the file server is sending data to many clients at the same time, or when there's a lot of traffic on the backbone between the server and your Internet access point.

If you don't see any change in the progress bar at the bottom of the Internet Explorer window, or if the RD light on your modem (or the modem icon in the Windows taskbar) stays dark for more than about a minute, the Refresh command can sometimes get the download moving again. It doesn't always work, but it's generally worth a try.

Source

Select the Source command to display the HTML source code for the current Web page. When you enter the Source command, Internet Explorer loads the code into the Notepad text editor.

If you know something about HTML code, you can use the Source command to give yourself a better idea of how and why the current page looks the way it does, or even to make some changes to the appearance of the page. If you're creating your own Web pages, you might want to use code from an existing page as a model for your own design.

Options

The Options command opens the Internet Properties dialog box, which controls a variety of Internet Explorer features and functions. You can also set these options from the Internet Properties dialog box in the Windows Control Panel or by using the Properties command in The Internet icon's right-click menu.

General Tab

The General tab, shown in Figure 9.11, contains commands that change the way Internet Explorer displays Web pages and other documents. The General tab options are described next.

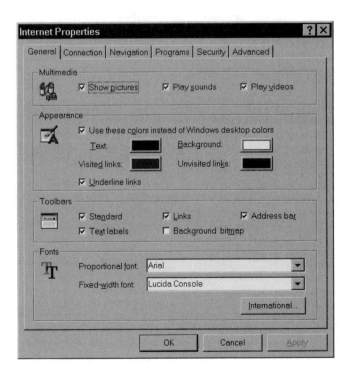

FIGURE 9.11:
Use the General tab to change the appearance of Web pages in Internet Explorer.

Multimedia

Multimedia options specify whether Internet Explorer includes imbedded pictures, sounds, and video clips when it downloads Web pages.

Show Pictures When the Pictures option is active, Internet Explorer will automatically download all pictures and other graphic elements embedded in Web pages. When it is not active, Internet Explorer leaves spaces in Web pages for pictures, as shown in Figure 9.12. To see an image when Show Pictures is turned off, click on the icon within the picture frame.

> **TIP**
>
> Turning off pictures can make a huge difference in the amount of time needed to download a new Web page, especially when the page contains large or complex images. The same page might take less than ten seconds to download without pictures, but more than a minute or two when all of the pictures and other graphic devices come along with the text. Therefore, many people browse with pictures turned off in order to move more quickly from one page to the next.

Play Sounds A growing number of Web pages include audio clips that download along with the text and pictures. If your computer has a sound board and speakers, the audio plays automatically when the download is complete.

The vast majority of these embedded sounds are, choose one or more: irritating, dumb, and irrelevant to the visual content of the page. After the first three or four times you hear them, fanfares, frog sound effects, synthesizer riffs, and crickets are not particularly entertaining. And a hearty disembodied voice suddenly saying, "Welcome to the Hoo-Hah Enterprises Web Page!" can be enough to make you drop your coffee cup into your lap.

Audio takes even longer to download than images, so you may want to seriously consider turning them off. If your computer doesn't have a sound board, it's a no-brainer—don't waste your time downloading sounds you can't play.

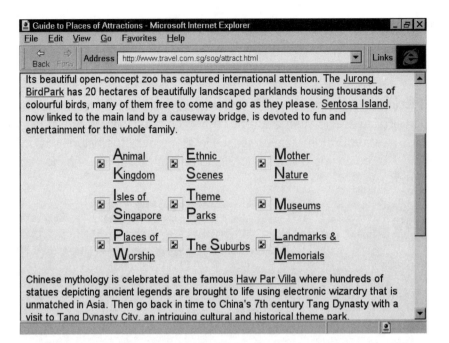

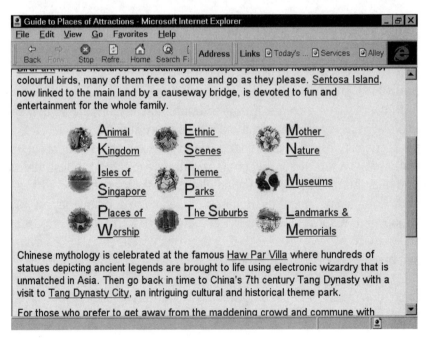

FIGURE 9.12: Turn off Show Pictures to download Web pages without graphic images.

Play Videos Animations in Web pages can be short video clips, cartoons, moving text, and animated icons. They all take extra time to download, so you can instruct Internet Explorer to ignore them when it opens new Web pages.

If you omit video when you open a Web page, you can download and view an animation later by clicking on the icon that replaces it.

Appearance

Use These Colors Instead of Windows Desktop Colors The Custom Colors options control the default text and background colors that Internet Explorer uses for Web pages that don't include their own background and text color attributes.

When the Use These Colors option is not checked, Internet Explorer will use the Window text and background colors specified in the Windows Display Properties dialog box. To open the Windows Display Properties dialog box, open the Control Panel and click on the Display icon, or place your cursor over a blank spot on your desktop and click the right mouse button.

To use different colors for Web pages, place a checkmark in the Use Custom Colors checkbox and click on the Text or Background button to choose a new color. As a general rule, black and other dark colors work best for text, and white and other light colors make the best backgrounds.

Links The Links options control the way Internet Explorer identifies hypertext links in Web pages. As you know, shortcuts appear in Internet Explorer in a different color from other text. After you visit a Web page, Internet Explorer keeps that page's URL in its History list, so it can distinguish between new sites and the ones you've already seen.

A Web page can specify the colors for links within their pages. If no color is specified, Internet Explorer will use the default settings. The Visited Links button sets the default colors for links to URLs that you have visited before. The Unvisited Links button controls the default color for links to new URLs. To change the color of either kind of link, click on the button and select a new color from the choices in the Color dialog box.

Underline Links When the Underline Links option is active, Internet Explorer displays hypertext links as <u>underlined text</u>. When the option is not active, links appear in the same type style as other text, but they're in the colors specified by the Visited and Unvisited Links options (or the colors specified by the designer).

Toolbars

The Toolbars options specify which toolbars will be visible in the Internet Explorer screen. When an option is not active, the toolbar controlled by that option is hidden.

Standard The Standard toolbar contains icon buttons that duplicate some of the most frequently used menu commands.

Text Labels When the Text Labels option is active, the Standard toolbar includes captions that identify the functions of each command button. When it is not active, no captions are visible, but a tool tip appears when you move your cursor over a command button.

Links The Links toolbar contains five quick links to URLs specified in the Navigation Options tab.

Address Bar The Address bar shows the URL of the current Web page.

Background Bitmap When the Background Bitmap option is active, all visible toolbars include a pattern under the text and icons. When the option is not active, the background is a solid color.

Fonts

Some Web pages include font attributes that instruct Internet Explorer to use a particular typeface for text and headlines, but many other pages leave the choice of a font to the browser. If a Web page does not include font attributes, Internet Explorer will use the typefaces specified in the Fonts fields.

Proportional Font Internet Explorer uses the typeface specified in the Proportional Font field for most headlines and body text in Web pages. These fonts are called "proportional" because some letters (like *m* and *w)* are wider than others (like *i* and *f)*.

The default proportional font is Times Roman, which is an excellent typeface for ink on paper, but other fonts are easier to read from a video screen. Arial is one good choice, but you may want to experiment with other typefaces before you decide to permanently change your default.

Fixed-Width Font Web pages use fixed-width fonts for text with characters that must maintain a constant width, such as tables or columns of numbers. The default fixed-width font is Courier, which looks like the output of a typewriter, but Lucida Console is a better choice for on-screen reading.

If the list of installed languages includes more than one character set, you can change to a different set by selecting the one you want and clicking on the Apply button. To install a new character set, click on the Add button.

International The International button opens a dialog box that specifies the character set that Internet Explorer uses to display text in Web pages. In most cases, you won't want to change the character set unless you're trying to download Web pages in foreign languages.

Connection Tab

Figure 9.13 shows the Connection tab. Windows automatically configures the options in this tab when you use the techniques described in Chapter 3 to set up Dial-Up Networking. When AutoDial is active, Internet Explorer (and every other 32-bit Winsock-compliant application program) will automatically set up a dial-up networking connection the first time the application tries to send or receive data through the Internet. The Connection tab options are described below.

Connect to the Internet As Needed If you're connecting to the Internet through a modem and a dial telephone line, the Connect As Needed... option should be active. If you connect to the Internet through a LAN or a direct high-speed network connection, the Connect As Needed... option should be turned off.

Use the Following Dial-Up Networking Connection If you have more than one Internet access account, or if you have created separate Dial-Up Networking connection profiles for different locations, you can use the drop-down list in this field to set one of these connection profiles as your default.

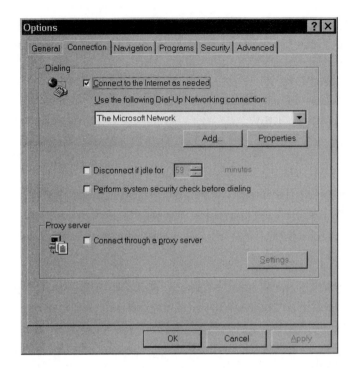

FIGURE 9.13:
The Connection tab controls connections to the Internet through a modern and telephone line.

You don't need to change your default to use a different connection, but you must configure the connection profile before you start Internet Explorer or any other application program. To use a different connection profile, follow these steps:

1. Open the Dial-Up Networking folder from the My Computer window.
2. Double-click on the connection profile you want to use.
3. When the Connect To dialog box appears, enter your user name and password, and then click on the Connect button.

Add Click on the Add button to create a new Dial-Up Networking profile.

Properties Click on the Properties button to change the telephone number, modem configuration, or server configuration in the current Dial-Up Networking profile. The Connection Properties dialog box that appears when you click on the Properties button is shown in Figure 9.14. This dialog box is identical to one that appears when you select the Properties command from the right-click menu in the Dial-Up Networking window.

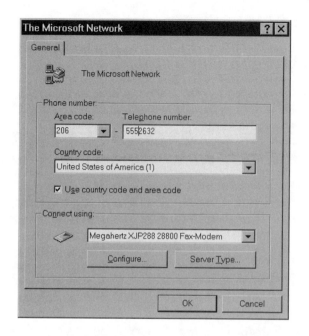

FIGURE 9.14:
Use the Connection Properties dialog box to change the characteristics of a Dial-Up Networking profile.

Disconnect If Idle If the Disconnect If Idle for _ option is active, Dial-Up Networking will hang up the modem connection if you don't send or receive any data for the number of minutes in the Disconnect If Idle field.

When the connection has been idle for the period of time specified, the information window in Figure 9.15 will appear, and your computer will beep once. After another 30 seconds, you will lose your connection unless you click on the Cancel button.

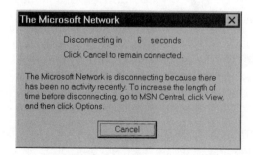

FIGURE 9.15:
Click on the Cancel button to interrupt Auto Disconnect.

It's a good idea to keep Auto Disconnect turned on, especially if you're using an ISP who charges by the hour (or by the minute) for connect time. There's no good reason to pay for a connection when you're not using it. Even if you have unlimited access time, you should disconnect when you're not using the link, because you're tying up an incoming telephone line and a modem at your ISP's access point. If you're not using the line, it's a courtesy to other users to let them get to it.

> **NOTE** The idle time counter does not reset itself when you send or receive data through Netscape Navigator, Winsock FTP, and many other Internet application programs, so you might see the Disconnecting in xx Seconds warning, even if your connection hasn't been idle. If that happens, just click on the Cancel button and go on with what you're doing. If you expect to do any large FTP file transfers, you should turn off Auto Disconnect, so you don't lose the link when you leave your desk for a few minutes to get a cup of coffee.

Perform System Security Check Before Dialing If your computer is connected to a LAN, it might be possible for unauthorized users to obtain access to files, printers, and other network resources through your Dial-Up Networking connection to the Internet at the same time that you're using Internet Explorer or some other Internet client program. It's not likely that anybody will try to break into your network this way, but it's possible. You can protect your network from unauthorized access by using the Advanced tab (described later) to add a proxy server to your Internet connection.

When the Perform Security Check option is active, Dial-Up Networking looks for unprotected LAN access, and issues a warning before it connects you to the Internet.

Connect through a Proxy Server When you connect your PC to the Internet, you also connect all the other computers on the same LAN as yours. Without some kind of protection, somebody outside your LAN could upload copies of private files without permission. A proxy server is a computer that acts as a filter (sometimes called a "firewall") between your LAN and an Internet connection. When the Connect through a Proxy Server option is active, all incoming and outgoing Internet commands and data pass through the proxy server on their way to or from the Internet, rather than going directly to their ultimate destination. If your computer is not connected to a LAN, you don't need to worry about a proxy server.

Change Proxy Settings When the Connect through a Proxy Server option is active, you can click on the Settings button to open the dialog box shown in Figure 9.16. The Servers fields identify the addresses and port numbers that your network uses as proxy servers for each type of address. You can obtain the information you need for these fields from your network administrator.

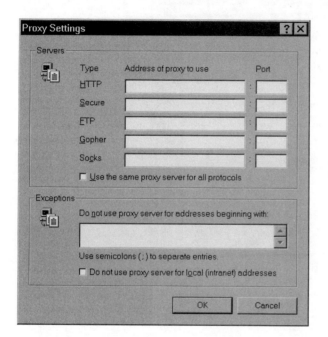

FIGURE 9.16:
Use the Proxy Settings dialog box to connect to the Internet through proxy servers.

If you want to connect directly to certain computers on the Internet without going through the proxy server, type the addresses of those computers in the Exceptions field, separated with commas. You can also bypass complete domains (such as .edu) or port numbers.

Once again, talk to your network administrator or help desk before you try to set up your system to work with a proxy server. You're probably not the first person on the LAN to try to do this, so the network experts can tell you exactly what you need to do to make this work properly.

Navigation Tab

The Navigation tab contains options that control permanent links to Web pages and other URLs. Figure 9.17 shows the Navigation Options dialog box.

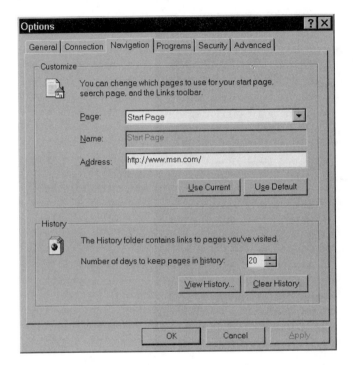

FIGURE 9.17:
Use the Navigation options to change your Start page, Search Page, and Quick Links.

Start Page The Start page is the Web page that Internet Explorer loads automatically when you start the program and when you click on the Home command button in the toolbar.

Search Page The Search page is the page that loads when you select the Search button. You can use the Start and Search Pages dialog box to define the current Web page as either the Start page or the Search page.

Quick Links Quick Links are commands in the Links Toolbar that take you directly to a specified Web page or other URL.

Changing a Destination To define a new Start page or Search page, or to create a new Quick link, follow these steps:

1. Jump to the page you want to specify as the new Start Page, Search Page or Quick Link.
2. Open the Options dialog box, and choose the Navigation tab.
3. Select the type of page you want to change from the drop-down list in the Page field.
4. Click on the Use Current button.
5. If you're changing one of your Quick Links, look at the Name field to confirm that the name (which will appear in the Links toolbar) clearly identifies the new Web page.

History When you visit a Web page, Internet Explorer places a shortcut to that page in the History folder. You can open your History folder from the Go menu. You can control the size of the History folder with the Number of Days to Keep Pages option. To delete all shortcuts from the History folder, click on the Clear History button.

Programs Tab

The Programs tab, shown in Figure 9.18, specifies the default Mail and News applications and provides a link to the Windows file register.

Mail and News Internet Explorer does not include a built-in e-mail manager or newsreader. Therefore, if a Web page contains a link to mail or news, Internet Explorer must open a separate program to handle the link. You can use Microsoft's own Internet News and Internet Mail programs, or client programs supplied by other software developers. To link an external Mail or News program to Internet Explorer, choose the program from the drop-down list of avaialble programs.

Viewers Internet Explorer uses the Windows 95 file register to open files after it downloads them. The File Types button opens the same dialog box as the one that appears when you open the File Types tab in a Windows folder, as shown in Figure 9.19. Chapter 8 explains how to associate file types with MIME types and application programs.

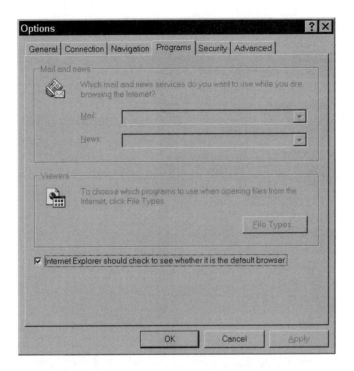

FIGURE 9.18:
Use the Programs Options dialog box to control links between Internet Explorer and other programs.

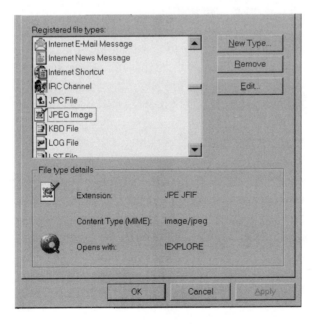

FIGURE 9.19:
Use the File Types dialog box to change file and MIME type associations.

Internet Explorer Should Check to See Whether It Is the Default Browser
The default Web browser is the program that Windows uses to load and display Web pages from shortcuts in folders and menus. If you double-click on a shortcut to a Web page in a window, a menu, or your desktop, Internet Explorer will start the default browser.

If Internet Explorer is your only Web browser, it's automatically the default. But if you have more than one Web browser on your PC, such as Internet Explorer and Netscape Navigator, things can get confusing, because both programs use the default browser to open Web pages from the list of favorites (Netscape calls them bookmarks). Therefore, if the current browser is not the default, you might unexpectedly start some other browser rather than loading the page you want in the current browser.

To avoid this kind of confusion, the Check for Default option should always be active, and you should always make the current browser the default.

Security Tab

The path between your PC and a server may pass through a dozen or more intermediate computers. In theory, every one of those computers offers an opportunity for somebody to read the commands and data you're sending and receiving. Theft of data doesn't happen that often—sending your credit card number through the Internet is probably no more dangerous than giving the card to the cashier in an all-night gas station—but you still may want to think twice before you send credit card numbers, passwords, or other account codes that might cost you money if they made their way into the wrong hands.

Theft of data is not the only potential risk you face when you use the Internet. It's also possible for content providers to download viruses to your system, or to store "cookies" on your system that provide specific information that they can use to personalize the data that they return to you. The Security tab, shown in Figure 9.20, allows you to display warnings before Internet Explorer sends or receives data that might be a security problem or an invasion of your privacy.

Privacy In order to reduce the danger of unauthorized access to valuable information, some Internet servers use security protocols that transmit data in encrypted form. When you connect to one of those servers with Internet Explorer, you will see a padlock in the status bar, like the one in Figure 9.21.

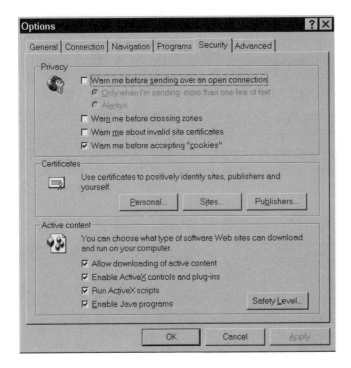

FIGURE 9.20:
Use the Security Options dialog box to control privacy and security warnings.

FIGURE 9.21: A padlock in the status bar indicates that Internet Explorer has received the current Web page from a secure server.

The options in the Security Options dialog box don't have much to do with secure servers, but they do allow you to hide or display warning messages when you send or receive data from a site that is not secure. These options control the warning messages, but they don't make any difference in the security of the actual transmission.

Warn Me Before Sending Over an Open Connection

The Warn Me Before Sending options determine if and how often Internet Explorer displays a warning message before you send data to a site that doesn't use security protocols.

Warn Me Before Crossing Zones

When the Warn Me Before Crossing Zones option is active, Internet Explorer displays a warning message before it receives data from a Web page located on a secure server.

Warn Me About Invalid Site Certificates

One part of the security protocol is an authentication certificate that includes several pieces of information that identify the server, including its address. When a Check Security option is turned on, Internet Explorer compares the address in the certificate to the address to which you instruct it to send data. When the Warn Me About Invalid Site Certificates option is active, Internet Explorer will display a warning message if the two addresses don't match.

Warn Me Before Accepting "Cookies"

Cookies are blocks of information that a web server stores on a client system to personalize the data that it sends to that system. If you prefer not to allow a server to use a cookie, you can instruct Internet Explorer to display a warning before it stores the cookie on your hard drive.

Certificates Use the Certificates options to specify the types of security certificates that Internet Explorer will accept.

Active Content Some Web pages can automatically download and run programs that will run on your PC. This feature is intended to enhance performance by adding animation, interactivity, and other special functions to otherwise static words and pictures, but it also opens up a possible way for viruses or other damaging programs to enter your computer. Use the Active Content options to display a warning about possible problems before a doubtful page downloads or to automatically reject pages that might contain a security problem.

Click on the Safety Level button to restrict access to Web sites that might have a potential security problem.

Unless you receive warnings about possible security problems from your system administrator, you should make all of the Active Content options active, and choose the Normal safety level.

Advanced Tab

The Advanced tab, shown in Figure 9.22, is a catch-all for options that don't fit any of the other tabs.

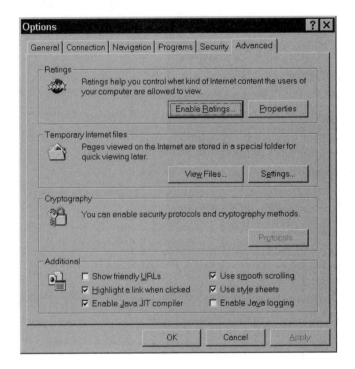

FIGURE 9.22:
The Advanced tab contains options that don't fit any of the other tabs.

Ratings Some Web pages may include content that contains language or pictures that some users may find objectionable. Other people may not want their children exposed to sex, nudity, violence or strong language. Therefore, Internet Explorer contains a set of tools that you can use to reject pages that contain particular types of material.

The Ratings options allow you to set the specific levels of sex, violence, and other material that you want to filter, and to turn the filter function on and off.

Internet Explorer includes a rating system created by the Recreational Software Advisory Council (RSAC) that many Web site developers include in their pages. Different users may have different personal standards for what they consider objectionable, For example, some parents might not want their children to see Web pages that disagree with their religious or political beliefs. To replace the RSAC ratings with some other set of acceptable options, click on the Properties button. When the Content Advisor dialog box appears, select the Advanced tab and click on the Rating Systems button.

To set the acceptable levels of content, click on the Ratings tab and move the sliders to set the ratings, as shown in Figure 9.23.

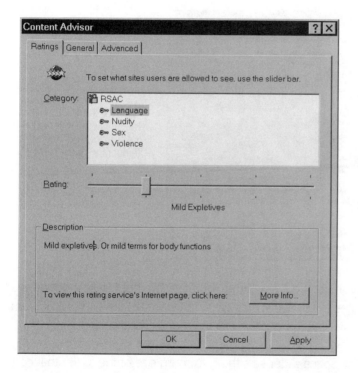

FIGURE 9.23:
Move the sliders to change each content rating.

Temporary Internet Files Every time you view a Web page in Internet Explorer, the program stores a copy of that page on your hard drive as a temporary file. When you return to a page you've recently seen, Internet Explorer will try to load the page from the temporary local file rather than downloading another copy through the Internet. As a result, it generally takes a lot less time to reload a page than to download a new page. However, the version of a page in a temporary file remains the same, even if the original has changed. The Temporary Internet Files options allows you to instruct Internet Explorer to download a new copy of every Web page that you view at least once during your Internet Explorer session.

View Files Click on the View Files button to open the Temproary Internet Files folder.

Settings Click on the Settings button to open the dialog box shown in Figure 9.24.

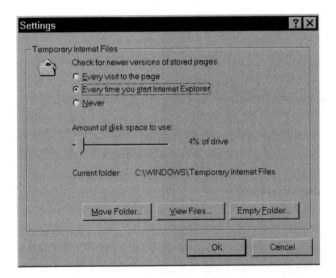

FIGURE 9.24:
The Settings dialog box controls the size, location, and use of the Temporary Internet Files folder.

It's a good idea to select the Every Time You Start Internet Explorer option, so that you won't miss updates to familiar Web pages. To download a new version of a page at any time, click on the Reload button in the Internet Explorer toolbar.

The Amount of Disk Space slider sets the maximum size of the folder that contains your temporary Internet files, expressed as a percentage of the total size of your hard drive. If you increase the amount of space available, you may reduce the amount of time needed to view Web pages, but you won't have as much space available on your hard drive for other files and programs.

Cryptography When they become available, cryptography methods and protocols will allow you send or receive secure data through Internet Explorer. Click on the Protocols button to specify the cyptography protocols you want to use.

Additional

Show Friendly URLs

The Show Friendly URLs option controls the format that Internet Explorer uses to display addresses in the status bar when you move your cursor over a link. When Show Friendly URLs is active, the program shows the address of the destination in this form: www.name.com/path.htm, or possibly just *path.htm* if the link points to another file in the same directory or folder as the current page. When the option is turned off, you will see the complete URL in the status bar, like this: http://www.name .com/path.htm.

Highlight a Link When Clicked

When Highlight a Link When clicked is active, you will see a dotted-line box around a text or graphic link when you click on it once.

Enable Java JIT Compiler

Java is a programming language that downloads simple application programs along with data. When you download a Java file through Internet Explorer, the JIT (Just In Time) compiler creates the necessary Java program if the Enable Compiler option is active.

Use Smooth Scrolling

When Smooth Scrolling is active, Internet Explorer scrolls the content of a web page at a defined speed.

Use Style Sheets

If a web page includes an HTML style sheet, Internet Explorer will use the style sheet if this option is active.

Enable Java Logging

When the Enable Java Logging option is active, Internet Explorer will create a log of Java activity.

Go Menu Commands

The commands in the Go menu instruct Internet Explorer to move to a different Web page.

Back

Use the Back command to return to the page that was visible immediately before the current page.

Forward

After you use the Back command, you can use the Forward command to return to the next page in the current series.

The Back and Forward commands are easier to use than to describe. If you start at Page A and jump to Page B, you can use the Back command to return to Page A, and then use the Forward command to go to Page B again.

Start Page

The Start Page is the Web page that Internet Explorer automatically opens when you start the program. Use the Start Page command to return to that page.

Search the Web

The Search Page is generally a Web page that provides access to one or more Internet search tools. To jump to your Search Page, select the Search the Web command.

Today's Links

The Today's Links command is a link to a Microsoft Web page that contains pointers to other new and interesting Web sites.

History List

The Go menu includes a list of Web pages that you have recently visited, as shown in Figure 9.25. To return to one of the pages in the History list, select the description of that page.

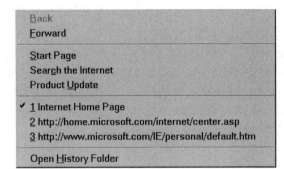

FIGURE 9.25:
The Go menu includes a list of recently visited Web pages.

Open History Folder

The Open History Folder command loads the History folder into Internet Explorer and changes the commands in the menu bar and toolbar. As Figure 9.26 shows, the command set in the History folder window looks more like a Windows folder window

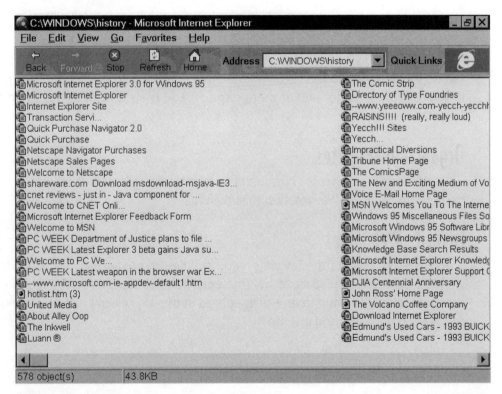

FIGURE 9.26: The History folder contains shortcuts to the last couple of hundred Web pages you've visited.

than an Internet Explorer Web page. Each item in the History folder is a shortcut to a Web page. To jump to a page, double-click on the shortcut.

The default arrangement of shortcuts in the History folder shows the names of Web pages in alphabetical order, with items displayed as list entries. You can change the order of the list. However, since all the shortcuts are the same type and size, the only other arrangement that makes any sense is Arrange by Date, which places the shortcuts in chronological order, with the most recent items at the top of the list.

You can also replace the list with large or small icons, or by a detailed list that shows the date and time you visited each site.

Favorites Menu Commands

The Favorites menu contains just two commands, plus shortcuts to items on your list of Favorite sites. Chapter 7 contains detailed information about working with favorites.

Add to Favorites

Use the Add to Favorites command to place a shortcut to the current Web page in your Favorites folder and, if there's space, add the shortcut to the list in the Favorites menu.

Organizing Favorites

Use the organize favorites command to open a dialog box that you want to use to move items in your Favorites list to subfolders.

Favorite Web Pages

As Figure 9.27 shows, the Favorites menu includes links to as many of the shortcuts in the Favorites folder as space allows (the exact number depends on the size of your monitor screen). To jump to one of the pages in the list, select it just as you would select any other command in a menu.

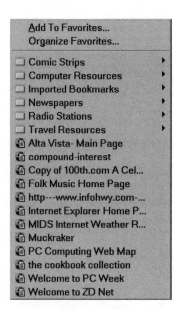

FIGURE 9.27:
The Favorites menu lists as many shortcuts in the Favorites folder as space allows.

Help Menu

The Help menu in Internet Explorer is like the Help menu in most other Windows programs. It contains a Help Topics command that provides access to Internet Explorer Help, and an About command that opens an information window with the version number and other information about the program.

The Microsoft On The Web commands opens a submenu that contains links to a handful of Microsoft Web sites where you can obtain additional software, technical support, and additional information about Internet explorer and other Microsoft products.

Right Mouse Button Commands

Internet Explorer displays a context-sensitive command menu when you click the right mouse button. "Context-sensitive" means that the specific set of commands changes, depending on the exact location of the cursor. A few of these commands are duplicates of the ones in the menu bar, but most are available only from a right-click menu. Several of the right-click commands can make it easy to lift out individual elements of a Web page and use them for other purposes.

Save Background As

Many Web pages, like the one shown in Figure 9.28, use pictures or textured patterns as a background. To save a copy of the background image as a file, move your cursor over the background and select the Save Background As command from the right-click menu.

FIGURE 9.28: Use the Save Background As command to store a local copy of a Web page's background image.

Set As Wallpaper

If you *really* like a picture or a background image on a Web page, you can use it as your Windows desktop wallpaper. The Set As Wallpaper command automatically saves the image in your \windows directory as a bitmap image file called Internet Explorer wallpaper.bmp, and defines that image as your current desktop wallpaper.

If you decide to keep an image as your wallpaper, you should rename the file to something that describes its content rather than the source. Otherwise, you will overwrite the file image the next time you use the Set As Wallpaper command.

To change your wallpaper back to the original pattern or image, or to go back to a solid-color desktop background, follow these steps:

1. From the Windows desktop, move your cursor over the wallpaper and click your right mouse button.
2. Select the Properties command from the right-click menu.
3. When the Display Properties window appears, choose the Background tab to display the dialog box shown in Figure 9.29.
4. Choose the image you want to use as wallpaper from the list in the Wallpaper field or click on the Browse button to find an image in a different folder.
5. The picture of a monitor screen will show you how this image will appear as wallpaper. If you want many copies of the image to fill the screen, choose the Tile option. For one copy of the image in the center of the screen, choose Center.
6. Click on the OK button to accept this wallpaper image and close the dialog box.

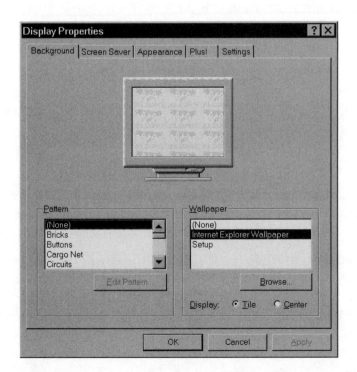

FIGURE 9.29:
Use the Background tab to add or change your desktop wallpaper.

Copy Background

Use the Copy Background command to place a copy of the current Web page's background image in the Windows Clipboard. To load the image into another program, open the second program and use the Paste command.

Select All

The Select All command in the right-click menu is identical to the one in the Edit menu. Use this command to select all of the text in the current Web page. After you select the text, you can use the Copy command in the Edit menu to copy the text to the Windows Clipboard.

Create Shortcut

Use the Create Shortcut command to place a shortcut to the current Web page on your desktop. This command also appears in the File menu.

Add to Favorites

Select the Add to Favorites command to include this Web page in your list of favorites.

View Source

The View Source command is identical to the Source command in the View menu. Use this command to load the HTML source code for the current Web page into a text editor.

Refresh

The Refresh command is a duplicate of the Refresh command in the View menu. Use this command to obtain a new copy of the current Web page from the server.

Properties

If your cursor is over text or background when you open the right-click menu, the Properties command opens a Properties window that contains information about the current Web page. If the cursor is over a picture or graphic image, the Properties window contains information about the image file. If the cursor is over a text link, the Properties window will provide information about the target URL for that link.

Open

The Open command appears in the right-click menu when your cursor is over a link. The Open command loads the destination of the current link into Internet Explorer, just as if you had clicked on the link with your left mouse button.

Open in New Window

The Open in New Window command starts a second Internet Explorer window and loads the destination of the current link into that window. Loading a Web page into a new window can allow you to read the text of the current page while you wait for the next page to appear, or to compare the contents of several pages.

Save Target As

Use the Save Target As command to download the target of the current link and store a copy as a file without loading it into Internet Explorer.

Copy Shortcut

The Copy Shortcut command places a copy of the current link (the link itself, not the target Web page) on the Windows Clipboard. From there, you can use the Paste command to add a Web link to a document created with a word processor or another application program.

Save Picture As

The Save Picture As command appears in the right-click menu when the cursor is over a picture or other graphic image. To save the image as a bitmap file, select the command and use the browser to choose the folder where you want to store the file.

Show Picture

When you turn off Show Pictures in the Appearance Properties dialog box, or if you interrupt a download before Internet Explorer has transferred all of the images in a Web page, you will see an empty box in place of each missing picture. The Show

Picture command instructs Internet Explorer to download the image file for the current cursor location.

Toolbar Commands

Most of the commands in Internet Explorer's Standard toolbar are duplicates of commands in the menus, but a few are not available anywhere else. The Standard toolbar is shown in Figure 9.30. The toolbar commands are described in the following sections.

FIGURE 9.30: The Internet Explorer Standard toolbar includes many of the commands you will use most frequently.

When you move your cursor over a toolbar command button, the icon changes from black and white to color.

Back

The Back button is an arrowhead pointing to the left. Click on the Back button to return to the Web page that was visible immediately before you jumped to the current page. When the Back command tool tip appears, it includes the name of the previous Web page.

Forward

After you use the Back command to retrace your steps, you can use the Forward button to return to the next page in the current string. As with the Back button, the tool tip for the Forward button includes the name of the next page.

Stop

Use the Stop button to interrupt the current file transfer.

Refresh

When a download is in progress, the Refresh command instructs Internet Explorer to restart the file transfer from the beginning. When a download is not in progress, the Refresh command obtains a new copy of the current URL. Even though Internet Explorer has placed a copy of the current Web page in the local cache, the program will get a new copy from the server.

Home

Click on the Home button (with a picture of a house on it) to jump to your Start page. To choose a different Web page as your Start page, use the Options command in the View menu.

Search

The Search button opens your Search Page. The icon on the Search button is a magnifying glass suspended over the Earth. To change you Search Page, open the Explore menu and select Options.

Favorites

Click on the Favorites button to open your Favorites menu. This menu includes the Open Favorites Folder command, the Add to Favorites command, and shortcuts to the sites in your list of favorites.

Print

Click on the Print command button to print a copy of the current Web page.

Font

The Font command changes the size of the text in the current Web page. To step through several font sizes, click on the Font command button several times. There are a total of five font size steps from smallest to largest. Internet Explorer will continue to use the new font size until you change the font size again.

Address Field

The address field shows the URL of the current Web page. To jump to a new page, type a URL into the address field and press the Enter key.

If you're jumping to a Web page, you can type the address without the URL heading; Internet Explorer will add "http://" to the address to create a URL. When you want to move to any other kind of Internet resource, such as a gopher menu, an FTP archive, or any other file or server whose URL has some other type of code, you must type the complete URL.

The address field is also a drop-down list of Web pages that you have viewed during the current Internet Explorer session. To return to a Web page, open the drop-down list, select the URL you want to view, and press the Enter key.

Quick Links

Quick Links are links to the Web pages that have been specified in the Navigation Options dialog box.

Please don't be intimidated by the fact that it takes so many pages to describe all of the commands in Internet Explorer. The basic structure of the World Wide Web and the architecture of Internet Explorer both make navigating the Web relatively easy. After you know how to click on a link or type a URL in the address field to jump to a new site, almost everything else is fine tuning.

In the next chapter, we'll talk about using add-on programs that integrate multimedia audio and video animation effects with Internet Explorer.

Chapter 10

USING MULTIMEDIA TOOLS WITH INTERNET EXPLORER

FEATURING

- Listening to sound clips and live connections
- Playing Wave files on Windows Sound Recorder
- Using RealAudio, StreamWorks, and True Speech players for compressed audio files
- Using MPEG format players
- Running other multimedia players

When the earliest graphic Web browsers appeared, they combined text, graphic designs, and still pictures into integrated pages. Today, many Web sites offer animation, sound and video recordings, and interactive images along with their words and pictures. You can use the World Wide Web to listen to live or pre-recorded radio programs, watch movies and videos, view the output of live video cameras, and move around "virtual reality" stages.

Internet Explorer recognizes some types of audio and video files, but others require separate add-on programs. For a sample of integrated audio and animation, take a look at the page that Microsoft has created to demonstrate Internet Explorer's multimedia functions at http://www.microsoft.com/ie/showcase/ howto_3/volcano3.htm. Figure 10.1 shows a static screen capture from that page, but you'll need to download it to your own computer to see the smoking, rotating coffee cup and hear the jungle drums.

FIGURE 10.1: The Volcano Coffee Web page is a Microsoft demonstration that includes sounds and animated picture.

Embedded Audio and Video Files

The drums that play in the Volcano Coffee demonstration are in an embedded audio file. An embedded audio file is a prerecorded audio clip, usually in .wav format, that is internally linked to a Web page. Internet Explorer will automatically download and play an embedded audio file just as it downloads and displays a graphic image file. Web designers use embedded audio for background sound effects and music, recorded greetings from the owner of the Web site, and similar enhancements to the information on your screen.

As a general rule, .wav files and other embedded audio formats, which must be downloaded before they play, provide much better sound quality than RealAudio and other live formats, but they take a lot longer to receive. Just as audio through a telephone doesn't sound as good as audio on a full-fidelity digital compact disc, live audio through the Internet won't come close to the quality of a recording that you can download and play from your hard drive.

Embedded audio files can add a lot to a Web page, but they do increase the amount of time required to download and display the page. If your computer doesn't have a sound card, or if you have a slow connection to the Internet, you should turn off Sounds in the General tab of Internet Explorer's Options dialog box.

Plug-in and Add-on Programs

There are at least a couple of dozen software developers trying to create sound and video file formats for the Internet. All of these folks are hoping that theirs will become the universal standard, so they'll be able to retire at the age of 32 and buy their own island in the Caribbean. In the meantime, there are Web sites that use many different formats, so you will need to download separate playback programs for each of them.

The distinction between add-in programs, which make an audio player or a video viewer part of a Web page, and external programs, which open the player or viewer in a separate window, is very important to Web page designers and software developers. But as a user, you're probably more concerned about content than display format. The content of an audio clip or a movie is about the same whether you see it as part of a page or separately.

Because it has such a huge share of the total browser market, there are a lot more integrated plug-ins for Netscape Navigator than for Internet Explorer, but as Microsoft gains market share, you can expect to see many new third-party programs that will integrate specialized services into Internet Explorer pages. In the meantime, the latest version of Internet Explorer can work with plug-in programs designed for Netscape Navigator.

Most Web sites that include audio, video, or other special functions also provide links to playback programs. For example, KING-FM, a radio station that uses RealAudio to send its programs to the Internet, has a link from its Web site (http://www.king.org/) to the RealAudio home page, as shown in Figure 10.2.

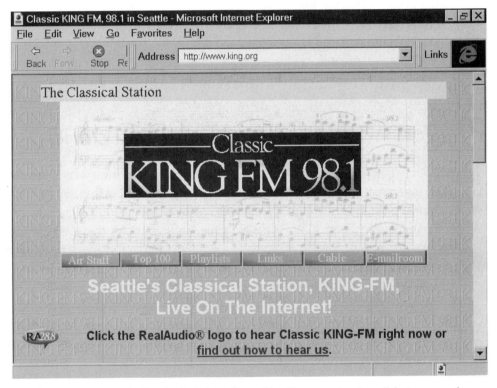

FIGURE 10.2: Most Web sites that include audio or video files or services have links to sources for playback programs.

In this chapter, we'll describe many of the most common audio and video formats, but new ones are bound to appear in the next few months. The procedure for downloading and installing them is about the same:

1. Jump to the format developer's Web site.
2. Download the player or viewer program.
3. Run the Setup program.
4. If it doesn't occur automatically, create a new file association for the new program and file format.

For both audio and video, you should try to use the fastest possible connection between your own computer and the rest of the Internet. It takes a *lot* of bits to make up a minute of high-fidelity audio, and even more than that for full-motion video. It's possible to download live audio with a 14.4 kbps modem, but the sound quality will not be as good as you would get with a faster connection. For most video, a 28.8 kbps connection is a practical minimum.

What You Need for Audio

In order to listen to sounds that you download through the Internet, your computer must have a sound card. If you already use a sound card with games or other programs, Internet Explorer and the add-in audio players that work with it should automatically find and use the existing sound card without any additional configuration. If you don't have a sound card, you'll need to install one before you can listen to sound files with any kind of decent audio quality (there are some utilities that play sound files through your computer's built-in speaker, but the quality is pretty terrible). Even the least expensive sound card and separate speakers will sound a lot better than the internal speaker, which was intended for nothing more than the occasional beep or click.

Sound cards come in a range of prices and quality levels. Any SoundBlaster compatible card will work with Internet Explorer, but the more expensive models that use wave table synthesis may sound better, because they use prerecorded samples of actual musical instruments rather than the synthesized audio that less expensive sound cards produce. In practice, wave table synthesis seems to make more of a difference when you're listening to music from CDs and .wav files than with the "live audio" formats used on the Internet.

You'll also need a pair of speakers. The rule here is simple: you get what you pay for. You can spend less than $20 for a pair of cheap speakers, or more than $200 for super-duper, high-quality speakers with separate subwoofers and built-in amplifiers. You can also find speakers built into keyboards, monitors, and platforms that hold your computer or monitor, but separate pieces are generally a better choice unless you have very limited space (and even then, there's nothing to stop you from putting the speakers on the floor under your desk). Speakers in the $50 to $100 (per pair) range should be adequate for most of the sounds currently distributed through the Internet, but if you plan to listen to a lot of music—either from CDs or downloaded files—you might want to consider something more expensive.

As an alternative to speakers, you can plug a pair of headphones directly into your sound card, but unless you wear the headphones all the time, you might miss the sounds embedded in some Web pages (which may not necessarily be a bad thing). If you're in an office where random noises are likely to distract other people, headphones may be the most considerate option.

Sound Clips and Live Connections

Web sites can offer two kinds of sounds: prerecorded sound clips and "live" continuous feeds direct from radio stations and other program sources. When you're looking for a sample track from a new CD, you will want to download the music file and play it back from your hard drive; but when you want the latest news or a continuous stream of background music, it makes more sense to listen to a live connection.

Some Web sites offer the same sound clips in more than one format. If you have a choice between .wav or .au files and files that use RealAudio, StreamWorks or True Speech, the trade-off is between high-quality recordings that will take a long time to download and compressed files that download more quickly, but with sound quality someplace between a telephone and an AM radio.

NOTE   If you want to listen to sounds embedded in Web pages, the Sounds option must be active in the General tab of Internet Explorer's Options dialog box. To ignore sounds and reduce the amount of time needed to download new Web pages, remove the checkmark from the Sounds checkbox.

One final point before we start to describe individual audio formats: don't expect live audio transmitted through the Internet to sound as good as the same programs on your FM radio or CD player. The quality will improve as the technology advances, but today, the best you can expect is something which sounds like a cheap AM radio in the next room, especially if you're trying to listen through a 14.4 kbps modem. If you listen to a radio station like KPIG (for country music) or KING-FM (for classical music) as background music while you explore the World Wide Web, a 28.8 kbps modem, or even an ISDN or faster Internet connection, will provide substantially better sound quality, but it still won't be perfect.

Playing WAV, AU, and AIFF Files

Wave audio (.wav file format) is the closest thing to a standard audio format in Windows 95. Inspired by the Apple Macintosh, Windows 95 can use .wav files to provide annoying sounds that accompany many commands and messages. The CD-ROM version of Windows 95 includes a large assortment of these sounds, and fortunately, a "no sounds" option that keeps the computer quiet.

Wave audio is also one of the two standard formats for embedded audio files within Web pages. When Internet Explorer receives one of these pages, it plays the sound file automatically. The same format is also used for some sound clips that you can download separately. Wave audio files can sound extremely good when you play them through good speakers, but they take a very long time to download. It might take as long as 25 minutes or more to receive a 5-minute .wav file.

Using the Windows Sound Recorder

The Sound Recorder applet supplied with both Windows 3.1 and Windows 95 is the default program for creating and playing .wav files through your sound card. You may find other programs that offer easier-to-use and more flexible editing facilities, but for playback, Sound Recorder is entirely adequate.

As Figure 10.3 shows, Sound Recorder should be associated with .wav files. Unless you change the file association, Internet Explorer will automatically load separate .wav files into Sound Recorder.

The control buttons in the Sound Recorder window are designed to look and work like the ones on a tape recorder. To play a sound file in Sound Recorder, click on the Play button (the one with the arrowhead pointing to the right), as shown in Figure 10.4.

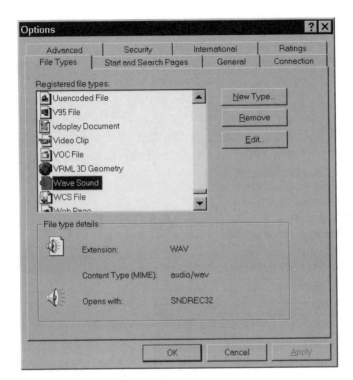

FIGURE 10.3:
The default association for .wav files is the Sound Recorder program.

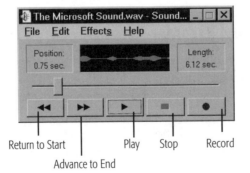

Return to Start   Play   Stop   Record

Advance to End

FIGURE 10.4:
The Windows Sound Recorder applet plays .wav files through your computer's sound card.

Using the Internet Explorer Audio Player

Internet Explorer can also recognize two other audio file formats without an audio player: .au files and .aiff files. Because the Windows 95 Sound Recorder doesn't recognize those formats, Internet Explorer uses its own audio player, as shown in Figure 10.5. The Internet Explorer audio player arranges the controls slightly differently from Sound Recorder, but its performance is about the same.

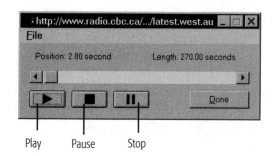

Play   Pause   Stop

FIGURE 10.5:
The Internet Explorer audio player is a simple playback utility.

Playing Compressed Audio

Wave audio files and the other standard audio file formats can provide extremely high-quality sound, but they're very large. Full CD-quality digital audio requires about five megabytes per minute for each channel. Therefore, it would take at least five minutes to download a one-minute .wav file through a modem. A six-minute radio newscast would take half an hour. Obviously, this creates certain practical problems when you want to listen to a continuous program stream.

There are two ways to solve these problems: either increase the speed of the connection or decrease the size of the files. It might be possible to replace your modem and telephone line with a high-speed digital connection, but that's extremely expensive. The alternative is to use *compression* to squeeze the audio signal into a smaller package before sending it, and a complementary program to *uncompress* the signal at the receiving end.

At least three different software developers are trying to promote their products as the Internet audio compression standard. From a listener's point of view, the three systems are similar, but they each use a different compression technique, so you need a separate player for each system. Because the software developers are anxious to sell their servers to program suppliers, they all give away the players necessary to listen to their file formats. Once you have installed and configured the players, Internet Explorer will identify the format used on a particular server and automatically open the correct player for programs from that source.

The first and most widely used of the three audio compression formats is RealAudio, from Progressive Networks in Seattle. Microsoft includes the RealAudio client program with Internet Explorer. Many broadcasters, including ABC Radio, National Public Radio, and the Canadian Broadcasting Corporation, offer archives of newscasts and other programs in RealAudio format. Many other program suppliers are producing and distributing special events in RealAudio format.

Most Web sites that use RealAudio also have links to the Progressive Networks home page, shown in Figure 10.6.

When you install RealAudio Player, the setup routine will automatically configure Internet Explorer (and other Web browsers that you may have on your system) for RealAudio, and place a link to the RealAudio home page in your Favorites list.

Some program sources, such as Radio Telefis Eireann (RTE) in Dublin, Ireland, shown in Figure 10.7, let visitors choose between RealAudio files transmitted as streaming audio, which plays directly from the server, and file transfer for later playback. If you have the time to spare, the file transfer option is likely to provide better sound quality, because the server will be able to resend data packets that don't make it through the network on the first attempt.

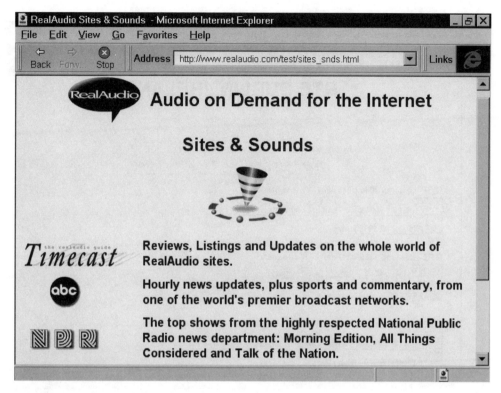

FIGURE 10.6 There are links to the RealAudio home page from many other sites that use RealAudio servers.

RealAudio Player Controls

The RealAudio Player, shown in Figure 10.8, allows you to control the way that your audio file is played back.

The RealAudio player includes these controls:

- The Play/Pause button has two functions. When the arrowhead symbol is solid, clicking on this button starts the player. The Pause control (with the two vertical lines) works slightly differently, depending on whether you're playing audio from a live program source or a prerecorded audio file. When you're listening to a live program, the Pause button will interrupt the sound; when you click on the Play button again, it will return to the server and pick up the current output from the source. When you're listening to a recorded file, the Pause button will halt the playback without losing the current position in the recording; click on the Play button to start where you left off.

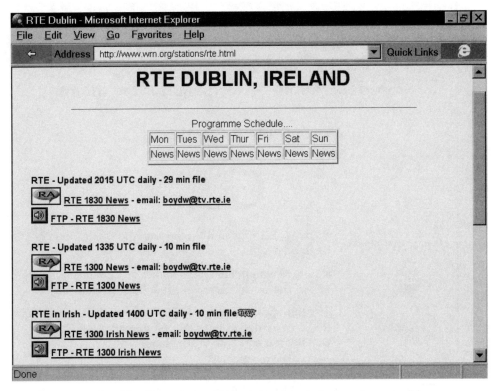

FIGURE 10.7: RTE Dublin offers a choice of either immediate playback or storage to disk.

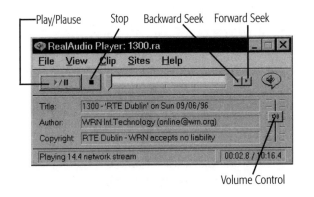

FIGURE 10.8:
The RealAudio Player controls playback of audio files.

- Click on the Stop button to stop the current playback. If you're listening to a recording, the player will return to the beginning of the item.
- The slider control works only when you're listening to a recording. To advance to a later portion of the file, move the slider to the right. To return to an earlier section, move the slider to the left.
- The Backward Seek button is the small button next to the slider with an arrowhead pointing to the left. When you're listening to a recorded file, click on the Backward Seek button to return to the beginning of the current file.
- The Forward Seek control is the small button next to the Backward Seek button with the arrowhead pointing to the right. Click on the Forward Seek button to move to the end of the current file.
- The Home button is a link to the Progressive Networks home page, and it also shows you the current activity on the player program. When the speaker is spinning, the player program is contacting a server and moving data to a local buffer. When the player program is playing, there are animated sound waves coming out of the speaker. And when the player loses a data packet, a red lightning bolt appears.
- The volume control makes the sound louder when you move the slider up, and quieter when you move the slider down. If the sound level is still too low when you move the volume control slider all the way up, double-click on the speaker in the Windows taskbar to open the Volume Control window, shown in Figure 10.9. If the volume is *still* too low, open the Control Panel and select Multimedia to increase Playback Volume in the Audio Properties dialog box.

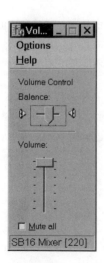

FIGURE 10.9:
Use the Windows Volume Control to increase the playback level.

- The times shown in the lower-left corner of the RealAudio Player window are the elapsed playback time and the total duration of the current file. When you're listening to a live program, the elapsed time counter starts when the connection starts, but the total duration remains at 00:00.0.

RealAudio Player Menu Commands

RealAudio Player includes five menus: File, View, Clip, Sites, and Help. These menus are described in the following sections.

File Menu The File menu contains these commands:

- Select the Open Location command to jump to another RealAudio server. When the Open Location dialog box appears, type the URL of the new site and click on the OK button.
- Use the Open File command to load a file into RealAudio Player from your own hard drive. Use the browser window to find and select the file you want to play.
- The Open Recent command opens a submenu that shows the Real-Audio sites or local files you have played most recently. To return to one of those sites or files, select the name from the submenu.
- Choose the Exit command to shut down RealAudio Player.

View Menu The View menu includes these commands:

- Select the Info & Volume command to display or hide the volume control and the Title, Author, and Copyright information fields.
- Select the Status Bar command to display or hide the status bar at the bottom of the RealAudio Player window.
- The Preferences command opens a tabbed dialog box that configures the RealAudio Player.
- Use the Statistics command to open the Connection Statistics window shown in Figure 10.10.
- Select the Always on Top command to keep the RealAudio Player window visible, even if you open another window.

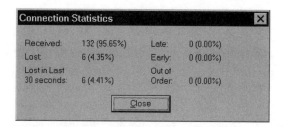

FIGURE 10.10:
The Connection Statistics window contains information about the current RealAudio session.

Clip Menu The Clip menu includes the Previous Clip and Next Clip commands. Some RealAudio files contain more than one audio clip. To move back to an earlier clip in the current file, select the Previous Clip command. Select the Next Clip command to move forward within the current multi-clip RealAudio file.

Sites Menu The commands in the Sites menu are links to Progressive Networks Web pages.

Help Menu The Help menu contains the typical Help commands. Use the Contents command to open RealAudio Player Help. Select the About command to open an information window that shows the version number and copyright information for RealAudio Player.

Using StreamWorks

The strongest competitor to RealAudio is Xing Technologies' StreamWorks, which can transmit both audio and slow-scan video. StreamWorks offers both live streams of continuously broadcast programs and on-demand programs of previously recorded material. You can download the free StreamWorks client software from http://www.xingtech.com/ (or win.xingtech.com/streams/info/swSites.html).

During installation, StreamWorks will add the MIME type application/x-xdma to your list of file associations, and associate it with the file name extensions .xdm and .xdma. Internet Explorer will automatically open the StreamWorks Player when you link to an .xdm file.

One nice feature of StreamWorks is its ability to run in background, so you can listen to one of the StreamWorks radio stations while you're using Internet Explorer to visit other Web sites. Audio quality will suffer if you try to receive sound and other data through a slow modem, but it's decent through a 28.8 kbps modem or an ISDN connection.

The audio quality you receive from a StreamWorks server depends on the speed of your modem; most Web sites offer separate links for listeners with slower modems and faster, direct connections to the Internet. As for video, the best you can expect with a 28.8 kbps modem is about two frames per second (for comparison, broadcast television in North America is thirty frames per second). For full-motion, you'll need a very high-speed direct Internet connection.

> **TIP** Among others, Capitol Records, NBC, and many foreign broadcasters use StreamWorks to distribute programs through the Internet. There's a directory of active StreamWorks servers at http://www.xingtech.com/streams/info/swsites.html.

As an example, let's look at the Web site for KPIG, a radio station in Freedom, California, which provides its programming to a live StreamWorks broadcast at http://www.kpig.com. As Figure 10.11 shows, KPIG offers a choice of two links. Since we're using a modem connection to the Internet, choose the 10.5 kb/s option.

After a few seconds, Internet Explorer will open the StreamWorks window, shown in Figure 10.12, and automatically start playing the station through your sound card. If you were connected to a video server, you would see the picture in place of the "Audio Only" symbol. To increase or reduce the volume, click on the Setup button in the StreamWorks window or on the speaker icon in the taskbar to open the Windows Volume Control window.

While it's possible to use the StreamWorks Player to connect to program sources without using a Web browser, it's a lot more complicated than simply letting Internet Explorer automatically start the player and load data from the server. Your best approach is to let your browser do the work for you rather than trying to reconfigure the client program on your own.

FIGURE 10.11:   KPIG provides separate feeds for modems and high-speed connections to the Internet.

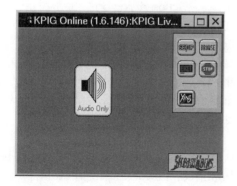

FIGURE 10.12:
The StreamWorks window appears when you're listening to a StreamWorks server.

Using True Speech

The third downloadable Internet audio format is True Speech, developed by DSP Group. It's not as common as RealAudio or StreamWorks, but there are a few interesting True Speech sites out there. It's easy enough to install and use, so you might as well add it to your bag of Internet tools. Unlike RealAudio and StreamWorks, the True Speech format is limited to playback of prerecorded sound clips; you can't use it to listen to live programs.

The True Speech player is available for free download from http://www.dspg.com/allplyer.htm.

Adding a True Speech File Association After you install the program, you should add it to Internet Explorer's list of file associations:

1. Open Internet Explorer's View menu and select the Options menu.
2. In the File Types tab, click on the New Type button to display the Add New File Type dialog box.
3. In the Description of Type field, enter **True Speech Audio.**
4. In the Associated Extension field, enter **.tsp.**
5. In the Content Type (MIME) field, enter **application/dsptype.**
6. Click on the New button.
7. When the New Action dialog box appears, type **Open** in the Action field and use the Browse button to find the Tsplay.exe or Tsplay32.exe file in the folder that contains the True Speech program files.
8. Click on the OK button to close the New Action dialog box.
9. Remove the checkmark from the Confirm Open After Download option.
10. Click on the OK button to close the New File Type dialog box.

To test the program, use Internet Explorer to open the sites.htm file in the True Speech folder, and then jump to one of the pages in the list of samples. When you click on a link to a True Speech audio clip, Internet Explorer should automatically open the True Speech Player and load the sound file into the player program.

True Speech Player Controls Figure 10.13 shows the True Speech Internet Player window. The bar graph moves across the bottom of the window to show the progress of the playback.

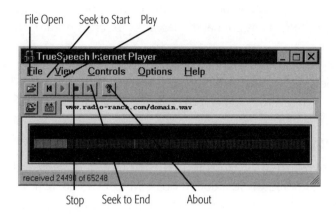

FIGURE 10.13:
The True Speech Player window shows the progress of a True Speech playback.

In most cases, you will want to use Internet Explorer to jump to True Speech files, but you can also download them directly from the True Speech Player using the toolbar commands. The toolbar includes these controls:

- Click on the File Open button to load and play a .wav or .tsp file located on your own hard drive.
- Click on the Seek to Start button to return to the beginning of the recording.
- Click on the Play button to start playing the current recording.
- Click on the Stop button to halt the current playback.
- Click on the Seek to End button to move to the end of the current recording.
- Click on the About button to display the version number and copyright information.

To jump to a True Speech site on the Internet, use the Open Location command in the File menu. The other menu commands are like those you have seen in other Windows programs.

Playing Video and Multimedia File Formats

Moving pictures and animated graphics can add a lot to the appearance of a Web page, but Internet Explorer may require additional software to display them. And like streaming audio, some formats use a separate player rather than placing the image within the Internet Explorer window.

The Internet is not the only place you can find videos and multimedia files. They also show up on many CD-ROMs as animated diagrams, excerpts from movies, and other short video clips.

Internet Explorer can recognize some of the standard video formats, but many others require separate viewers. As with audio players, you must download and install video and multimedia players before you can view the files encoded in those formats.

Using MPEG Players

MPEG (Moving Picture Experts Group) format is an international standard for encoding and decoding compressed, full-motion video. MPEG files are relatively large, but they do support full-screen images, which some other video formats can't handle without distorting or blurring the picture.

Because MPEG is a working group that includes people from more than one organization, it's not a proprietary format. Therefore, you can find MPEG players from several sources. Two good choices are MPEGPLAY, a $25 Australian shareware program available for download from ftp://ftp.NCSA.uiuc.edu/Web/Mosaic/Windows/viewers, and QuickTime for Windows, a program from Apple Computer that plays both MPEG and QuickTime movie files.

Because the Apple program doesn't recognize every version of MPEG format, MPEGPLAY is the better choice. Figure 10.14 shows the control window for MPEG-PLAY. When you open a file, it appears in a separate window. From the left, the control buttons are Open, Rewind, Stop, Advance One Frame at a Time, and Play.

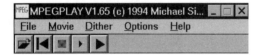

FIGURE 10.14:
MPEGPLAY uses separate windows for controls and images.

The MIME Type for MPEG movies is video/mpeg. The standard file name extensions are mpeg, mpg, and mpe.

Using the QuickTime Player

The QuickTime format was developed by Apple as a cross-platform format for video and multimedia files. It's widely used on CD-ROMs as well as Internet file servers. You can download the Apple QuickTime player for Windows from http://quicktime.apple.com.

The QuickTime Movie Player program, shown in Figure 10.15, plays both QuickTime movies and MPEG video files. By now, you will recognize the controls, which are similar to the ones you've seen in the other programs described in this chapter. From left to right, they're the volume control, the Start/Pause button, a slider that shows the progress of the playback, and Backward and Forward step buttons that move the file one frame at a time.

The MIME Type for QuickTime movies is video/quicktime. The standard file name extensions are .mov and .qt.

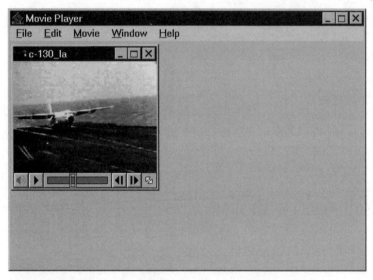

FIGURE 10.15: Apple's QuickTime for Windows plays both QuickTime and MPEG files.

Viewing Images in VRML Format

The person who came up with the name VRML (Virtual Reality Modeling Language) has a very different concept of "reality" from yours or mine. VRML is a graphic format that places a viewer "inside" a scene and allows him or her to change his point of view and relative location. Because the process of creating detailed VRML scenes is extremely complex, many of them tend to resemble a surrealistic set of child's blocks rather than anything more complicated or recognizable. For example, Figure 10.16 shows a VRML representation of the Boston Marathon's finish line.

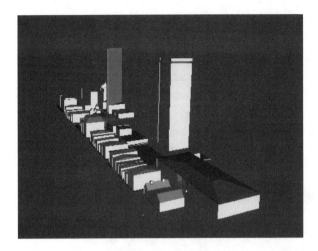

FIGURE 10.16:
VRML format places you "inside" a scene.

ActiveVRML is a Microsoft add-on program that displays interactive animation within Internet Explorer. To download and install ActiveVRML, jump to the Internet Explorer home page at http://www.microsoft.com/ie and follow the links to ActiveVRML. The setup routine will automatically configure Internet Explorer to recognize VRML images embedded in Web pages and separate VRML files.

Interactive Multimedia with Shockwave

Macromedia's Shockwave is an interactive multimedia format that many Web site developers use to include movies and interactive graphics in their pages.

Macromedia has promised plug-in Shockwave software for Internet Explorer, but it wasn't yet available when this was written. When it becomes available, you will be able to download the free Shockwave plug-in from http://www.macromedia.com/shockwave/plugin/plugin.cgi.

Viewing VDOLive Video

CBS News and a few other broadcasters use the VDOLive video format to distribute some of their programs through the Internet. A plug-in viewer may appear later, but for the moment, the best way to view VDOLive videos is with the separate viewer available for free download from http://www.vdolive.com, as shown in Figure 10.17.

After you download the viewer, create a file association for VDOLive Videos, with the MIME Type video/vdo and the file name extension vdo.

FIGURE 10.17:
VDOLive format is used
by several broadcasters
for video to the Internet.

Using StreamWorks for Video

If you have a fast connection to the Internet, you can use StreamWorks for real-time video as well as audio. The section on audio add-on programs earlier in this chapter contains detailed information about installing and using StreamWorks. The same MIME type works for StreamWorks video as for audio.

Summary: Audio and Video Formats

If and when Microsoft begins to catch up with Netscape's overwhelming share of the Web browser market, many more software developers will introduce plug-in audio and video programs for Internet Explorer. As they appear, you can expect Microsoft to provide links from http://www.microsoft.com/ie to the developers' home pages, where you will be able to download the programs. It's too soon to know which formats will become the standards, so you may end up with half a dozen or more of them taking up space on your hard drive, just because you wanted to listen to live news from Kuala Lumpur and Tulsa, and watch cartoons from Zagreb and Vancouver. When you begin to run out of space on your hard drive, you should consider deleting the players you don't use, since you can always download another (possibly newer and better) copy when you need it again.

If you can't find a source for a player on the Microsoft Web site or the site that offers files in an obscure format, try the Netscape list of plug-ins at http://www.netscape.com/com-prod/products/navigator.version_2.0/plugins/index.html. Many of the software developers with links on that page will also have versions that work with Internet Explorer.

Chapter 11

INTERNET NEWS

FEATURING

- **Understanding how Internet newsgroups operate**
- **Getting news with Microsoft Internet News**
- **Using Free Agent as a newsreader**
- **Participating in newsgroups through MSN**
- **Reading Internet news with AOL**

News, the system that exchanges public messages through the Internet, has actually been around longer than the Internet itself. Usenet, as it was originally called, began when users of two computers at universities in North Carolina started to move messages through a dial-up telephone link between their two campuses. Today, most news moves across the Internet, but there are still a few isolated users who send and receive their messages through computers that are not connected to the Internet, using a technique called UUCP (Unix to Unix CoPy), and even by exchanging floppy disks or magnetic tapes. In spite of these exceptions, the exchange of public messages organized by topics has come to be called "Internet news."

News is one of the most popular and widely used Internet services. Participants use news for fast and efficient distribution of information about academic subjects, current events, business, hobbies, and other special interests. Each topic is discussed in a separate message stream, called a newsgroup. There are newsgroups devoted to more than ten thousand separate topics, ranging from computer languages to popular television programs, and from cars for sale to particle physics. You might see two or three hundred new messages a day in the most popular newsgroups, but other, more obscure subjects may only get three or four messages a week.

Some newsgroups are intended for worldwide distribution; others are focused on a specific geographic region, college campus, or corporation. However, many local or regional newsgroups are distributed beyond their own borders. It's not uncommon, for example, to see a message in the Seattle.eats newsgroup from somebody who's planning to visit the area and wants to find a good seafood restaurant.

What Happens in Newsgroups

If you can think of a topic, there's probably a newsgroup devoted to it. In some newsgroups, the most common messages are questions and answers or requests for help: "I just found a 1934 Crosley radio at a swap meet—can anybody tell me where to replace the missing knob?" is a typical message in the newsgroup devoted to collecting and restoring antique radios and phonographs.

Because the same questions tend to come up again and again, many newsgroups contain lists of "frequently asked questions," or FAQs. It's a good idea to look for a FAQ among the recent messages, or post a message asking for a pointer to a place where you can download it, before you send your own beginner's questions to a newsgroup.

In other groups, much of the traffic is devoted to discussions of current events related to the topic of the news group. Many groups contain ongoing conversations in which one or more readers post replies to an earlier message, and then other people reply to *those* messages.... These continuing series of online replies to replies to replies are known as *threads*.

Each newsgroup has its own style. Some groups tolerate and even welcome newcomers; others are like the big table in the back of a local coffee shop, where the same half dozen regulars have been gathering every day for years. After you have followed a newsgroup for a few weeks, you will begin to recognize the names and reputations of some of the regular participants and some of the shared in-jokes and local customs.

If you have experience with online services such as CompuServe or America Online, or with non-Internet bulletin board services (BBS), the general form of Internet news will probably seem familiar to you. Discussions in other systems' conferences and forums have many features in common with Internet news. But since Internet news reaches many more users than any single online service, there are many more topics and a wider variety of users than you can find in other online communities.

In most newsgroups, anybody can post a message that will automatically be distributed to every other subscriber. In order to weed out off-topic messages and prevent *ad hominem* attacks and other distractions, a few newsgroups are moderated; all messages pass through the moderator before they go back out to the newsgroup. A good moderator can keep discussions on track, send answers to common questions by e-mail, and generally keep things flowing well. Bad moderators, who insist on advancing their own opinions at the expense of those who disagree with them, or who join in attacks, usually get either replaced or ignored pretty quickly.

Newsgroups are a very important part of the culture of the Internet, because they encourage people to join online communities of people who share the same interests. Unlike the World Wide Web, which is still primarily a one-to-many communications medium, News is more of a many-to-many channel, where everybody can participate on a more-or-less equal footing.

Whether this is a good thing is a matter of opinion. In many newsgroups, the "noise" level of irrelevant comments and uninformed opinion is pretty high. Just because you see an article in a newsgroup, that does not mean it's automatically true or correct.

As you participate in newsgroups, it's important to remember that your postings may go to readers around the world. You can't assume that everybody who receives your messages shares your own culture and values. For example, if you're discussing the Internet itself, don't try to claim that the First Amendment protects your online freedom of speech; the American Constitution doesn't apply outside the borders of the United States. The same thing applies to assumptions about religion. Just because you live in a small midwestern city where everybody is either Presbyterian or Catholic, you might be exchanging messages with Hindus in Bombay or Jews in New York and Jerusalem, who might be offended by your well-meaning Christmas or Easter greetings.

If you're not prepared to defend your opinions, you may want to think twice before posting them. There's an excellent chance that somebody, someplace, will disagree and let you know about it in no uncertain terms.

In the rest of this chapter, you will find an explanation of the way Internet news operates and descriptions of several news client programs, including Microsoft's Internet News, Free Agent, and the newsreaders within Microsoft Network and America Online.

How News Is Organized

Every newsgroup has a unique name that identifies the topic of discussion within the newsgroup, and the general category, or *domain*, that includes this topic. For example, the rec.gardens newsgroup is part of the rec (short for recreational) domain.

Many topics have been divided into subtopics, each with a separate newsgroup, such as rec.gardens.roses, devoted to gardening information for people who grow roses. In some cases, the subtopics have been divided into still more specific groups, like rec.food.drink.coffee and rec.food.drink.tea.

The most widespread newsgroups are the seven original Usenet domains, and the alternative domains that don't fit the Usenet categories. The Usenet domains are:

comp   Computer-related topics

news   Topics related to Usenet news

rec   Hobbies, arts, and recreational activities

sci   Science and technology (except computers)

soc   Politics and society

talk   Debates and controversies

misc   Subjects that don't fit one of the other six categories

The alternative domains include:

alt   A catch-all for alternative topics, including oddball subjects like alt.alien.visitors and alt.happy.birthday.to.me, and conferences whose originators didn't want to bother with the bureaucratic procedure involved in creating a new Usenet newsgroup

bionet News about the biological sciences

biz   Business topics, including advertisements, which are not allowed in most other domains

clari   News from the commercial Clarinet service, supplied by the Associated Press and Reuters

k12   Newsgroups for and about schools and teachers

There are also several hundred other domain names, including geographic headings, institutions (such as specific universities or corporations), and network services. These secondary domains are not distributed as widely as the major ones, but your news server will probably support at least a few of them.

When you create an article for a newsgroup, or a reply to somebody else's article, you send it from a client program called a newsreader to a news server, probably at your Internet Service Provider (ISP). The news server assigns a unique identity number to your article, and then passes it along to all the other news servers that support the newsgroup where you posted the article.

To read news articles, you must instruct your newsreader program to complete these steps:

1. Download a list of newsgroups from the server.
2. Select the newsgroups that you want to read.
3. Download a list of available articles in a newsgroup.
4. Select and download individual articles.

With a couple of important exceptions, almost all news servers use the standard NNTP (Network News Transport Protocol) to exchange articles with newsreader client programs. Therefore, you can use just about any newsreader program with any server. Later in this chapter, you can find descriptions of two quite different newsreaders.

Unfortunately, the major exceptions are Microsoft Network and America Online. If MSN is your only ISP, the only way you can read news is through the MSN online service. You can find instructions for finding Internet news on MSN at the end of this chapter.

Using Microsoft Internet News

Microsoft Internet Mail and News is part of the Microsoft Internet Starter Kit, and it's also available for free download from http://www.microsoft.com/ie/ imn.htm. The initial release is strictly for Windows 95, but additional versions for other platforms may appear later. The Internet Mail and News package actually contains two separate programs. This section describes the newsreader; you can find information about the mail client in the next chapter.

Before you try to use Internet News, remember that it does not work with an Internet connection through MSN. If MSN is your only access, look in the "Obtaining News from MSN" section later in this chapter.

Both the Internet News and Internet Mail programs are integrated into the Windows Explorer, so you can open the programs from within the Explorer window and jump between news (or mail) and any other folder.

Configuring the Newsreader

Internet News will ask you to identify your news server and information about your account when you run the program for the first time. You can obtain this information from your ISP's technical support group (most good ISPs send new customers an information sheet that contains the addresses you need to configure news, mail, and other Internet client programs on your local system).

To change the configuration, or to add another news server, follow these steps:

1. Open the News menu and select the Options command.
2. Click on the Server tab to display the dialog box shown in Figure 11.1.
3. To change an existing news server configuration, double-click on the name of the server in the News Server(s) list. To obtain news from a new server, click on the Add button. Either way, the dialog box in Figure 11.2 will appear.
4. Type the exact address of your ISP's news server in the News Server Name field.

FIGURE 11.1:
Use the Server tab of the Options dialog box to add or change your configuration.

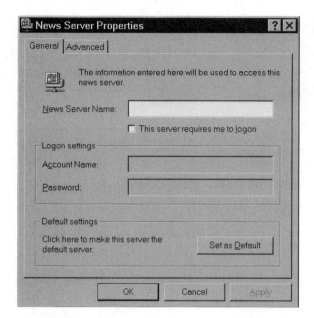

FIGURE 11.2:
The News Server Properties dialog box contains details about the server that supplies news to the newsreader client program.

5. If your ISP has advised you that you must send the news server your name and password, place a checkmark next to This Server Requires Me to Logon, and type your login name and password in the Logon Settings fields.

6. If you want this server to be your default, click on the Set as Default button.

In most cases, the default settings in the Advanced tab are the ones you need. Don't change them unless your ISP tells you to do so.

Reading News Articles

There are two steps involved in reading news articles through Microsoft Internet News: subscribing to a newsgroup and downloading individual articles.

The first time you run Internet News, the program will automatically download a list of newsgroups that are available from your news server.

To join a newsgroup, follow these steps:

1. Click on the Newsgroups icon in the frame along the left side of the News window, or select the Newsgroups command from the News menu. The Newsgroups window, shown in Figure 11.3, will appear.

2. Scroll through the list of newsgroups to select the one you want to join. If you're looking for something specific (rather than just browsing for interesting-sounding groups), you can type all or part of a name or description in the search field at the top of the window.

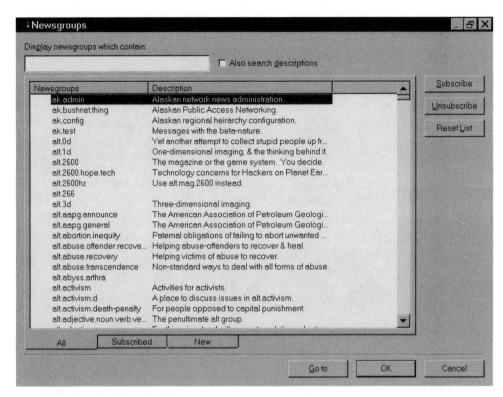

FIGURE 11.3: Use the Newsgroups dialog box to join a newsgroup.

3. Click on the Subscribe button or double-click on the name of the group to add the selected newsgroup to your subscription list.

4. To see a list of articles in a newsgroup, select the name of the group and click on the Go To button at the bottom of the Newsgroups window.

Once you have opened a newsgroup, you can read an article by selecting it from the list, as shown in Figure 11.4. To sort the list of articles in a different order, click on a column heading. When you select an article, the text appears in the preview pane, which is normally below the article list.

To load the article into a separate window, as shown in Figure 11.5, double-click on the description in the list.

Viewing Subscribed Newsgroups

The complete list of newsgroups is enormous, but when you subscribe to a newsgroup, Internet News adds it to the list that appears when you click on the Subscribed tab in the Newsgroups window.

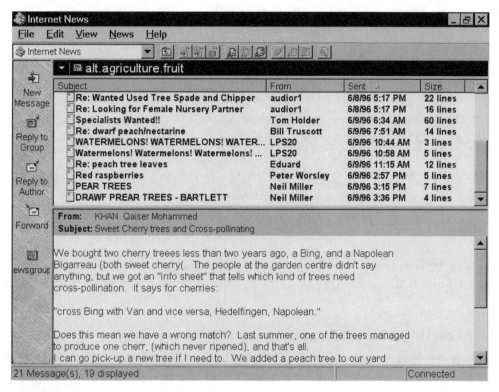

FIGURE 11.4: To read an article, select it from the list.

When you download and read an article, the newsreader program marks this message as "read." The newsreader displays message descriptions for unread articles in **boldface type**, and articles you've already read in normal type. The next time you download a list of new articles, the newsreader will ignore the ones you've already seen if you select the Unread Messages Only command in the View menu.

In many cases, you will want to scan subject descriptions, but you won't want to bother actually reading every message. You can use the Mark As Read, Mark All As Read, and Mark As Unread commands in the Edit menu to change the status of news articles in the message list.

Sending Messages to a Newsgroup

Eventually, you will probably want to participate in a newsgroup more actively, by sending your own messages for other people to read. Internet News includes the most important commands in the icon bar at the left of the message window. You can hide the icon bar and move the commands to the toolbar with the Icon Bar command in the View menu. The following sections describe the commands for sending messages.

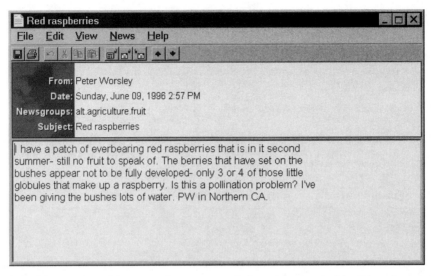

FIGURE 11.5: An article appears in a separate window when you double-click on its description in the list.

Creating a New Message

The New Message command in the icon bar and the New Message to Newsgroup command in the Message menu both open the new message window shown in Figure 11.6.

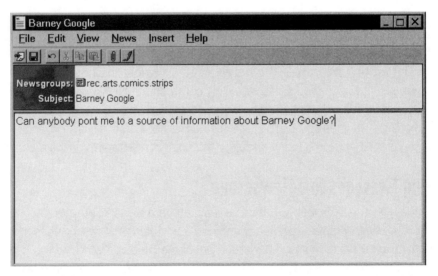

FIGURE 11.6: The new message window includes space for the destination and text of your message.

The program will automatically insert the name of the current newsgroup in the Newsgroups field. If you want to send this message to a different group, you can delete the default and type a different name, or use the Choose Newsgroups command in the News menu.

Type a brief description of this message in the Subject field. This description will appear in the list of articles when other users join this newsgroup.

Click in the bottom half of the New Message window to begin typing the text of your article. You can use the standard Windows Edit commands to cut, copy, and paste text between this window and other Windows documents.

Replying to Messages

Use the Reply to Group command on the icon bar, or the Reply to Newsgroup command in the News menu, to add your own comments to an existing message thread.

Use the Reply to Author command to send a private e-mail message to the originator of the current article. This is a good alternative to the Reply to Group command when somebody has posted a request for very specific information that may not be of general interest to other people participating in the newsgroup. For example, if you participate in one of the genealogy newsgroups, you might see an article requesting information about your grandmother's family name. Since nobody else reading the newsgroup is likely to care about your answer, you should send your reply directly to the originator only.

Forwarding Messages

The Forward command copies the current news article into an e-mail message, so you can send a copy of the article to somebody who may not have seen it in the newsgroup. If you wish, you can add your own comments to the beginning or end of the message, or insert them within the original text.

Hiding the Desktop Icons

Like Internet Explorer, Internet News automatically places a command icon on your desktop when you install the program. And like Internet Explorer, News won't allow you to delete the icon easily.

If you don't want the icon on your desktop, you must use the Desktop tab of the Tweak UI program to hide it. You can download a free copy of Tweak UI from http://www.microsoft.com/windows/software/powertoy.htm.

Using Free Agent

Microsoft's Internet News is an okay newsreader, but it's not your only choice. There are several third-party programs that offer different feature sets and screen layouts from the Microsoft product. One of the best is Free Agent, which has the added benefit of being free. You can obtain a copy of Free Agent from http://www.forteinc.com/agent/. Forte also offers another newsreader with even more and better features, but you'll have to pay for that one.

One of Free Agent's nicest features is that it allows you to arrange the screen in just about any imaginable layout. Figure 11.7 shows the default layout. When you're concentrating on a particular section of the screen, you can expand it to fill the window by clicking on the sizing icon in the upper-right corner of each pane.

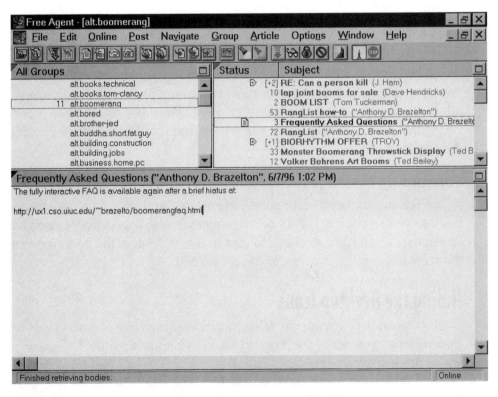

FIGURE 11.7: Free Agent can display lists of groups and articles and the text of the current article at the same time.

As Figure 11.8 shows, you can also organize the screen in many other ways: horizontal or vertical rows, or one big pane and two little ones.

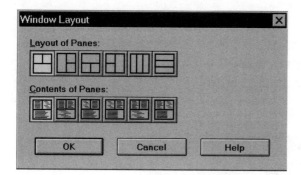

FIGURE 11.8:
You can organize information in Free Agent in almost any layout.

The first time you run the program, Free Agent automatically loads the current list of newsgroups from your server. To update the list, use the Get New Groups command in the Online menu. To get another complete list, use the Refresh Groups List command.

Once you have a copy of the list of groups, you can obtain a list of articles within a particular group, or subscribe to a group by double-clicking on the name of the group. To switch between a list of all groups, a list of new groups, and your own list of subscribed groups, click on the title bar at the top of the Groups pane. After you have loaded a list of articles, double-click on a description to see the text of that article.

Free Agent is a lot more flexible than Microsoft's Internet News, but it has one important drawback for Windows 95 users: it's a 16-bit program, which means that it won't automatically use AutoDial to connect your computer to the Internet. Therefore, you must set up your Dial-Up Networking connection before you start Free Agent. This isn't a big deal, but it can catch you by surprise if you don't think about it. If this makes a difference to you, there's a 32-bit version of (non-free) Agent that does not have this problem. Check the Forte Web site (www.forteinc.com/agent) for details.

Obtaining News from MSN

Because MSN doesn't use an NNTP news server, it's not possible to use Microsoft Internet News or Free Agent with an Internet connection through MSN. This is likely to change as Microsoft converts MSN from a proprietary online service to an Internet access provider, but for the moment, you can't get there from here.

This does not mean that you can't participate in newsgroups through MSN. You can, but you must treat newsgroups as if they were MSN forums.

Finding Newsgroups

A few shortcuts to Internet newsgroups show up in some of MSN's category areas, but the easiest way to find them is through The Internet Center. As Figure 11.9 shows, the Internet Newsgroups folder contains several subfolders that eventually take you to individual newsgroups.

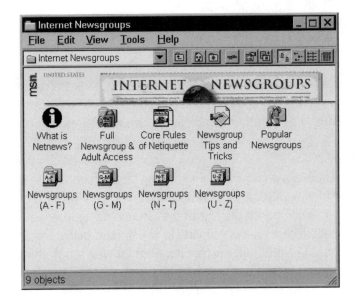

FIGURE 11.9:
MSN has organized Internet newsgroups to fit its own system of folders and messages.

Finding a specific newsgroup in MSN is not always easy. There are four folders that list newsgroups alphabetically, with a subfolder within the alphabetical folders for each domain. If all of the newsgroups you want to read are in the major Usenet domains, you can use the Popular Newsgroups folder instead of the alphabetical listings.

You may notice that there's no folder in the alphabetical list for the alt domain, which contains many of the most interesting and timely newsgroups. In the interest of protecting underage readers from possibly objectionable material, MSN has placed an extra step in the way of access to newsgroups and other areas on MSN that contain "adult content." Without the alt newsgroups, you're missing an important part of the "feel" of Internet news. While it's true that the alt domain is home to some news-groups that are not appropriate for children, it also includes many groups like alt.books.isaac-asimov, where people discuss the work of the famous science fiction author, and alt.christnet, a gathering place for Christian ministers. Fortunately, it's simple enough to gain full access.

Before they'll let you see any alt newsgroups, you must complete the Full Newsgroups Access EForm, shown in Figure 11.10. You can download this form from the Full Newsgroup & Adult Access folder or the Popular Newsgroups folder.

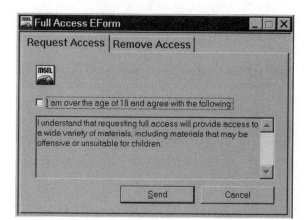

FIGURE 11.10:
Place a checkmark in the I Am Over 18 box and click on the Send button for full access to all newsgroups.

Reading News

Reading news through MSN isn't very different from using a separate newsreader program. First select a newsgroup, and then choose the messages within the groups that you want to read.

Figure 11.11 shows a list of articles in the rec.music.folk newsgroup. The default listing displays them sorted by date, but it will probably be easier to follow a thread if you click on the Subject column header to rearrange the list in alphabetical order by topic. To read an article, double-click anywhere on the line that contains the description of that item.

If you want to read everything in a newsgroup, the easiest method is to open the first item, and then use one of the command buttons in the Message window toolbar to advance through the list of messages.

If you have only a passing interest in reading news, MSN can meet your needs. And if you're already active in MSN forums, it's nice to use the same commands for both MSN forums and Internet newsgroups. But the Internet News and Free Agent newsreaders are both easier to use. If newsgroups are one of the primary reasons you're

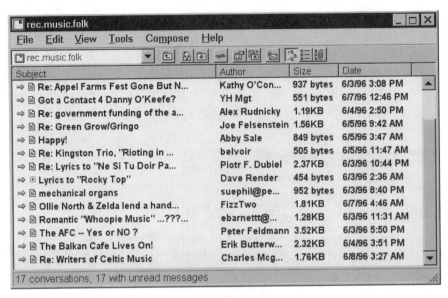

FIGURE 11.11: MSN lists news articles in message lists.

interested in the Internet, you'll probably be happier with a separate newsreader program and a different ISP.

Reading News on AOL

If you're an AOL subscriber, you can read Internet news by following these steps:

1. Log on to AOL and go to the keyword Newsgroups. The window shown in Figure 11.12 will appear.

2. To add a newsgroup to the list of My Newsgroups, click on the Add Newsgroups button, select a domain, and click on the List Topics button. When the list of groups within a domain appears, double-click on the name of the subdomain or newsgroup you want. After a window appears for the newsgroup, click on the Add button.

3. To open a newsgroup in the My Newsgroups list, click on the Read My Newsgroup button and choose it from the list. To read an article, double-click on the listing for that item. The text of the article will appear in a window like the one in Figure 11.13.

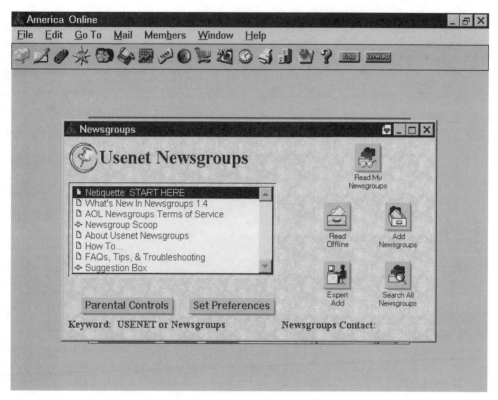

FIGURE 11.12: The Newsgroups window is AOL's gateway to Internet news.

NOTE Don't worry if the AOL screens shown here don't look exactly like the ones you see on your own computer. The commands are the same in earlier software releases. If you haven't received AOL's Version 3.0 software, go to the Keyword Upgrade or Preview to download it, or call AOL's customer support at 800-827-6364 to request a copy on disk.

As a newsreader, AOL is less flexible than the programs that obtain news from NNTP servers. It's easy to use, but it lacks many features that are in Free Agent and Internet News.

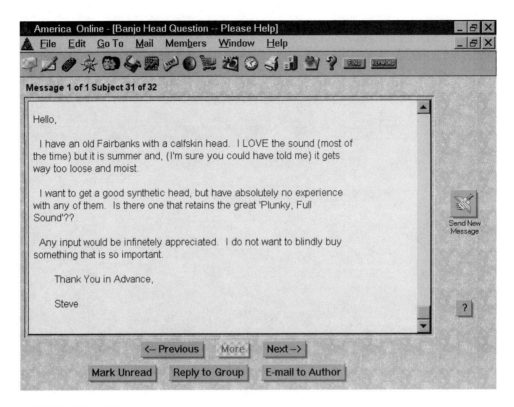

FIGURE 11.13: AOL displays Internet news articles in separate windows.

Whichever newsreader you choose, a warning is in order: you can waste an incredible amount of time keeping up with Internet news. If you participate in more than a handful of active groups, it's easy to spend several hours a day reading new articles, writing replies, and keeping up with the private e-mail that you exchange with the people you met in those groups.

When you begin to feel that most of your closest friends are the regulars in your favorite newsgroups, you should realize that you're on the way over the edge. It's time to turn off the computer for a day or two and remind yourself that there's another world out there. Go for a walk; spend more time with your family; read a book. In spite of what your net.friends may tell you, there's more to life than an alternative reality based on typing.

Internet news is a many-to-many communications medium. In the next chapter, you'll learn about sending and receiving one-to-one messages through electronic mail.

Chapter 12

SENDING AND RECEIVING E-MAIL

- **Understanding how e-mail works**
- **Using links to e-mail addresses in Internet Explorer**
- **Exchanging e-mail through Microsoft Exchange**
- **Sending and receiving e-mail with Internet Mail**
- **Using Eudora as your e-mail manager**

Electronic mail is both the simplest and most widely used Internet service. You can exchange messages with just about anybody who has access to the Internet or any other network with an e-mail gateway to the Internet.

When the system is working properly, most messages should arrive at their recipients' computers anywhere in the world within a few minutes after you send them; in practice, it's not uncommon for messages to be delayed because of heavy network traffic or equipment problems between the sender and the receiver. Even so, it's almost always faster and less expensive to send messages by e-mail rather than by using the postal system.

How E-Mail Works

Like the other Internet services we've looked at, e-mail is yet another client-server system, called Simple Message Transfer Protocol (SMTP). As Figure 12.1 shows, you use a mail client program to send a message to a post office server (an SMTP server), which identifies the recipient's address and sends it to the mail server that handles mail for that address (a POP3—Post Office Protocol No. 3—server). The mail server stores the message in a mailbox until the recipient's client program requests it.

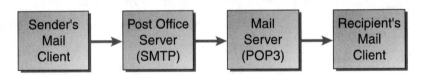

FIGURE 12.1: Internet e-mail moves from the sender to the recipient through a series of clients and servers.

If the sender or the recipient has an account on a system that does not use SMTP, such as a Novell MHS (Message Handling Service) e-mail network or an online service like AOL or CompuServe, there's an additional step between the post office server and the mail server: a gateway that converts the address information from SMTP format to the format used by the other system, or from the other format to SMTP.

All e-mail client programs perform at least five separate functions:

- They include a method for creating new messages.
- They send messages to a post office server.

- They receive messages from a mail server.
- They display messages.
- They store copies of inbound and outbound messages.

Many mail clients include additional features and functions, such as message filters and address books, but every mail program will handle the above basic services.

Address Formats

In order to make this worldwide message exchange work properly, everybody must use a consistent address format. Unlike the post office, where a human mail sorter will know what to do with a letter that has the city on the top line of the address and the recipient's name at the bottom, like this:

New Bedford, Massachusetts 01347

349 Oak Street

Elizabeth Borden

The computers that handle e-mail are unforgiving; if an address is formatted incorrectly, the message won't get through.

The standard format for an Internet e-mail address is:

name@address.domain

The *name* part identifies the recipient's e-mail account, and the *address.domain* part specifies the recipient's mail server. The *domain* is a code that identifies either the type of organization that owns the mail server (such as .com for commercial businesses, .edu for educational institutions, or .gov for government agencies), or the geographic location (such as .ca for Canada or .fr for France).

So, for example, bugs@carrot.com might be an e-mail address for a user with the account name "bugs" on a commercial system called "carrot.com." Every e-mail address is unique; there's only one computer with the address "carrot.com," and just one user on that system with the account name "bugs."

| TIP | When spoken, the @ symbol is read as "at" and the period as "dot." So bugs@carrot.com would be spoken as "bugs at carrot dot com." |

E-Mail Client Programs

You have several options for sending and receiving Internet e-mail:

- Directly from Internet Explorer, using e-mail links in Web pages
- The Microsoft Exchange client supplied with Windows 95 and similar client programs available for other operating systems
- The Microsoft Internet Mail and News program
- A third-party mail program, such as Eudora by Qualcomm, or the Mail program included with Netscape Navigator

If you're using Windows 3.1, there's no built-in mail program supplied with Internet Explorer, but you can use the 16-bit versions of Eudora, Microsoft Internet Mail (when it becomes available), or any other third-party mail client program.

Sending E-Mail from Internet Explorer

Internet Explorer does not include a general-purpose e-mail client, but it does recognize links to e-mail addresses. When you click on an e-mail link, Internet Explorer opens your e-mail client program and creates a new message, as shown in Figure 12.2 , with the recipient's address already in the To field. To send a message to the person identified in the link, type the text in the body of the editor and click on the Send button in the toolbar.

Using the Microsoft Exchange Client

The Exchange client is a "universal inbox" that can process many different kinds of messages through the same window. The Exchange client is a front-end program for Microsoft's Messaging Application Program Interface (MAPI). If you use other messaging services along with your Internet e-mail (such as fax, voice mail, or e-mail through an online service such as CompuServe or Microsoft Network), or if you're exchanging data with a Microsoft Exchange server, you can use the Exchange client as a single control point, regardless of each message's source or destination. It's also possible to use OLE (Object Linking and Embedding) commands to send e-mail through MAPI directly from application programs such as word processors and spreadsheets.

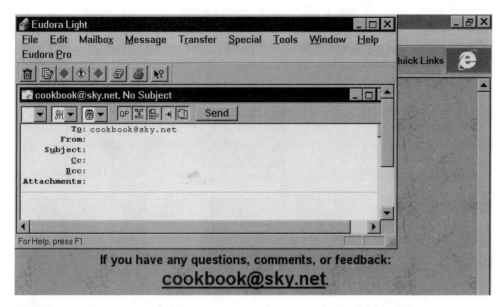

FIGURE 12.2: Use your e-mail client program to send a message from a link in a Web page.

As Figure 12.3 shows, the Windows 95 Messaging Subsystem separates message handling into three separate functions: message manager client applications such as the Exchange client, the MAPI interface, and individual drivers for specific information services. As long as the MAPI interface is in place, it's a simple matter to mix and match front ends and messaging services.

Windows 95 comes with Exchange drivers for several messaging services, including MSN, Microsoft Fax, Microsoft Mail, and Internet Mail. Many other drivers for additional messaging services are available from service providers and software developers, including AT&T Mail, WinFax, CompuServe, Prodigy, Netscape, and several voice messaging systems. When America Online starts to bundle Internet Explorer with software, you can expect to see a MAPI messaging service driver for AOL as well.

If you use Microsoft Network as your e-mail service provider, you can use the "Internet Over The Microsoft Network" driver included with Windows 95 to process your Internet e-mail through the Exchange client. If you use some other ISP that uses SMTP and POP3, you will need a separate Internet E-Mail driver, which is available from Microsoft as a free download from http://www.microsoft.com/windows/software/inetmail.htm.

When you use Internet Explorer to download a messaging service driver from Microsoft, the program may automatically install and load the new driver when the

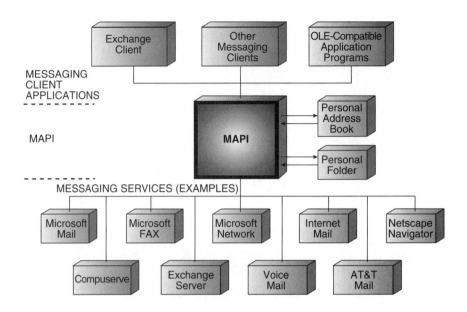

FIGURE 12.3: The Windows 95 Messaging Subsystem uses a modular architecture.

download is complete. If installation does not happen automatically or when you obtain driver software from other suppliers, either by download or on diskette or CD-ROM, follow these steps to add a new messaging service to your Exchange client:

1. Start Microsoft Exchange from the Windows Start ➤ Programs menu.
2. Open the Tools menu and select the Services menu.
3. Click on the Add button to display the Add Service to Profile dialog box, shown in Figure 12.4.

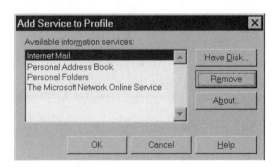

FIGURE 12.4:
Use the Add Service to Profile dialog box to install a new messaging service.

4. If the name of the service you want to add is visible in the list of Available Information Services, select it; if it's not on the list, click on the Have Disk button.

5. If you're loading the messaging service from a disk, place the disk in your drive and use the Browse button to specify the directory that contains the driver software. Click on the OK button to load the software.

6. The new messaging service will now be in the list of Available Information Services. Select it and click on the OK button to add this service to the current Exchange Profile.

Configuring the Internet Mail Messaging Service

If you're using the "Internet Over MSN" as your e-mail service, you will automatically configure it when you load the software. When you install the Internet Mail messaging service for other ISPs, the program will ask for configuration details; you can change this information later by following these steps:

1. Start the Exchange client.

2. Open the Tools menu and select the Options command.

3. Click on the Services tab and select Internet Mail from the list of active services.

4. Click on the Properties button to display the dialog box shown in Figure 12.5. Fill in the fields in this dialog box as described below.

General Tab

The options in the General tab identify the account and mail servers that the Exchange client will use to send and receive mail:

- **Full Name:** Exchange will use the name you specify as your full name in the From fields of all your outgoing messages.

- **E-mail Address:** Your e-mail address is the address where you want people to send replies to your messages. If you have more than one e-mail address, it's sometimes useful to send messages through one account but use another as your e-mail address for replies; the address in this field doesn't need to be the one used by this messaging service.

- **Internet Mail Server:** The mail server is the computer that holds your mail in a mailbox until your mail client program downloads it. If your e-mail address is bugs@carrot.com, your mail server is probably mail.carrot.com, but you should confirm this with your ISP or network help desk. The name you specify must be exactly correct, or you won't be able to receive your mail.

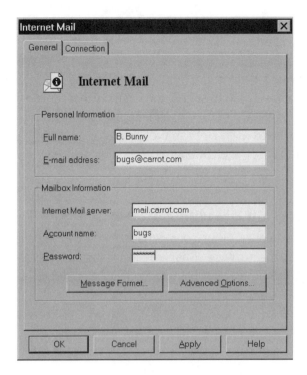

FIGURE 12.5:
Use the Internet Mail dialog box to change the address of your mail server.

- **Account Name:** An outbound (POP3) mail server accepts messages only from users who have an account on that server. Therefore, your mail client program must log you into the server whenever you want to send mail. Your account name is usually the same as the *name* part of your *name@address* e-mail address. When you set up your account, your ISP or system administrator will tell you what account name to use. It's probably the same name you use when you connect your computer to your ISP's network server.
- **Password:** Your ISP or network administrator will give you a password when you set up your e-mail account.
- **Message Format:** Exchange can use either MIME or UUENCODE format for outgoing messages. In most cases, the only time this makes any real difference is when you attach a binary file to a message, in which case you should make sure that the recipient can decode the format you use to send the file. If the recipient isn't sure which format is correct, try UUENCODE first. To use MIME format, place a checkmark in the option box; to use UUENCODE, make sure there is not a checkmark in the box.

- **Character Set:** The only time you need to worry about the Character Set options is when you're sending messages in Norwegian or Swedish, or in a language that doesn't use the Roman alphabet, such as Greek or Russian.
- **Advanced Options:** If the SMTP server has a different address from your POP3 server, click on the Advanced Options button to specify the name of the SMTP server. If both inbound and outbound mail use the same server, leave this field blank.

Connection Tab

The options in the Connection tab control the way the Exchange client connects to your mail server:

- **Connecting to Internet Mail:** If you're connected to the Internet through a LAN, choose the Connect Using the Network option. If you use Dial-Up Networking, choose the Connect Using the Modem option, and select a connection from the drop-down list.
- **Transferring Internet Mail:** If you don't want your mail server to automatically download all your mail to the Exchange client when you check for new mail, place a checkmark in the Work Off-line and Use Remote Mail option box. When this option is active, you will be able to use Exchange's Remote Mail feature to scan a list of messages and select the ones you want to download and read, rather than downloading everything whenever you connect.

Creating and Sending E-Mail through Exchange

Every entry in the Exchange client's address book has a messaging service assigned to it. When you send a message, the program automatically sets up links to the correct service for each recipient and uses the appropriate set of protocols to send and receive messages. Therefore, you can send the same message to people who use different services by choosing their names from your address book.

Figure 12.6 shows the Exchange client's message editor. To create a message, either type the recipient's e-mail address in the To field or click on the To button to choose one or more names from your address book. Type a description of the message in the Subject field, and the body of your message in the large box in the bottom of the window. The text-editing functions in Exchange will be familiar if you have used other Windows text editors.

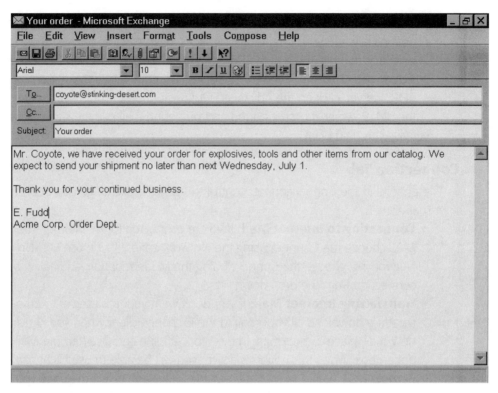

FIGURE 12.6: Use the message editor window to create e-mail messages in Exchange.

Receiving and Reading Messages with Exchange

Every time you open the Exchange client, and at intervals you can specify, the MAPI connects to each active messaging service, checks for new messages, and places them in your Inbox folder, as shown in Figure 12.7. You can move a message to a different folder by dragging and dropping the description. The Exchange Viewer shows unread messages in **boldface type**. After you read a message, the listing changes to normal type.

To read a message, double-click on its description in the message list. As Figure 12.8 shows, the message view window includes the usual set of editing functions, so you can add your own annotations to a message.

The Exchange client has features that make it easy to send and receive e-mail, faxes and voice mail through more than one service at the same time, but if Internet e-mail is the only message service you use, it may be more trouble than

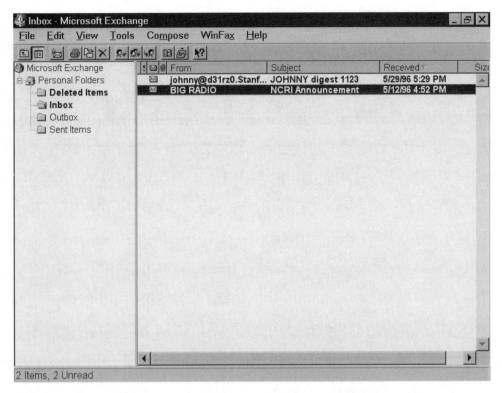

FIGURE 12.7: The Exchange Viewer displays a list of messages in each folder in your folder list.

it's worth. The mail manager in Microsoft's Internet Mail and News and third-party programs like Eudora don't have Exchange's multiple-messaging service features, but they handle Internet e-mail at least as well as the Exchange client. Like much of life, it all comes down to a matter of personal taste.

Exchanging E-Mail with Microsoft Internet Mail

Internet Mail is the SMTP client program that comes with the Microsoft newsreader described in the previous chapter. Internet News and Internet Mail use similar screen layouts, and both are closely integrated with the Windows 95 Explorer. You can download both programs from Microsoft's Web site at http://www.microsoft.com/ie/platform/imn.htm.

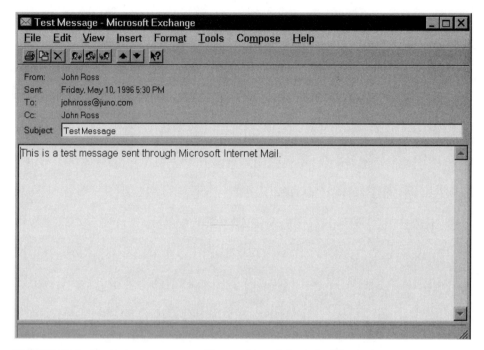

FIGURE 12.8: The Exchange message editor provides a full set of editing tools.

Because Internet Mail depends on SMTP and POP3 protocols, it won't work through a connection to Microsoft Network; if you use MSN to reach the Internet, you'll need the Exchange client to handle your e-mail.

Figure 12.9 shows the main Internet Mail window. The top part of the window contains a list of messages in the current folder; the text of the currently selected message appears in the preview pane at the bottom of the window. To change to a different folder, click on the title of the current folder to open a drop-down list, and then choose the folder you want to open.

The icon bar on the left side of the Mail window includes several of the program's most frequently used commands. If you prefer, you can move the icon bar to any of the other borders by dragging and dropping. To hide the icon bar completely and move the commands to the toolbar, remove the checkmark from the Icon Bar command in the View menu.

The preview pane isn't the only place you can read a message. To open a message in a separate window, double-click on the entry for that message in the message list.

Newly received messages appear first in the Inbox folder, but you don't have to leave them there. To create a new folder, use the Folder command in the File menu.

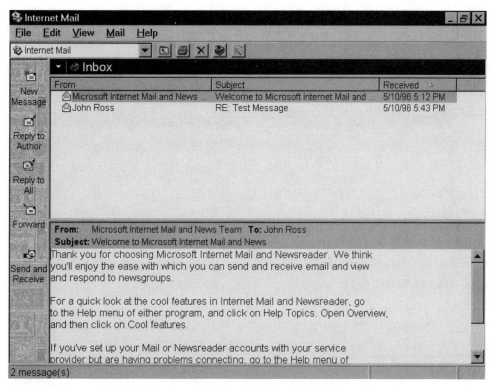

FIGURE 12.9: The main Internet Mail window contains a list of messages in the current folder and the text of the currently selected message.

To move the currently selected message to a different folder, open the Mail menu and choose the Move To command to select the target folder.

Sending and Receiving Messages with Internet Mail

To create a new e-mail message, use the New Message command in the icon bar or the Message menu to open the New Message editor window shown in Figure 12.10. When the message is complete, use the Send Message command in the File menu or the toolbar to place the message in your Outbox folder.

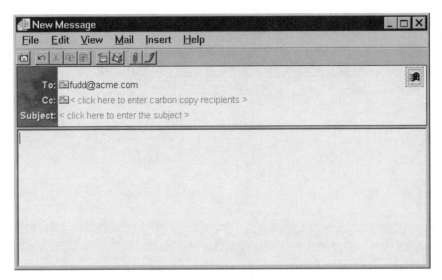

FIGURE 12.10: Use the New Message editor to compose e-mail messages.

When you're ready to upload outgoing messages to your post office server, click on the Send and Receive icon in the icon bar, or use the Send and Receive Mail command in the Message menu.

While Internet Mail is connected to the server, it will also check for new messages that may have arrived at the mail server since the last time it was connected. If you prefer, you can configure the program to automatically look for new messages on a regular schedule by selecting the Options command in the Mail menu. As Figure 12.11 shows, the Check for New Messages option in the Read tab allows you to set a time interval for message checking.

Internet News and Internet Mail are quite obviously a matched set of applications; if you're comfortable with one of them, you'll have no trouble using the other along with it. They're both relatively easy to use, and both have the basic features and functions you need to send and receive messages and articles.

Attaching Files to Messages

To send a text file or a data file along with your message in Internet Mail, use the File Attachment command in the Insert menu. This opens a file browser from which you can select the file you want to include.

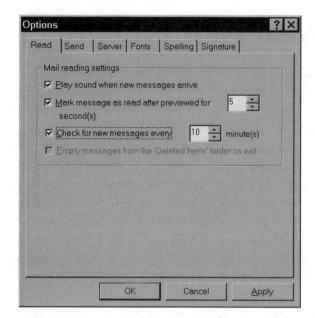

FIGURE 12.11:
Use the Check for New
Messages option to automatically
download new messages on
a regular schedule.

When you send or receive a message that includes one or more attached files, the message editor displays a shortcut icon to each file, as shown in Figure 12.12. You can treat these icons just like other Windows icons: double-click to open a file and drag-and-drop to move the icon to the desktop, a folder, Windows Explorer, or a message window.

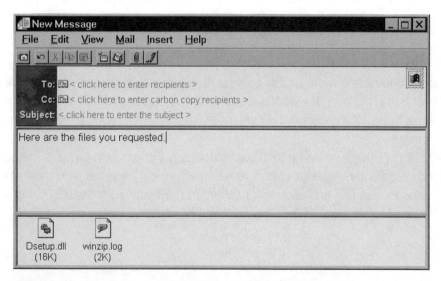

FIGURE 12.12: Internet Mail places shortcuts to files in a separate window.

Managing E-Mail with Eudora

It won't surprise you to learn that Microsoft is not the only place you can go for an Internet e-mail manager program. One of the best alternatives is Qualcomm's Eudora. Originally developed at the University of Illinois in 1988, Eudora is now used by about ten million people. If you don't care about close integration with Windows 95, you might find that Eudora's additional features make it a better mail program than either of the Microsoft products. If you're still using Windows 3.1, Eudora is the clear choice.

Qualcomm offers two versions of the program: Eudora Light, which you can obtain free from http://www.qualcomm.com/prodtech/quest/light.html, and Eudora Pro, which is sold as a shrink-wrapped product from software retailers or directly from Qualcomm. Both versions are fully functional e-mail managers, but the commercial version has several added features, including automatic message filtering, spell checking, and support for the Windows 95 MAPI interface that can integrate Eudora with the Exchange client and other application programs.

The Windows versions of Eudora come with separate programs for Windows 3.1 and Windows 95. When you install the program, it determines which platform you're using and loads the appropriate software. There's also a Macintosh version available from the same sources.

Eudora displays each mailbox and each inbound and outbound message in a separate window, as shown in Figure 12.13. You can move a message from one mailbox to another by using the commands in the Transfer menu.

Configuring Eudora

Eudora requires the same kind of configuration information as other mail programs: your own e-mail address, the addresses of your mail server and POP3 server, and so forth. All of these settings are in the Options dialog box, which you can reach from the Tools menu.

Most of the other Eudora options control the way the program displays messages on your screen and the details of its interaction with the mail server. The most essential options for sending and receiving mail are in the Getting Started, Checking Mail, and Sending Mail sections of the Options dialog box.

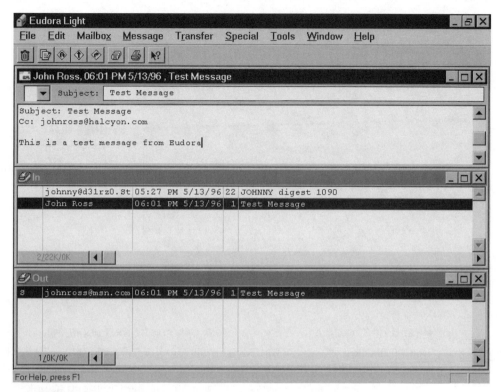

FIGURE 12.13: Eudora displays messages and mailboxes in separate windows.

Receiving Messages with Eudora

Eudora can automatically connect to your POP server and check for new mail on a regular schedule, or if you prefer, only when you enter a manual Check Mail command. The Checking Mail Options dialog box, shown in Figure 12.14, includes two options that control the way Eudora retrieves mail for you:

- **Check For Mail Every _ Minutes:** To check for new messages automatically, type the number of minutes you want Eudora to wait between downloads in this field. Unless you expect to receive a really huge volume of mail, you'll want to set an interval of at least 10 or 15 minutes. If you prefer to check for mail manually, set the interval to 0 minutes.

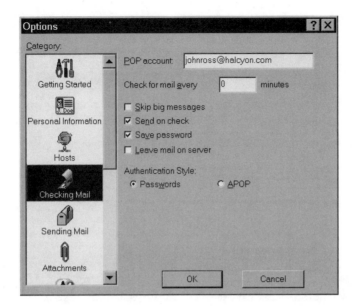

FIGURE 12.14:
The Checking Mail options control the way Eudora downloads mail from your POP server.

- **Send on Check:** If the Send on Check option is active, Eudora will automatically upload any messages waiting in the message queue to the mail server every time it checks for new mail. If the option is not active, you'll need to use the Send Queued Messages command in the File menu to upload outbound mail.

Sending Messages with Eudora

To create an e-mail message, choose the New Message command in the toolbar or the Message menu. When the window shown in Figure 12.15 appears, fill in the To and Subject fields, and type your message in the lower portion of the window. If you want to send a file along with your message, use the Attach File command in the Message menu to specify the name and location of the file. Use the Attachments category in the Options dialog box to specify the type of formatting you want to apply to this file.

When you create a new message, you can either send it to your mail server as soon as it's finished or place it in a message queue for later transmission. To change the configuration, open the Tools menu and select the Options command, and then click on the Sending Mail icon. The Immediate Send option is the first item in the Sending Mail dialog box.

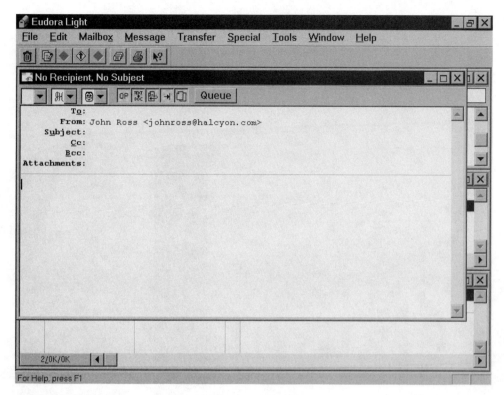

FIGURE 12.15: Type the details and text of your messages in the new message window.

If the Immediate Send option is active, Eudora will connect to your mail server and upload each message as soon as you click on the Send button. If Immediate Send is not active, you must either use the Send Queued Messages command in the File menu or make the Send on Check option active and wait for the next time Eudora checks for new mail.

In the long run, it really doesn't matter which mail client program you decide to use—once you learn how to use any of these programs, you'll be able to send and receive your mail without thinking about the command set or the screen layout. And of course, those messages are the whole point of e-mail in the first place.

Chapter 13

OTHER INTERNET TOOLS

FEATURING

- **Using WS_FTP and other FTP clients**
- **Running telnet programs, such as Windows 95 Telnet and HyperTerminal**
- **Using Internet diagnostic tools, such as ping and tracenet**

Internet Explorer and other Web browsers are excellent general-purpose tools for moving data though the Internet to your own computer, but they're not always the best ones to use. This chapter contains information about other, more specialized tools that you might want to use along with Internet Explorer. Some of these tools perform specific tasks more quickly and efficiently than Internet Explorer; others allow you to do things that you can't do with a Web browser.

Some of these tools are supplied with Windows 95, and others are available from other software developers or as shareware or freeware through the Internet. You can also find programs that perform some of these functions in commercial suites of Internet tools, including IBM's Internet Connection, NetManage's Internet Chameleon, and similar packages from FTP Software, WRQ, Frontier Technologies, and other companies. But there's really not much reason to spend the money for these utilities unless you also need other network connectivity tools, such as servers and special-purpose network drivers.

All of the programs described in this chapter are Winsock-compliant, so you can use the same network connection that you use for Internet Explorer. Remember to use only 16-bit programs with Windows 3.1.

The people who develop many of these programs seem to release new versions about three times a week. One of the best places to keep up with new and improved Internet tools is the Web site called The Ultimate Collection of Winsock Software (TUCOWS), at http://www.tucows.com. TUCOWS includes ratings and descriptions of most new programs within a few days of their release, along with direct links to the developers' own home pages and sources for the programs.

Using FTP Clients

FTP is the Internet's standard method for moving text files, data files, and binary program files from one computer to another. As you read in Chapter 8, you can use Internet Explorer for some FTP file transfers, but it's often faster and easier to use a dedicated FTP client instead of the Web browser.

There's an FTP client supplied with Windows 95 (in your Windows folder), but it uses a command line rather than a graphic interface. Don't waste your time with it. Much better FTP clients with point-and-click or drag-and-drop capabilities are available from online sources.

Each FTP application has a different screen layout, but the process of finding and downloading a file is essentially the same for all of them:

1. Connect your client program to an FTP server.

2. Log on to the server. Almost all public FTP servers accept the login name "anonymous," with your e-mail address as the password. If you have an account on the server, you can use your own login name and password to get access to files that may not be available to anonymous users, or to upload files from your computer to the server.

WARNING Some very popular servers will accept only a limited number of connections at the same time, so that the file transfer speed doesn't become impossibly slow. If you can't get through the first time you try to connect to a server, try again later, or look for another source for the file you want to download.

3. Move to the directory on the server that contains the file you want.
4. Specify the folder or directory on your own computer where you want to place the downloaded file.
5. Transfer the file from the server to your own computer. Some clients ask you to specify whether each file is ASCII text or binary data before you start the download.
6. Disconnect from the server.

WS_FTP

WS_FTP has been available for several years, but it's still one of the best FTP clients around. The developer, John Junod, now of Ipswitch, Inc., continues to offer new and improved versions. The program is free to government and academic users, and to individuals for their own noncommercial use. Other users can evaluate the program free for 15 days, and then order the commercial version from the developer.

You can obtain the latest versions of WS_FTP from the Ipswitch Web site at http://www.ipswitch.com/pd_wsftp.html. There are separate versions of the program for Windows 3.1 (16-bit) and Windows 95 (32-bit).

WS_FTP displays the contents of a directory in your own computer (the "local system") on the left, and a directory at the distant FTP server (the "remote system") on the right. The remote system is usually the source of your file transfers, and the local directory is usually the destination.

To move to a subdirectory within the current directory, double-click on its name. To move to the parent directory that contains the current directory, double-click on the two dots (..) at the top of the list. To move to a completely different directory on the same computer, type the new path in the field directly above the list of files.

The 32-bit WS_FTP package contains two separate programs: a four-window version that lists local folders and remote directories separately from individual files, as shown in Figure 13.1, and a two-window version that shows directories and files in the

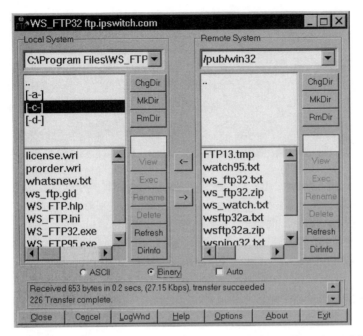

FIGURE 13.1: The four-window version of WS_FTP shows directories and files separately.

same window with icons that identify file types, as shown in Figure 13.2. The free versions of both programs work the same, but the commercial version of the two-window program supports drag-and-drop file transfers.

Connecting to an FTP Server with WS_FTP

To connect to an FTP server, follow these steps:

1. Click on the Connect button at the bottom of the WS_FTP window. The Session Profile dialog box shown in Figure 13.3 will open.

2. Open the drop-down Profile Name list to select a host, or type the full address of the server in the Host Name field.

3. For anonymous FTP, place a checkmark in the Anonymous Login option box. WS_FTP will use the address you specified during installation as your password. To log in to a server on your own account, type your user ID and password in the fields that request them.

4. If you know the full path of the directory on the server that contains the file you want, type the path in the Remote Host field. If you leave this field blank, WS_FTP will connect you to the server's root directory, and you can move to the right place one step at a time.

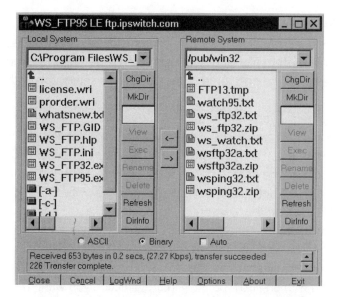

FIGURE 13.2:
The two-window version lists directories and files in the same windows.

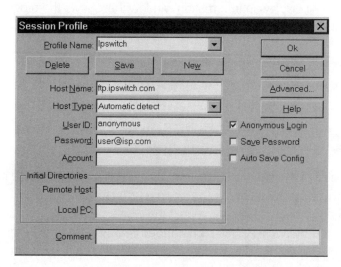

FIGURE 13.3:
Use the Session Profile dialog box to connect to an FTP host.

5. Click on the OK button. WS_FTP will display the commands and responses that it exchanges with the server at the bottom of the screen.

Transferring a File with WS_FTP

When the connection is in place, you will see the contents of the current directory on the server in the Remote System file list on the right side of the WS_FTP window. To move a file from the server to the host, or from the host to the server, follow these steps:

1. Find the name of the file you want to transfer in one of the directory lists.

2. Make sure the correct file type is specified; either ASCII for text files or Binary for data files. You can assume that any file with a file name extension .txt or .lst, and files called read.me or readme are ASCII text; most others are probably binary. If you're not sure about a file, try it as binary first. Or if it's a relatively small file, click on the View button to load it into a text editor; if it appears as plain text, you can use the editor's Save command to store it. If it appears as gibberish, it's probably a binary file.

3. Select the file or files you want to transfer.

4. Click on the button with an arrow pointing in the direction you want to move the file. WS_FTP will display an information window that shows the progress of the file transfer.

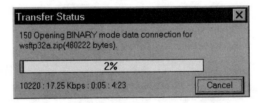

After you have copied all of the files you want from this host, click on the Close button at the bottom of the window to break the connection. To look for files from another host, click on the Connect button and repeat the whole process.

The commercial version of WS_FTP has some added features that may make it worth the added cost, even if you qualify for free use of the Limited Edition. Among other things, it supports drag-and-drop file transfer between directories, and it will resume where it left off when you reconnect after an interrupted file transfer.

Other FTP Clients

If you prefer a drag-and-drop FTP client, or if you want to see a graphic display of the distant FTP server's file structure, you might want to take a look at one of the other FTP programs listed at the TUCOWS site. For example, Figure 13.4 shows the main screen of CuteFTP, which can display descriptions of files along with their sometimes cryptic names. To transfer a file, you can either drag-and-drop or double-click on the file name.

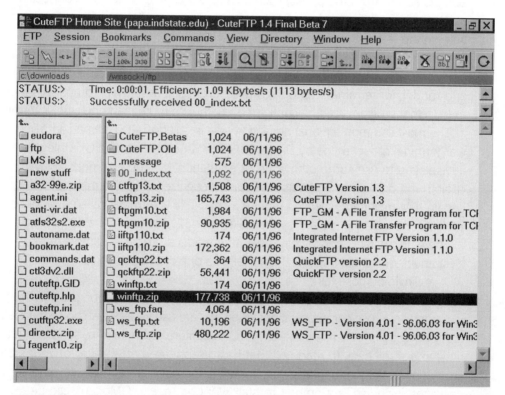

FIGURE 13.4: CuteFTP is a drag-and-drop FTP client program.

CuteFTP is shareware, which means you should pay for it if you decide to continue using it after a 30-day evaluation. You can obtain the latest version of CuteFTP from http://papa.indstate.edu:8888/CuteFTP/, or via anonymous FTP from papa .indstate.edu/winsock-l.ftp.

Using Telnet Clients

Telnet makes your computer a remote terminal that sends commands and receives data through the Internet to and from a distant host. When you type on your own keyboard, those keystrokes go directly to the host, just like keystrokes from a keyboard plugged directly into the host. The most common uses for telnet are remote access to a distant computer where you have an account and connection to a computer that accepts access from the public, such as a library catalog. Once the connection is in place, a telnet client program should be transparent; you should be able to concentrate on the responses you receive from the host.

Because telnet makes your computer appear to a telnet host as if it's a terminal, telnet clients are also known as *terminal emulation* programs. Because different brands and models of terminals send slightly different signal formats to host computers, many telnet programs can be configured to emulate more than one type of terminal.

The most common terminal emulation type is called VT-100, named for a very popular terminal model made by Digital Equipment Corporation (DEC). Unless the host advises you to use some other kind of emulation, VT-100 is almost always a good choice. The only common hosts that don't recognize VT-100 terminal emulation are certain IBM mainframes, which require a special IBM terminal called a Model 3270. You'll need a separate telnet program called a TN3270 to log in to a 3270 host.

There are many Windows telnet client programs available, and most of them do at least an adequate job. In general, they fall into one of two categories:

- Single-purpose telnet clients
- Telnet clients included with general-purpose communication programs

General-purpose communications programs are usually a better choice than telnet-only applications, because they allow you to capture incoming text, send and receive files, and scroll back to read text that has disappeared off the top of your screen, among other things. The latest versions of all the popular Windows communications packages, including ProComm, Crosstalk, WinComm, and QModem, can be used as Winsock-compliant telnet clients. HyperTerminal, the communications program supplied with Windows 95, does not support telnet, but you can get a free upgrade that adds this feature from Hilgraeve, the software developer who created the program for Microsoft. Hilgraeve's Web site is at http://www.hilgraeve.com/htpe.html.

Windows 95 Telnet

If you're using Windows 95, you probably have Microsoft's Telnet program in your \Windows directory. To start the program, follow these steps:

1. Open the Start menu and select the Run command.
2. Type **telnet *host address*** in the Open field. For example, to connect to The Well, type **telnet well.com**.

If you use the program often, you should place a shortcut to it on your desktop, add it to your Start menu, or both.

Figure 13.5 shows the Telnet window as it appears when you start the program. To set up a connection after Telnet is already running, open the Connect menu and select the Remote System command.

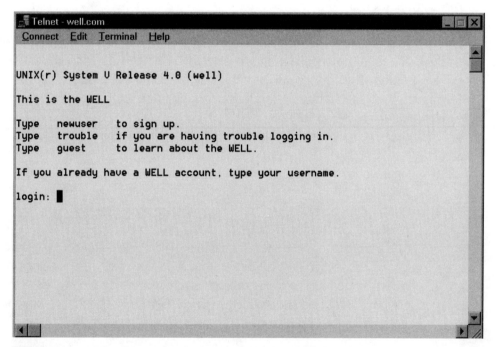

FIGURE 13.5: Microsoft Telnet is a simple terminal emulation program.

Once the connection to a telnet host goes through, you're at the mercy of that host. If you have an account on the host, you should already know how to log in, as well as how to send commands and receive data. If you're connecting to a host that welcomes public access, it should automatically display the information you need to get started.

The Microsoft Telnet client and most other single-purpose telnet programs do not include one very important feature: you can't use them to upload or download binary program files between your PC and the telnet host. If you're using telnet to connect to a file library, you'll need a client program that supports file transfer protocols, such as XModem, ZModem, or Kermit.

HyperTerminal

In addition to Microsoft Telnet, Windows 95 also includes a terminal emulation program called HyperTerminal that can connect to other computers through a modem and telephone line. HyperTerminal was created for Microsoft by Hilgraeve, who also makes a family of commercial connectivity products for Windows, OS/2, and other platforms, called HyperACCESS.

The version of HyperTerminal that comes with Windows 95 does not include a telnet client, but Hilgraeve has released a free upgrade that adds telnet and several other useful features to the original program. Hilgraeve calls this upgrade HyperTerminal Private Edition. The free HyperTerminal Private Edition upgrade is available on Hilgraeve's Web site, at http://www.hilgraeve.com/htpe.html, or the HyperTerminal bulletin board at 313-243-9957.

To connect to a new telnet host through HyperTerminal Private Edition, follow these steps:

1. Open your Start menu and choose the Programs menu. Select Hyper-Terminal from the Accessories submenu to open the HyperTerminal window.
2. Double-click on the hypertrm.exe icon to start HyperTerminal.
3. When the Connection Description dialog box, shown in Figure 13.6, appears, type a description of the telnet host in the Name field and choose an icon for this connection profile. Click on the OK button to close the dialog box.
4. When the Connect To dialog box appears, open the drop-down list in the Connect Using field and select the TCP/IP (Winsock) option. The other fields in the dialog box will change to the ones shown in Figure 13.7.

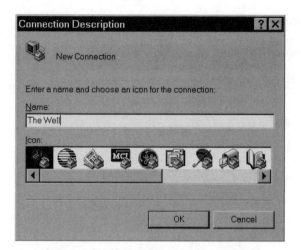

FIGURE 13.6:
Type a description of the telnet host in the Name field.

FIGURE 13.7:
When you select a TCP/IP connection, HyperTerminal asks for the address of a telnet host.

5. Type the address of the telnet host in the Host Address field and click on the OK button.

6. If you're not already connected to the Internet, HyperTerminal will start Dial-Up Networking and connect you to the host, as shown in Figure 13.8. Follow the instructions that appear on your screen to log in to the remote host.

7. When you're finished using the remote host, disconnect and use HyperTerminal's Exit command to shut down the program. The program will ask if you want to save the current session. If you ever expect to return to this host, click on the Yes button.

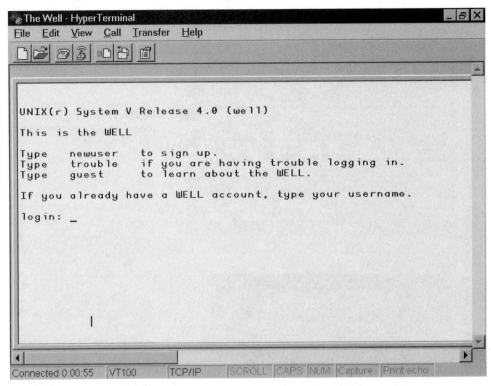

FIGURE 13.8: HyperTerminal can connect to a telnet host through your Winsock connection.

The next time you want to connect to the same host, just select the icon for that connection profile in the HyperTerminal folder. Like any other Windows 95 file, a connection profile can have a shortcut from your desktop or your Start menu.

Telnet Clients for Windows 3.1

If you don't have Windows 95, neither Microsoft Telnet nor HyperTerminal will do you much good. Fortunately, there are plenty of other good telnet programs for Windows 3.1.

If you have a communications program like ProComm or Crosstalk, you can use it for telnet connections as well as dial-up links. Look for specific instructions in the online Help under the heading "TCP/IP."

If you prefer, you can use one of the single-purpose telnet clients that are available through the Internet. For a full set of features, take a look at CRT, from Van Dyke Technologies (http://www.vandyke.com/vandyke.crt/) or NetTerm from InterSoft

International (http://starbase.neosoft.com/~zkrr01/netterm.html). Two simple ones are EWAN (Emulator Without A Name) and YAWTEL (Yet Another Windows TELnet), both available through TUCOWS (http://www.tucows.com).

Running Diagnostic Tools

When the Internet is working properly, you don't notice any of the intermediate circuits, switchers, routers, or network interconnection points. The only thing you need to know is that your computer is receiving data from a server someplace out there in cyberspace. But when you can't connect to a particular host, or if data transfer seems to slow down to a crawl, it can be useful to have a better idea of what's happening between your own system and the rest of the network.

When you talk to your ISP's tech support center, they might ask you to try "pinging a host" or "running a traceroute" to a server you're trying to reach. Ping and traceroute are common Internet tools for testing the system.

Ping

Ping (Packet InterNet Groper) is a tool that sends a message to a distant host and asks the host to send back a reply. When the ping client receives the reply, it displays the total duration of the exchange. Many ping clients repeat the whole process up to five or ten times and calculate an average response time. Therefore, ping can tell you two things: is the distant computer alive, and how good is the connection?

When a ping request times out or fails completely, you can assume that there's a problem someplace between the two computers: either the distant computer is not connected to the network or your own system or ISP has a problem. If the reply takes more than about 600 milliseconds from a host on the same continent, there's probably a problem with the network, such as a very heavy demand for resources or a network server not working properly somewhere along the path between you and the distant system.

In Windows 95, the ping utility is a DOS program. To send a ping request, follow these steps:

1. Open the Start menu and select the MS-DOS Prompt command in the Programs submenu.

2. At the C:\WINDOWS> prompt, type **ping *host*** and press the Enter key. In place of *host*, type the address of the system to which you want to send the ping request.

As Figure 13.9 shows, ping sends four echo requests and shows the success of each attempt. The section that says *time=xxxms* shows the number of milliseconds needed for each reply.

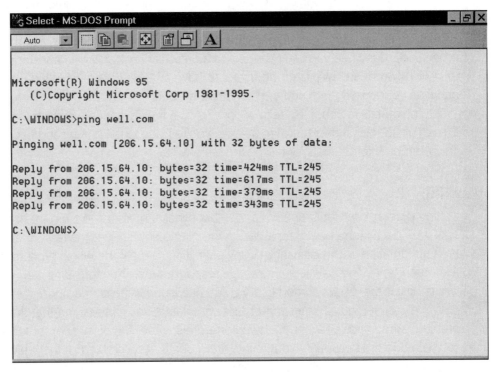

```
Select - MS-DOS Prompt

Auto

Microsoft(R) Windows 95
   (C)Copyright Microsoft Corp 1981-1995.

C:\WINDOWS>ping well.com

Pinging well.com [206.15.64.10] with 32 bytes of data:

Reply from 206.15.64.10: bytes=32 time=424ms TTL=245
Reply from 206.15.64.10: bytes=32 time=617ms TTL=245
Reply from 206.15.64.10: bytes=32 time=379ms TTL=245
Reply from 206.15.64.10: bytes=32 time=343ms TTL=245

C:\WINDOWS>
```

FIGURE 13.9: The Windows ping program shows the result of a ping request in a DOS window.

Traceroute

Traceroute is a standard Internet tool that identifies all of the intermediate steps between an origin and a destination. This can be fascinating information if you want to understand how data moves through the Internet, but most of us won't use it very often.

The traceroute program in Windows 95 is another DOS program. To run a traceroute test, follow these steps:

1. Open a MS-DOS window from the Start menu.
2. At the C:\WINDOWS> prompt, type **tracert *host***, using the address of the distant system in place of *host.*

As the program steps through each link, it will display the name of each network server and the amount of time needed to obtain an echo from that server. For example, Figure 13.10 shows a traceroute test from an ISP to The Well in San Francisco.

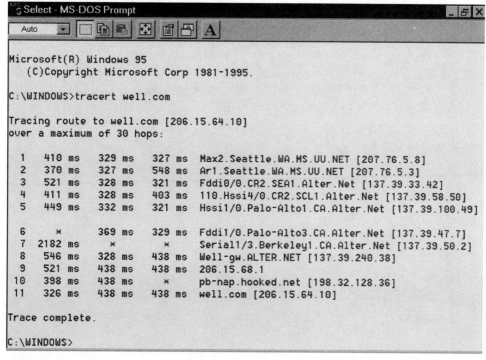

```
MS
 ⌄ Select - MS-DOS Prompt                                          _ ⯐ X
Auto     ▼   □ ⬚ ⬚   ⊠ ⛶ ⬚   A

Microsoft(R) Windows 95
   (C)Copyright Microsoft Corp 1981-1995.

C:\WINDOWS>tracert well.com

Tracing route to well.com [206.15.64.10]
over a maximum of 30 hops:

  1    410 ms    329 ms    327 ms  Max2.Seattle.WA.MS.UU.NET [207.76.5.8]
  2    370 ms    327 ms    548 ms  Ar1.Seattle.WA.MS.UU.NET [207.76.5.3]
  3    521 ms    328 ms    321 ms  Fddi0/0.CR2.SEA1.Alter.Net [137.39.33.42]
  4    411 ms    328 ms    403 ms  110.Hssi4/0.CR2.SCL1.Alter.Net [137.39.58.50]
  5    449 ms    332 ms    321 ms  Hssi1/0.Palo-Alto1.CA.Alter.Net [137.39.100.49]

  6       ×      369 ms    329 ms  Fddi1/0.Palo-Alto3.CA.Alter.Net [137.39.47.7]
  7   2182 ms       ×         ×    Serial1/3.Berkeley1.CA.Alter.Net [137.39.50.2]
  8    546 ms    328 ms    438 ms  Well-gw.ALTER.NET [137.39.240.38]
  9    521 ms    438 ms    438 ms  206.15.68.1
 10    398 ms    438 ms       ×    pb-nap.hooked.net [198.32.128.36]
 11    326 ms    438 ms    438 ms  well.com [206.15.64.10]

Trace complete.

C:\WINDOWS>
```

FIGURE 13.10: Traceroute identifies all of the intermediate network servers between your system and a specified host.

WS Ping

WS Ping is a graphic program that combines ping and traceroute functions into a single Windows 95 program. It was created by the same developer as WS_FTP. If you use either of these functions more often than about once a month, the program is worth having, especially since it's free for government, academic, and noncommercial home use. You can download the program from ftp.ipswitch.com/pub/win32.

Figure 13.11 shows the main WS Ping screen. To run a ping or trace route test, type the address of the target computer in the Host field and click on the button that describes the type of test you want to run.

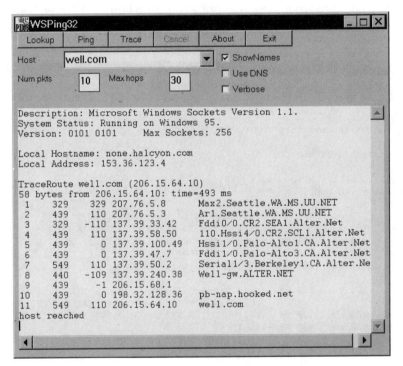

FIGURE 13.11: WS Ping combines ping and traceroute into a single program.

Time Synchronizers

Time synchronizers are Internet client programs that connect your computer to a time server and reset your local clock to match the time provided by the server. For example, Figure 13.12 shows a time synchronizer called Dimension 4, which is available as freeware from http://www.thinkman.com/~thinkman/4d.htm.

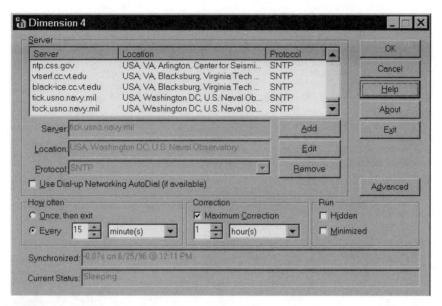

FIGURE 13.12: Dimension 4, available as freeware, is a time synchronizer that allows you to obtain the correct time from any of a variety of servers.

To synchronize your clock to a time server, click on the name of a server from the list, and then click on the OK button. All the servers on this list are synchronized to international time standards, so you will obtain the correct time from any of them. As a general rule, it's a courtesy to other network users to choose a server as close to your own geographic location as possible.

When you run the program, it will set your clock and display an information message like the one shown here, which tells you how much of an adjustment was necessary.

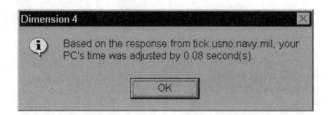

You won't use the programs in this chapter as often as you use Internet Explorer, but when you need to perform a specific task, you'll be glad to have the right tool for the job.

Appendix A

KEEPING INTERNET EXPLORER UP-TO-DATE

Microsoft and Netscape have drawn their respective swords to do battle for control of the market for Web browsers and servers. Both companies are spending millions of dollars (and pounds, yen, marks, and zlotys, no doubt) to promote their respective products.

One result of this competition is a continuing game of "dueling features." If one company introduces a neat new function in its browser, you can be pretty certain that the other will match it in the next release.

Fortunately, both products are distributed through online channels at little or no cost. Internet Explorer is free for everybody; Netscape Navigator is free to students and employees of nonprofit organizations, and available for free evaluation to most others for 90 days (and by the time that 90-day evaluation period is up, Netscape will probably have a new version for you to evaluate).

It's a good idea to check in at Microsoft's Internet Explorer home page every few weeks to find out if they are offering a newer version than the one you already have. You can jump directly to the Microsoft Web site from Internet Explorer by selecting the Product Update command in the Go menu. If you're using Netscape Navigator or some other browser, you can use the Internet Explorer site's URL: http://www.microsoft.com/ie.

The Internet Explorer Web site offers a choice of several versions of the program, as well as several sources in different locations. To download an update, choose the operating system you want to use with Internet Explorer and the nearest download site, and click on the link.

When the download is complete, you should go ahead and install the update over your existing version of Internet Explorer. Your list of favorite pages, your home page, and your search page will carry across from the older release, but you might have to readjust the character sets and other options if you don't use the defaults.

Appendix B

INTERNET EXPLORER KEYBOARD SHORTCUTS

If you're unable to use a mouse, or if you just prefer not to move your hand away from the keyboard, Internet Explorer allows you to enter many commands directly from the keyboard. This appendix contains a list of the program's keyboard shortcuts.

Moving around a Web Page

To step forward through images, links embedded in text, links embedded in images, and the address bar, press the Tab key. To move backward, press the Shift key and the Tab key at the same time. As you move from one location to the next, you will see a border appear around the currently selected item.

Other Keyboard Shortcuts

Jump to the currently selected link	Enter
Display a right-click menu	Shift+F10
Jump forward to another frame	Ctrl+Tab
Jump backward to another frame	Shift+Ctrl+Tab
Move backward to the previous page	Alt +← or Backspace
Move forward to the next page	Alt +→ or Shift + Backspace

Refresh the current page	F5 or Ctrl+R
Stop downloading the current page	Esc
Open a new page in the current window	Ctrl+O
Open a new window	Ctrl+N
Save the current page	Ctrl+S
Print the current page	Ctrl+P
Cut the selected text or image and place it in the Clipboard	Ctrl+X
Copy the selected text or image to the Clipboard	Ctrl+C
Paste the contents of the Clipboard	Ctrl+V
Select all	Ctrl+A
Find text on the current page	Ctrl+F
Close Internet Explorer	Ctrl+F4

Appendix C

SOME MAJOR WEB SITES

This book is all about using Internet Explorer and other tools for finding and using information and resources on the Internet, but those tools are not really the point; the information and resources you retrieve are a lot more important than the path you use to get to them.

In this appendix, you can find descriptions of some good starting points for your Web explorations. It's not a definitive list, because there's no such thing on the Internet. By the time you read this, there will probably be thousands of new sites that hadn't existed a month or two earlier. But the sites described here will give you pointers to much of the best—and oddest—that the Internet has to offer.

General-Interest Guides

These Web sites are designed as home pages for Internet users, with links to many other interesting and/or useful sites. Some are maintained by Internet Service Providers; others are stand-alone services. Any of these sites would be a good choice as a home page that loads whenever you start Internet Explorer.

The Microsoft Network

www.msn.com

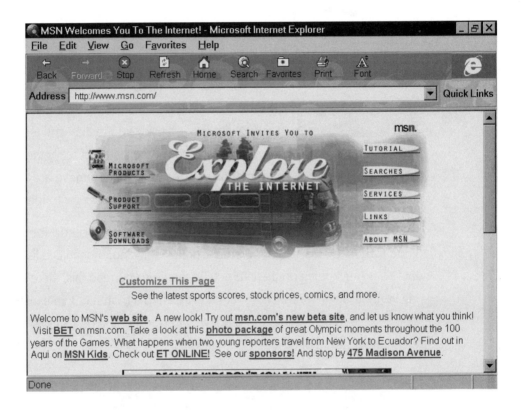

The Microsoft Network Web site is the default home page for Internet Explorer. It offers links to lists of other selected sites. You can also customize this page to include specific links to sites that you visit often, and to sources for news, weather, sports scores, and stock quotes (see Chapter 5).

Global Network Navigator

www.gnn.com/gnn/wic/index.html

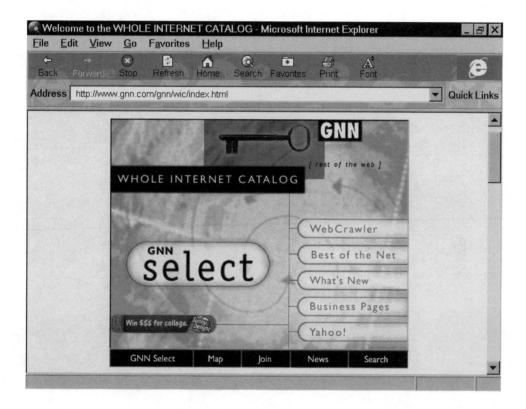

GNN's Whole Internet Catalog is another good starting point, with links to several search tools and directories of other sites.

Time Warner's Pathfinder

pathfinder.com

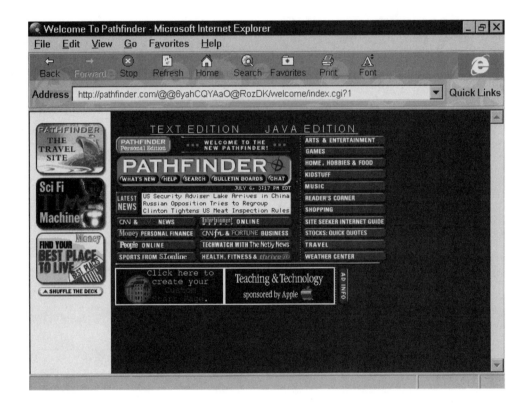

Pathfinder is Time Warner's huge Web site with separate sections for many of the company's magazines and other entertainment properties, including Time, Fortune, Atlantic Records, HBO, and various recent movies. It's a great place to find up-to-date news, sports, and entertainment information.

AT&T Business Network

www.bnet.att.com

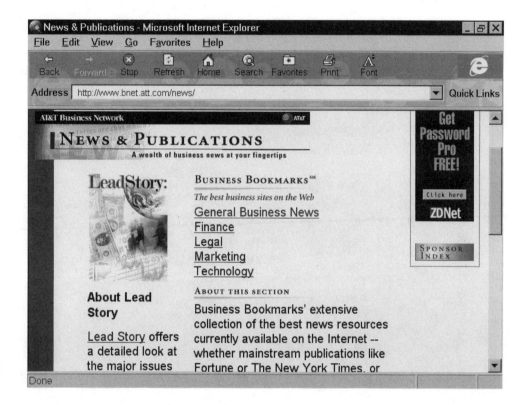

AT&T Business Network started out as a feature of Interchange, an online service that has gradually shifted its content to the Internet. BN's staff constantly monitors dozens of online newspapers, broadcasters, and wire services and provides direct links to the ones who provide the best coverage of each current story.

C|net

www.cnet.com

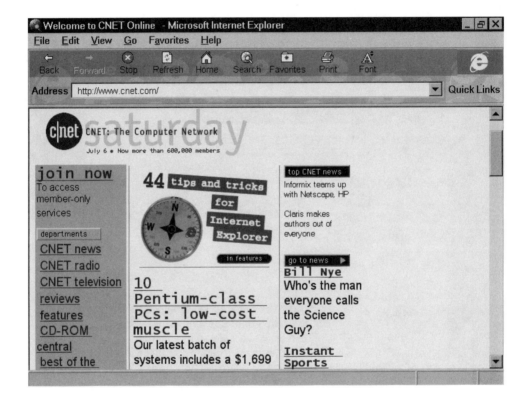

C|net is The Computer Network's online home. It includes links to news and reviews about personal computers, the Internet, and related topics, along with access to other c|net services such as Search.com and Shareware.com.

Magellan Internet Guide

www.mckinley.com

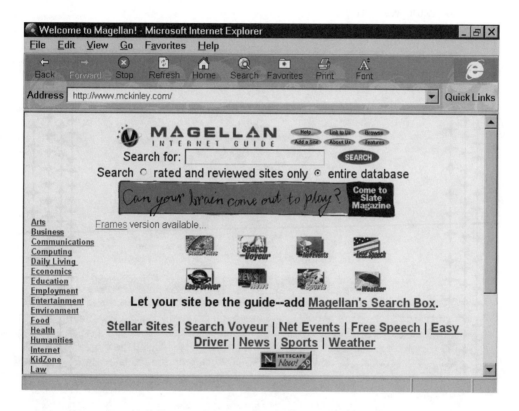

Magellan is the McKinley Group's guide to the Internet that provides ratings and reviews of many sites, along with a search engine.

Guides to Downloadable Software

The two sites listed here can begin to help you make sense of the huge number of programs and other files that are available for download through the Internet.

TUCOWS

www.tucows.com

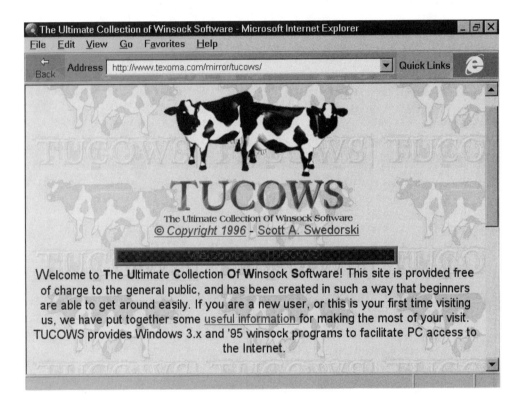

We've given you pointers to TUCOWS (The Ultimate Collection of Winsock Software) several times in this book. It's a large and growing set of reviews and links to browsers, plug-ins, client programs, and related utilities for the Internet.

Shareware.com

www.shareware.com

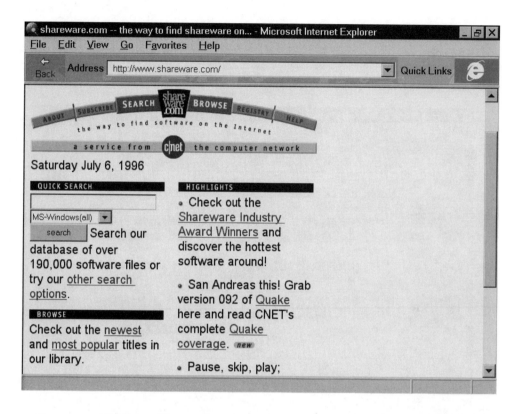

Shareware.com is another service from c|net. As the name suggests, this is a database of links to more than 190,000 free and inexpensive program files.

Interactive Search Tools

There are so many sources of information on the Internet that the process of finding any single item can be overwhelming. As an alternative to drilling through random links until you find what you want, an interactive search tool allows you to specify a name, keyword, or other description, and obtain pointers to the sites that match it. As a general rule, it's a good idea to run the same general search through more than one of these search engines, because each uses a somewhat different approach.

Search.com

www.search.com

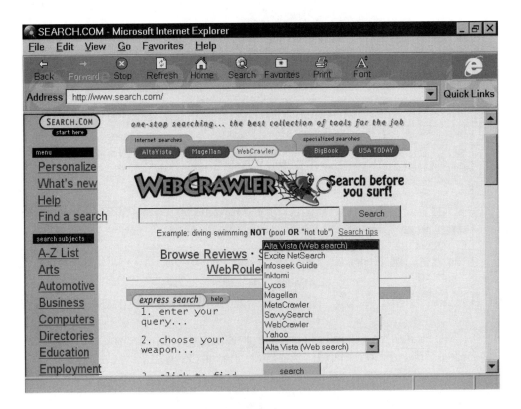

Search.com is a single access point for several hundred general and specialized Internet search tools. It's a good place to begin a "search for a search."

Yahoo

www.yahoo.com

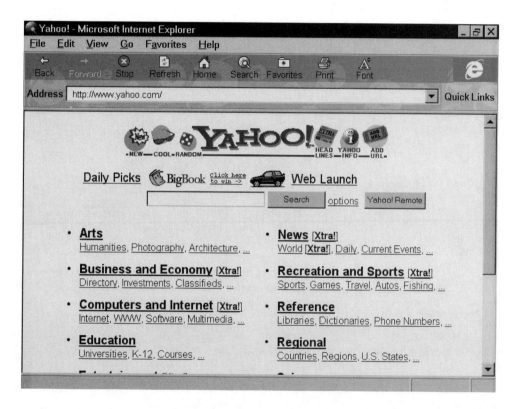

Yahoo has organized Web sites by topic and subtopic, with a search engine that finds links to specific sites. When you're looking for information on the Web related to a specific topic, Yahoo is a good place to start.

AltaVista

www.altavista.digital.com

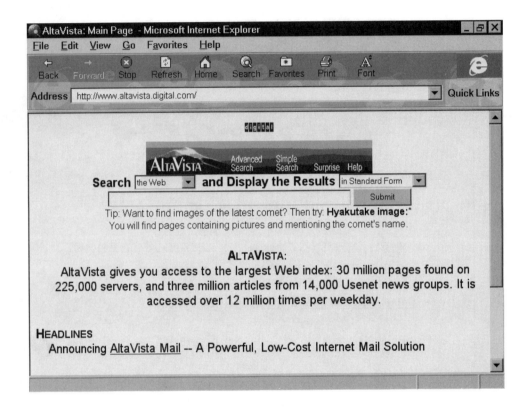

Digital's AltaVista searches through the complete text of more than 30 million Web pages. As a result, it usually finds many more matches than other search engines that limit themselves to categories or headings. It's not unusual to see an AltaVista search produce several thousand hits.

Glossary

GLOSSARY OF INTERNET TERMS

From *The ABCs of the Internet,* adapted from *The Internet Dictionary,* both by Christian Crumlish.

If you've run into some jargon in this book that you don't understand, you should find an explanation here.

> **NOTE** If you want a more thorough compendium of Internet jargon, terminology, and culture at your fingertips, get the *Internet Dictionary,* also from Sybex.

$0.02
Appended to the end of a **Usenet post,** this means "my two cents."

:-)
The basic **smiley** symbol; this is often used to mean "just kidding," "don't flame me," or "I'm being sarcastic," but it can also mean "I'm happy."

^]
This garbage symbol may appear on your screen, or in text-transferred files, from time-to-time. It's an uninterpreted Esc character. Ignore it.

acceptable use

Internet service providers require that all their users agree to some guidelines of acceptable use of Internet and Usenet resources. Acceptable use guidelines vary from provider to provider.

account

A form of access to a computer or **network** for a specific **username** and password, usually with a home directory, an **e-mail inbox,** and a set of access privileges.

address

1. The name of a computer (also called a **host** or **site** on the **Internet,** in the form `host.subdomain.domain;` 2. An **e-mail address** in the form `username@host.subdomain.domain;` 3. A **Web** address (**URL**) in the form `http://host.subdomain.domain/optional-path/optional-filename.html`.

address book

In some **e-mail** programs, a list of abbreviations for **e-mail address**es.

administrivia

Information regarding the administering of a **mailing list** or **moderated newsgroup** that is posted to the list or group.

AIFF

The Macintosh audio format on the **Internet.**

alias

An abbreviation for an **e-mail address,** sometimes called a *nickname.*

alt.

A quasi-**Usenet hierarchy** devoted to "alternative" topics. It is easier to create alt. groups than to create standard Usenet groups, and it's practically impossible to remove them.

alt.fan groups

Newsgroups devoted to a real-world or **Net** celebrity or villain.

America Online

A popular **online** service.

Amiga

A line of desktop PCs, famous for their handling of graphics and the evangelical zeal of their users. Many Amiga users include an **ASCII**-graphic double checkmark in their **.sigs.**

Anarchie

An **Archie** program for the Mac.

anon.penet.fi

The most well-known anonymous remailer service.

anonymous FTP

The most common use of **FTP**, the **Internet file transfer protocol. FTP site**s that allow anonymous FTP don't require a password for access—you only need to log in as anonymous and enter your **e-mail address** as a password (for their records).

anonymous remailers

A service that provides anonymity to users on the **Net** by allowing them to send **mail** and **Usenet post**s through the remailer.

*.answers

Moderated newsgroups dedicated to the posting of **FAQ**s. The "*" in *.answers stands for anything. *.answers newsgroups include `news.answers`, `alt.answers`, `rec.answers`, `misc.answers`, and so on.

AOL

America Online, a popular **online** service.

application

A program (or piece of software) that isn't a **shell,** environment, or operating system.

Archie

A **client/server** application that gives users access to databases that keep track of the contents of anonymous **FTP** archives.

ARPAnet

The legendary predecessor to the **Internet.**

article

A **Usenet post.**

ASCII

American standard code for information exchange. ASCII is a standard character set that's been adopted by most computer systems around the world (usually extended for foreign alphabets and diacriticals).

ASCII file

A file containing only straight text. ASCII files are easier and quicker to transfer.

asynchronous

Not happening at the same time. **E-mail** is an asynchronous form of communication.

attachment

Any **data file,** in any form, that your **e-mail** program will send along with your e-mail **message.**

.au

A **Unix** audio format.

autoselect

In **Usenet killfile**s, to select automatically—the opposite of to kill. A killfile comprises instructions to search for certain keywords and then either kill or autoselect the articles containing those words.

AutoSurf

A new **Mosaic** feature that will pull down and cache all of the pages at a site, letting you browse through them at your leisure.

.avi

A movie format native to the Windows platform.

B1FF

A legendary persona from the early days of **BBS**s, B1FF liked to talk about *kOOl warez–*, cool, pirated computer software.

back

1. In a **Web browser,** a command, often a shortcut button, for retracing your steps back to the previous page or **link;** 2. The command in a **Unix** paging program to go back one screen.

backbone

A large, fast **network** connection.

bandwidth

1. The amount of information that can pass through the wires in a certain amount of time; 2. A more general term for what everyone is encouraged not to waste on the **Net.**

baud

Usually confused with **bps** (bits per second), baud is technically the number of times per second that your **modem** changes the signal it sends through the phone lines.

BBS

A **bulletin board system.** Many BBSs are connected to the **Internet**.

Bcc line

The portion of an e-mail **message** header where you list the recipients who will be sent *blind* copies of the message. This means that the primary (and Cc:) recipients will not see the names of people receiving blind copies.

Big Dummy's Guide to the Internet

The former name of **EFF**'s excellent, free **Internet** guide.

binaries

Newsgroups that generally contain huge **post**s each comprising part of a large **binary file,** usually a program, image, or other special-format file, as opposed to a **text file.**

binary file

As opposed to a **text file,** a file that contains more than simple text. It must be copied literally, bit for bit, or it will be corrupted. Also called an **image file.**

binary transfer

A **file transfer** in which every bit of the file is copied (as opposed to a **text transfer,** in which the text is transferred to whatever format the receiving machine prefers).

BinHex

A form of file **compression** native to the Macintosh.

bitnet

A huge **network,** distinct from the **Internet,** but fully connected to it, used largely for **e-mail** and **Listserv mailing list**s.

bitnet.

A **newsgroup hierarchy** in the **Usenet** mold, comprising newsgroups that correspond to **bitnet** mailing lists.

biz.

A **newsgroup hierarchy** in the **Usenet** mold that expressly permits advertising (biz stands for *business*).

bookmark

In a **Web** or **gopher** browser, a record of a destination that allows you to immediately get back there at any time. (Also called Favorites or Favorite Places in some browsers, and items on a **Hotlist** in others.)

'bot

A **robotic** entity on the **Net** that automatically performs some function that people usually do.

bounce

When **e-mail** fails to reach its destination and returns to you, it is said to have bounced.

bozo filter

A **killfile** that allows you to filter out the bozos whose **Usenet post**s you don't wish to see.

bps

Bits per second, a measurement of **modem** speed.

browse

To skim an information resource on the **Net,** such as **Usenet, gopherspace,** or the **Web.**

browser

The program you use to read the **Web.**

BTW

By the way.

bulletin board

1. What some **online** services call their **discussion group**s; 2. A **bulletin board system.**

bulletin board system

A set of computers and **modem**s running **bulletin board** software that allow users to dial in, send **mail,** participate in forums, and (sometimes) access the **Internet.**

cancel an article

On **Usenet,** to delete an article after you've posted it. It takes a while for the article to vanish everywhere, because the cancel message must catch up with the propagating article.

cascade

A nonsensical series of one-line follow-up **post**s, each a play on the previous one and designed to create a huge triangle of >s on the screen.

cc:Mail

A network-oriented e-mail **client** program.

Central Search Page

Most of the **Web browser**s have a shortcut to one or more **directory** or search pages built in to the program.

CFV

Call for votes. A step in creating a **Usenet newsgroup** that comes after the **RFD** (request for discussion) step.

character-based browsers/readers

Internet programs, generally used in **Unix** systems, that can display only characters (and no graphics).

chat

Synchronous, line-by-line communication over a **network.**

client

An application that communicates with a **server** to get you information.

client/server application

An application whose process is distributed between a central **server** and any number of autonomous **client**s.

clueless newbie

A derogatory term for a beginner who POSTS IN ALL CAPS or betrays some ignorance of the **Net.** We were all clueless newbies once.

.com

An **Internet domain** that stands for *commercial.*

COM port
A communication port in your PC. Your **modem** plugs into one.

command line
The place in a character-based **shell,** such as a **Unix** or DOS shell, where you can enter commands directly (usually at the bottom of the screen).

commercial online service
A private, proprietary **network,** offering its own content and access to other network members, such as **CompuServe, America Online, Prodigy,** and **Microsoft Network.**

comp.
A **Usenet hierarchy** devoted to computers.

compress
1. (v) To squish a file; 2. (n) A **Unix** program that squishes files.

compression
The method of squishing a file or the amount of squishing.

CompuServe
A popular **online** service.

copyright
People debate how standing copyright law applies to articles posted to **Usenet** or to texts in general made available on the Internet. Some people attach copyright notices to their **post**s. *See also* **fair use.**

cracker
A **hacker** who breaks into computers.

Craig Shergold
See **Shergold, Craig.**

crosspost

To **post** a **Usenet** article to several **newsgroup**s at once. Crossposting takes up less disk space than posting it separately and repeatedly.

CU-SeeMe

A **protocol** that enables anyone with a video camera and enough memory to play video images in his or her computer to see other people on the **Internet.**

cyberspace

A term, popularized by author William Gibson, for the shared imaginary reality of computer **networks.** Some people use cyberspace as a synonym for the **Internet.** Others hold out for the more complete physical-seeming consensual reality of Gibson's novels.

daemon

In **Unix,** a program that runs all the time, in the background, waiting for things to do (possibly from Maxwell's Demon). When you post an article to a *.test newsgroup, daemons all over the world send you e-mail confirming they received your post.

data bits

One of the things you need to set to use your **modem.** Usually set to 7 or 8, it depends on the modem you're calling.

decoding

Retranslating a file from some encoded format to its original format.

decrypt

To remove the **encryption** from a file or e-mail **message** and make it readable.

DejaNews

A service for searching **Usenet** (at `http://www.dejanews.com/forms/dnq.html`).

delurk

1. (v) To **post** to a **list** or **newsgroup** for the first time; 2. (n) A first post to a newsgroup or list after the writer has **lurked** for a while.

dial-up account
An Internet **account** on a **host** machine that you must dial up with your **modem** to use.

digest
A collection of **mailing list post**s, sent out as one message.

digestified
Turned into a digest. Not all **mailing list**s are available in a digestified form.

Direct-Access ISP
A **service provider** (usually called an ISP, for **Internet service provider**) that offers direct **Internet** access, as opposed to an **online** service.

directory
A **Web site** where other Web sites are organized by topic and subtopic, something like a yellow pages phone book.

discussion groups
Any "place" on the **Net** where discussions are held, including **mailing list**s and **Usenet newsgroup**s.

domain
The three-letter code indicating whether the **address** is a business (**.com**), a non-profit organization (**.org**), a university (**.edu**), a branch of the government (**.gov**), a part of the military (**.mil**), and so on.

download
To transfer a file over a modem from a remote computer to your desktop computer.

.edu
An Internet domain. It stands for educational.

EFF
Electronic Frontier Foundation. Founded by Mitch Kapor and John Barlow, the EFF lobbies for the preservation of freedom on the cyberspace frontier.

EFF's Guide to the Internet

Formerly *Big Dummy's Guide to the Internet*, **EFF**'s excellent and free **Internet** guide. It is available via the **Web** (`http://www.eff.org/papers/eegtti/eegttitop.html`).

EFNet

The traditional **IRC** network.

Electronic Frontier Foundation

See **EFF.**

elm

A popular **Unix** mail program.

.elmrc

A setup file for **elm.**

emacs

A **Unix** operating environment that doubles as a **text editor.**

e-mail

Electronic mail, but you knew that already, didn't you?

e-mail address

An **Internet** address that consists of a **username** (also called a **login,** a **log-on name,** a **userID,** an **account** name, and so on), followed by an "at" sign (@) and then an address of the form `host.subdomain.domain`.

emoticons

Those little **smiley** faces people use to indicate emotions.

encoding

Any method of converting a file into a format for attaching to e-mail **messages.**

encrypt

To scramble the contents of a file or e-mail **message** so that only those with the **key** can unscramble and read them.

encryption

A process of rendering a file or e-mail **message** unreadable to anyone lacking the right encryption **key.**

Eudora

An **e-mail** program.

fair use

The legal doctrine that allows limited quotation of other people's work if the use of their work does not undercut its market value.

FAQ

1. Frequently asked questions; 2. A file containing frequently asked questions and their answers, also sometimes called a FAQL (Frequently Asked Question list). To find FAQ lists, look in the ***.answers newsgroup**s or the **FTP** archive at `rtfm.mit.edu`.

Fetch

An **FTP** program for the Mac

FidoNet

A **network** of **BBS**'s with **Internet e-mail** access.

file transfer

To copy a file from one computer to another.

File Transfer Protocol

See **FTP.**

film at 11

A common tag in **Usenet** follow-up posts mocking the timeliness of the news. Often follows **Imminent death of the Net predicted!**

finger

A **Unix** command that reports back on the status of a user or a **network.**

flame

1. An ill-considered, insulting e-mail or Usenet retort; 2. An insulting post.

flamebait

A **mailing list** or **newsgroup post** designed to elicit **flame**s. Flamebait can be recognized by the fact that it goes beyond the premises of the list or newsgroup. Nobody objects to provocative or even argumentative posts, but a post to the alt.fan.frank-zappa newsgroup saying that "Zappa was a no-talent, potty-mouthed dweeb" betrays a lack of legitimate interest in the subject at hand.

flamer

One who **flame**s or likes to flame others.

flame war

An out-of-control series of **flame**s and counterflames that fills up a list or news-group with noise. Traditionally, flame wars end when Nazis are mentioned.

FlashSession

An America Online process that enables its users to work **offline** and then send and receive **mail** and **newsgroup** articles and **download** files all at once, minimizing connect time.

FOAF

Friend of a friend.

follow a link

In graphical browsers, following a link entails positioning the mouse pointer over the link (the pointer will change to show you that you're over an active link) and then clicking once.

follow-up

A **post** that replies to and possibly quotes an earlier post.

follow-up line

In **Usenet** articles, if there is a follow-up line, follow-up articles will be posted to the **newsgroup**s listed there, and not necessarily to the original newsgroups. Always check the follow-up line before posting. Pranksters sometimes direct follow-ups to ***.test** groups, resulting in thousands of automated replies, stuffing the inbox of anyone hapless enough to follow up without editing the follow-up line.

FQA

Frequently questioned acronyms.

free-net

A free public **network** (also written as one word, *freenet*).

freeware

Free software available for downloading on the **Net.**

FTP

File Transfer Protocol, the standard **Internet** way to transfer files from one computer to another.

FTP site

A computer on the **Net** containing archives and set up for **FTP.**

FTPmail

A way to use **FTP** by **e-mail** if you don't have an FTP application.

full name

Your full name as it appears in e-mail **message**s and **Usenet post**s.

full-screen editor

A text editor that enables you to move the insertion point or cursor all over the screen, as opposed to a line-at-a-time editor that always keeps the insertion point at the bottom of the screen.

FUQ

Frequently unanswered questions.

FWIW

For what it's worth.

<g>

Indicates the author is grinning, similar to **:-).**

garbage characters

Nonsense characters that **modem**s sometimes spit out.

gate

Short for **gateway,** a computer that transfers files or **e-mail** from one **network** to another, or from a **newsgroup** to a list, and vice versa.

gated

Said of a **newsgroup** or **mailing list** that is connected to a mailing list or newsgroup, respectively.

gateway

1. A computer that connects one **network** to another, for the purpose of transferring files or **e-mail** when the two networks use different **protocols;** 2. A computer that transfers **post**s from a **newsgroup** to a **list,** and vice versa.

GIF

1. A **compress**ed graphics (image) file format (GIF stands for graphics interchange format) invented by **CompuServe;** 2. A file in the .gif format.

gnu.

A **hierarchy** in the **Usenet** mold devoted to the Free Software Foundation and to **emacs.**

gopher

A **client/server application** that performs **FTP** transfers, remote **login**s, **Archie** searches, and so on, presenting everything to you in the form of menus. This saves you from having to know (or type in) the **address**es of the **Internet** resources being tapped. You run a gopher **client** program to get information from a gopher **server** running at a gopher **site.**

gopherspace

A collective name for all of the **gopher** servers on the **Net,** so called because all the **server**s can connect to each other, creating a unified "space" of gopher menus.

.gov

An Internet domain that stands for government.

green-card lawyer

A derogatory term for people who **spam** the **Net** with unwanted advertisements and then go on TV to defend their actions.

<grin>

Equivalent to the **:-) emoticon.**

group

A **newsgroup.**

gunzip

The **Unix uncompression** program for gzipped files.

gzip

A file **compression** program.

^H

In the standard **VT100** terminal emulation, the Delete key is used to erase characters, and Backspace either backs up over the previous character (without deleting it) or produces this character on the screen. It's a sign that a **clueless newbie** has tried to erase something and failed.

hack

To dig into some computer activity, going beneath the surface and reinventing things when necessary.

hacker

A computer adept. Among hackers, anyone who can bend a computer to his or her will is a hacker. (People who break into computer systems are called **cracker**s.) In the rest of the world, people generally refer to those who break into computers as hackers.

Hayes-compatible

Modems that understand the Hayes AT instruction set are said to be Hayes-compatible. (Hayes is a name-brand modem maker.) If you're buying a modem, make sure it's Hayes-compatible. Most are these days, so that shouldn't be difficult.

hierarchy

1. In file storage, the arrangement of directories into a tree of parents and children; 2. In **Usenet,** the organization of **newsgroup**s into general areas, topics, and subtopics.

history

A record of your last so many actions. On the **Web,** a list of all the **page**s you've been to since you started your Web browsing program. The history list will actually show you only the pages you've visited in a straight line from your starting point. Any time you back up and then follow a different **link,** you will lose the original history path from that point onward.

$HOME

In **Unix,** a variable that means your **home directory.**

home directory

The directory you start off in when you log into your **Unix account.**

home page

1. The page you begin with when you start your **Web browser;** 2. The main page of a **Web site;** 3. A personal Web page.

host

A computer on the **Internet.**

HotJava

A **Web browser** made by Sun Microsystems.

hotlist

A **bookmark** list (especially in **Mosaic**).

HTML

Hypertext Markup Language, the **hypertext** language used in **Web page**s. It consists of regular text and tags that tell the **browser** what to do when a **link** is activated.

HTML source

The underlying source file that makes a **Web** document look the way it does in a **Web browser.**

HTTP

Hypertext Transfer Protocol. The Web **protocol** for linking one **Web page** with another.

hypermedia

Linked documents that consist of other media in addition to plain text, such as pictures, sounds, movies, and so on.

hypertext

Text that contains **link**s to other text documents.

hypertext link

A **link** from one text document to another.

Hytelnet

A **telnet shell** that helps you find the telnet **site** you want and then runs the telnet session for you. It contains a huge list of university and public library catalogs.

image file
A **binary file.**

IMHO
In my humble opinion.

Imminent Death of the Net Predicted
A parody of the perennial warnings that traffic on the **Net** has gotten to be too much. Often followed by **film at 11.**

IMNSHO
In my not-so-humble opinion.

IMO
In my opinion.

inbox
A file containing your incoming **e-mail.**

info
Many **Internet** providers have an info **address** (`info@host.subdomain.domain`).

Internet
The worldwide **network** of networks. The Internet is a way for computers to communicate. It is not a place; it's a way to go through.

Internet address
See **address.**

Internet Explorer
Microsoft's **Web browser.**

Internet Phone
A **protocol** that enables anyone with a microphone, speaker, and sound card in their computer to talk to other people on the **Internet.**

Internet Resources Meta-Index

A useful starting point on the **Web.**

Internet service provider (ISP)

A company that offers "just" access to the **Internet** and no local content (or only very limited local information and **discussion groups**).

InterNIC—

The Internet's Network Information Center, a repository of **Internet** information (a resource worth knowing about).

IP

Internet Protocol, the **protocol** that allows computers and networks on the Internet to communicate with each other.

IRC

Internet relay chat. A **protocol** and a **client/server** program that allows you to **chat** with people all over the **Internet,** in channels devoted to different topics.

Ircle

A Macintosh IRC program.

Java

A programming language from Sun that's a variant of C++. With a special Java-savy browser such as **HotJava, Netscape Navigator** 2.0, or earlier versions of Netscape with a Java **plug-in,** users can interact with fully operational programs inside the **browser** window.

JPEG

A **compress**ed file format for images (extension .jpg).

Jughead

An index of high-level **gopher** menus.

k12.
A **hierarchy** in the **Usenet** mold, devoted to kindergarten through twelfth grade education.

Kermit
A **protocol** for **download** and **upload file transfer**s.

key
In **encryption,** a code that allows you to **decrypt** encrypted text.

key encryption
A form of **encryption** that relies on **key**s.

keyword
A word used to search for a file, document, or **Web page.**

Kibo
The **username** of James F. Parry. Some say he is the first deity of the **Internet**. Also known as "he who greps," Kibo reportedly notes every mention of his name on **Usenet** and replies to worthy posts. (Grepping means searching a file or an entire directory for a specific word.) There is also an evil anti-Kibo named Xibo, whose legions are much fewer than the **troll**ing readers of `alt.religion.kibology`.

kibology
The religion (or is it a science?) of **Kibo.** Its main doctrine is that *You're Allowed.* Only Spot, Kibo's dog, is *Not Allowed.*

killfile
A file containing search instructions for automatically killing or **autoselect**ing **Usenet post**s. *See also* **bozo filter.**

Knowbot
An information service on the **Net** that, among other things, helps find **e-mail address**es.

kps

Kilobits per second, a measurement of **modem** speed.

LAN

A local-area **network.** A computer network usually confined to a single office or building.

lharc

A file **compression** program for DOS.

library catalogs

Most university and public library catalogs are available via **telnet** (and some via **gopher**). **Hytelnet** has an excellent index of library catalogs.

line-at-a-time

Said of programs that, as the name suggests, allow users to see only one line of type at a time.

link

On **Web page**s, a button or highlighted bit of text that, when selected, jumps the reader to another page.

list

A **mailing list.**

Listserv

A type of **mailing list** software that runs on **bitnet** computers.

local-area network

See **LAN.**

log in

To start a session on your **Internet account.**

login

A **username,** the name you **log in** with.

log out

To end a session on your **Internet account.**

LOL

Laughing out loud.

lurk

To read a **mailing list** or **newsgroup** without **post**ing to it. You should lurk for a while before posting.

lurker

One who **lurk**s.

Lynx

An excellent, text-based, **Unix browser** for the **Web,** developed at the University of Kansas.

^M

In **text file**s transferred from DOS to **Unix** as **binary** files, this character will sometimes appear at the end of each line. Get rid of it with the dos2unix program.

mail

On the **Internet,** synonymous with **e-mail.**

mail box

A folder or area in a **mail** program where **messages** are stored.

mailing list

A list of people with a common interest, all of whom receive all the **mail** sent, or **post**ed, to the list.

.mailrc

A resource file for **mail** programs, other than **elm.**

mail reader

A program that allows you to read and reply to **e-mail,** and to send out new e-mail of your own.

mail reflector

A computer that sends copies of **mail** to a list of **address**es.

majordomo

A type of **mailing list** software.

MAKE.MONEY.FAST

A chain letter still making its rounds on the **Net.** It's a classic Ponzi/pyramid scheme. As someone replied last time I saw this garbage reposted, "Don't make your first act of fraud one that includes your name and address at the top!"

message

1. An **e-mail** letter; 2. A comment sent to a specific person on **IRC** and not to the entire channel.

MIDI

Musical Instrument Digital Interface.

.mil

An **Internet domain** that stands for military.

MIME

Multipurpose Internet Mail Extensions, a **protocol** that allows **e-mail** to contain more than simple text. Used to send other kinds of data, including color pictures, sound files, and video clips.

mIRC

A Windows **IRC** program.

mirror site

Another **FTP site** that maintains the exact same files (updated regularly), in order to reduce the load on the primary site.

misc.
A **Usenet hierarchy** devoted to whatever doesn't fit in the other hierarchies.

modem
A device that connects your computer to a phone jack and, through the phone lines, to another modem and computer. (It stands for *mo*dulator/*dem*odulator.)

moderated
Lists and **newsgroup**s whose **post**s must pass muster with a **moderator** before being sent to the subscribers.

moderator
The volunteer who decides which submissions to a **moderated list** or **newsgroup** will be **post**ed.

more
The most common **Unix** pager program.

Mosaic
A **Web browser,** developed by **NCSA,** for graphical user interfaces.

MOTAS
Member of the appropriate sex.

MOTOS
Member of the opposite sex.

MOTSS
Member of the same sex.

motto!
A **follow-up post** on **Usenet** proposing the previous post as a motto for the group.

MPEG
A **compressed** file format for movies (extension .mpg).

MS Exchange

A Microsoft **e-mail** program.

MU*

Any one of a series of acronyms for multiuser role-playing game environments.

MUD

A multiuser **domain**/dimension/dungeon. A role-playing game environment that allows people all over the **Net** to play together in something like interactive text adventures.

MUSE

A multiuser simulation environment (for role-playing games).

my two cents

A tag appended to **Usenet** or **list post**s, indicating, "This is just my opinion," or "I just wanted to get my two cents in."

Ncftp

A more sophisticated **Unix FTP** program than FTP (File Transfer Protocol).

NCSA

The National Center for Supercomputing Applications, founded by the **NSF** in 1985; inventor of **Mosaic.**

NCSA Mosaic

The original graphical **Web browser,** developed at the National Center for Supercomputer Applications and distributed for free.

NCSA What's New Page

The unofficial newspaper of the **Web** (found at `http://www.ncsa.uiuc.edu/SDG/Software/Mosaic/Docs/whats-new.html`).

Net, the

Often used as an abbreviation for the **Internet** or for **Usenet,** the Net is really a more general term for the lump sum of interconnected computers on the planet.

.net
An **Internet domain** that stands for **network.**

net.celebrity
A celebrity on the **Net.**

net.cop
Someone accused of trying to control others' **post**s in **mailing list**s or in **Usenet newsgroup**s.

NetCruiser
Netcom's all-in-one **Internet** access software.

Netfind
An **Internet** resource for finding **e-mail address**es.

net.god
An apparently powerful being on the **Net.**

nethead
A Dead Head (serious fan of the Grateful Dead) on the **Net.**

netiquette
The traditional rules of civilized behavior **online.**

netizen
A citizen of the **Net.**

net.personality
A somewhat well-known person on the **Net.**

.netrc
A file of **FTP** archive **site** names, **username**s, and passwords, used by FTP and **Ncftp** to automate login to **FTP site**s.

Netscape Navigator

Hands-down the most popular **World Wide Web browser** program. It works very much the way **Mosaic** does, but with a number of additional features and improvements.

net.spewer

A new contributor to a group who spews hundreds of **post**s, following up every **thread** that's around and attempting to start new ones.

network

A linked-together set of computers and computer equipment.

newbie

A beginner. Not as derogatory as **clueless newbie.**

newsfeed

The packet of news articles passed along from one computer to the next on **Usenet.**

newsgroup

A **Usenet discussion group.**

.newsrc

The list of **subscribed** and **unsubscribed newsgroup**s for a **Unix newsreader.**

newsreader

A program used to read **Usenet** articles.

NewsWatcher

A **newsreader** for the Macintosh.

News Xpress

A **newsreader** for Windows.

NFS

Not to be confused with **NSF,** NFS is the Network File System **protocol,** developed by Sun Microsystems, for transferring files over a **network.**

NIC

A **network** information center.

Nn

A **Unix newsreader.**

node

Any computer on the **Internet,** a **host.**

noise

Useless or unwanted information (as in **signal-to-noise ratio**).

NSF

The National Science Foundation, maintainers of the **NFSnet.**

NSFnet

A high-speed backbone, crucial but not essential, to the Internet; maintained by the NSF.

Ob

A prefix added to an obligatory addendum to a **Usenet** or **list post.**

offline

Not currently connected to the **Net.**

offline mail reader

A **mail** program that connects to the **Net, download**s your **e-mail,** and then disconnects, allowing you to read, reply to, and send mail without being charged for very much connect time.

offline news reader

A newsreader that connects to the **Net, download**s all unread articles in all sub-scribed **newsgroups**, and then disconnects, allowing you to read, reply to, and **post** articles without being charged for connect time.

online

Currently connected to the **Net.**

.org

An **Internet domain** that stands for (nonprofit) organization.

page

A **hypertext** document available on the **World Wide Web.**

pager

A **Unix** program that presents text one screenful at a time.

parent directory

The parent for which the current directory is a **subdirectory.**

parity

One of the things you need to set to use your **modem.** It's usually set to None or Even, but it depends on the modem you're calling.

Pegasus Mail

A free **e-mail client** program.

pgp

A **shareware encryption** program (it stands for Pretty Good Privacy).

Pico

A **Unix text editor** based on the text editor built into the **Pine mail reader.**

Pine

A popular **Unix mail** program.

ping
A somewhat obsolete **Unix** command that checks on the status of another **network.**

pkunzip
The **uncompression** program for **pkzipped** files.

pkzip
A DOS file **compression** program.

.plan
A **text file** that is displayed when someone fingers (uses a program called Finger to see if you are **online**) your **e-mail address.**

platform
A type of computer or system.

players
Programs, also called **viewers,** used to display multimedia file formats.

plebiscite
Literally, popular vote. In a **newsgroup,** it means polling the readership.

plonk
A **follow-up post** that means, "I just put you in my killfile." (It's supposed to be the sound of the **bozo** falling into the **killfile.**)

plug-ins
Programs that can be plugged into a **Web browser** to add multimedia capabilities to it.

point at
To start a **client** program, such as a **Web browser,** by supplying it with an address, as in: "Point your Web browser at `http://ezone.org/ez` to see the latest episode of *Enterzone.*"

POP

1. Point of Presence, a local access number for a **service provider;** 2. Post Office Protocol, a standard way to **download** and **upload e-mail.**

POP server

A type of **mail server** that "speaks" **POP.**

post

To send a **message** to a **mailing list** or an article to a **newsgroup.** The word *post* comes from the bulletin-board metaphor, in which scraps of paper are posted to the board, to be read by anyone who comes by.

Postmaster

The human being responsible for information requests for a **mail server** (`postmaster@address`).

PPP

Point-to-Point Protocol, a **protocol** for an **Internet** connection over a **modem.**

private key

In **key encryption,** the **key** that allows you to **encrypt** your outgoing messages.

.project

A **text file** that might be displayed when someone **fingers** your **e-mail address**. Not all fingers check for a .project file. You can describe the project you're working on in it.

propagation

The process of dissemination for **Usenet post**s, as they are passed from computer to computer. Propagation delays are responsible for the sometimes confusing situation that occurs when you read a **follow-up** to a post that hasn't yet appeared at your site.

protocol

Any agreed-upon method for two computers to communicate.

/pub
A **Unix** directory often found on **FTP host**s.

public data network
A **network** that allows you to make a local call to connect to a national network.

public discussion area
See **discussion group.**

public key
In **key encryption**, the **key** that allows you to verify the **encrypted** signature of the person who has sent you **mail** or **decrypt** a **message** from that person, given out to anyone who asks.

query
A search request submitted to a database.

queue
A list of **messages** waiting to be sent.

QuickMail
An **e-mail client** program designed for **networks**.

QuickTime
A movie format originally on Macintoshes.

Real Audio
Progressive Networks' **streaming** audio format.

real name
Your full name as it appears on e-mail **message**s and **Usenet post**s.

real-time
The time it takes real people to communicate, as on a telephone.

rec.

A **Usenet hierarchy** devoted to recreation.

remote login

Logging into another computer over a **network.** *See also* **telnet.**

reply

An e-mail **message** or **Usenet post** responding to, and possibly quoting, the original.

repost

To **post** again. A subsequent post of the same information.

-request

Human-administered **mailing list**s have an address for sending administrative requests (such as subscriptions), with -request appended to the **username** for the list. The administrative address for the imaginary list `epictetus@netcom.com` would be `epictetus-request@netcom.com`.

RFC

Request for Comments. One of a set of documents that contain **Internet protocol**s, standards, and information, and that together, more or less define the Internet in an open way. The standards contained in them are followed carefully by software developers (both commercial and **freeware**). The name "Request for Comments" can be confusing, since the contents are settled, but they arrived from free and open discussion on the **Net.**

RFD

Request for Discussion. A stage in the creation of a new **Usenet newsgroup,** preceding the **CFV.**

Rlogin

A **Unix** program that allows you to log on to another Unix machine without needing to give your password.

Rn
A nonthreaded **newsreader** for **Unix**.

roboposter
A **'bot**, disguised as a person, that automatically **post**s and **repost**s huge numbers of articles to **Usenet**. Roboposters have rendered some **newsgroup**s without a **killfile** to filter out unwanted posters unreadable A reputed roboposter, using the human name of Serdar Argic, single-handedly rendered `soc.history` (and a number of other newsgroups) unreadable. His howling through the wires (ranting holocaust revisionism about the Turks and the "x-Soviet" Armenians) came to an unexpected halt in the spring of 1994.

root
The directory with no parent. An **Internet address** at a **network** usually monitored by a **system administrator.**

ROTFL
Rolling on the floor laughing.

RTFM
Read the fucking manual!

sci.
A **Usenet hierarchy** devoted to science.

search engine
A program, usually reachable through a **Web page,** used to search a Web **site,** the entire **Internet,** or some **domain** in between.

select articles
In **newsreader**s, to choose ahead of time (by their titles or authors) which articles you want to read.

semi-anonymity
Because you'll never see the vast majority of people whose **post**s you read on the **Net,** this creates a veil of semi-anonymity.

server

A **network** application providing information to **client** programs that connect to it. Servers are centralized repositories of information or specialized handlers of certain kinds of traffic.

service provider

A company that provides access to the **Internet.**

shareware

Software you're expected to pay for after evaluating it, if you decide to keep using it. It is available for a free trial and must be registered and paid for if you decide to use it.

shell

A computer operating environment.

shell account

An **Internet account** that gives you access to a **Unix shell.**

Shergold, Craig

If you get the chain mail telling you to send this poor kid (or someone with a very similar name, as in the popular misspelling, Shirgold) a get-well card, don't! He is the famous "dying boy" (no longer dying and no longer a little boy) who is said (in endlessly circulating chain-mail **post**s and **e-mail**) to be hoping to become the *Guiness Book of Records* champion for postcards received. (It was true once—ten years ago.) The hospital where he stayed still gets postcards.

.sig

A **signature** file.

signal-to-noise ratio

An engineering term adapted as a metaphor for the proportion of useful information to junk on a **list** or in a **newsgroup.**

.signature

A **signature file** (so spelled because of the convention used for **Unix** signature files).

signature

A few lines of text, usually including your name, sometimes your postal (snail mail) address, and perhaps your **e-mail address.** Many people also include quotations, jokes, gags, and so on. Signatures (also called sig blocks, signature files, .signatures, or .sigs) are a little like bumper stickers in this respect. Some e-mail programs do not support signature files.

signature file

A **text file** that is automatically attached to the end of your e-mail **message**s or **Usenet post**s, usually containing your name and other pertinent information about you.

site

An Internet host that allows some kind of remote access, such as a Web site, FTP site, gopher site, and so on.

SLIP

Serial Line Internet Protocol. A **protocol** for an **Internet** connection over a **modem.**

SlipKnot

A program made by MicroMind that provides graphical access to the **Web** for people with character-based **Unix accounts.**

smileys

Sideways smiley faces, such as **:-)**, ;^), and =%7o, used to indicate emotions or facial expressions.

SMTP

Simple Mail Transport Protocol. This **protocol** is what enables **Internet e-mail** to flow so freely.

snail mail

Internet slang for surface mail.

SO
Significant other.

soc.
A **Usenet hierarchy** devoted to society (and usually sectarian groups in it).

spam
To **post** (or **robopost**) huge amounts of material to **Usenet,** or to post one article to huge numbers of inappropriate groups.

spew
To **post** excessively.

stand-alone program
For **online** services, a program that runs separately from the main access program, but one that can use the connection established by the main program.

stop bits
One of the things you need to set to use your **modem.** Usually set to 1 or 2, but it depends on the modem you're calling.

streaming
When files are sent a little at a time and start playing almost immediately.

subdirectory
A **directory** that is the child of another directory.

subdomain
A named portion of an **Internet domain,** usually a **network,** university, or company. In one of my **e-mail address**es, xian@netcom.com, *netcom* is the subdomain.

subscribe
To join a **mailing list** or start reading a **newsgroup.**

surf

To **browse,** following tangents. You can surf either **Usenet** or **gopherspace,** but the **Web** is best for surfing.

synchronous

Happening at the same time. **Chat** is a synchronous form of communication.

sysadmin

A **system administrator.** Someone who runs or maintains a **network.**

sysop

A **system operator.**

system administrator

Someone who runs or maintains a **network.**

system operator

A type of **system administrator** who runs a **BBS.**

talk

One-to-one **synchronous** chatting over the **Net.**

talk.

A **Usenet hierarchy** devoted to discussion, argument, and debate.

tar

.1. (v) To lump a bunch of files together in an archive; 2. (n) The **Unix** program that does the said lumping

TCP

Transmission Control Protocol. A **protocol** that transmits information over the **Internet,** one small piece at a time.

TCP/IP

The **Internet protocol** using **TCP.**

telnet

A **protocol** for **remote login** and the name of most programs that uses that protocol.

*.test

Usenet newsgroups, such as misc.test, alt.test, etc. used for posting test **messages** to see if they propagate properly. If you **post** something to a *.test newsgroup, be prepared for a mailbox full of confirming replies to your post, sent back by **daemons** as your post propagates around the world.

text editor

A program for editing **text files;** less fully featured than a word processor.

text file

A file containing text only.

text transfer

A transfer of straight text over the **modem,** between the remote computer and a **text file.**

thread

A series of **post**s and follow-ups in a **newsgroup.**

threaded newsreader

A **newsreader** that organizes **post**s according to a **thread** and allows you to read your way up or down a thread.

time out

To fail, as a **network** process, because the **remote server** or computer has not responded in time.

Tin

A **threaded newsreader** for **Unix.**

Trn

A **threaded newsreader** for **Unix,** similar to **Rn.**

troll

To deliberately **post** egregiously false information to a **newsgroup,** in hopes of tricking dense know-it-alls into correcting you. Also, such a post itself. If you follow up a bizarre post to point out that Grover Cleveland Alexander was never president of the U.S., you may see an even more confusing reply to your post saying just "YHBT. YHL. HAND." This stands for "You have been trolled. You have lost. Have a nice day."

TrueSound

Microsoft's own **streaming** sound format.

TurboGopher

A **gopher** program for the Mac.

UL

An **urban legend.** The **Internet** is a perfect communication medium for tracking down and verifying or debunking urban legends.

uncompress

To unsquish a **compress**ed file. A **Unix** uncompression program.

uncompression

The process of unsquishing a file.

Undernet

A smaller, more community-oriented alternative **IRC network** than **EFNet.**

Uniform Resource Locator

See **URL.**

Unix

An operating system common to workstations and on which most **Internet protocol**s were developed.

Unix shell account

An **Internet account** that provides access to a character-only **Unix command line.**

unmoderated
Said of a **newsgroup** or **list** whose articles are not reviewed by a **moderator**.

unselect articles
To remove the selection tag from **Usenet articles** selected for reading.

unsubscribe
To remove yourself from a **mailing list** or to stop reading a **Usenet newsgroup.**

untar
To separate a **tar**red file into its component parts.

upload
To transfer a file over a **modem** from your desktop computer to a remote computer.

urban legends
Stories passed around and always attributed to a friend of a friend (a **FOAF**), frequently (but not always) based on a kernel of falsehood. The **Usenet newsgroup** `alt.folklore.urban` (and its less noisy cousin `alt.folklore.suburban`) are the homes of **UL** debunkers.

URL
Uniform Resource Locator. A **Web address.** It consists of a **protocol,** a host name, a port (optional), a directory, and a file name.

Usenet
1. The collection of computers and **network**s that share news articles. Usenet is *not* the **Internet** (although it overlaps); 2. The **hierarchy** of **newsgroup**s.

username
Also called a **login** or userID. The name a user **log**s **in** with. Also the first part of your **e-mail address** (up to the @).

UUCP
Unix to Unix Copy. A **protocol** and a program for intermittent **network** connections and file and mail transfers.

uudecode

1. (v) To turn a uuencoded file back into its **binary** form; 2. (n) The **Unix** program that does this.

uuencode

1. To convert a **binary file** into a text form that can be sent as part of an e-mail **message;** 2. The **Unix** program that does this.

vacation

A **Unix** program that sets up a return message to be sent to anyone who sends you mail, telling them you're on vacation.

Veronica

An index of **gopher** menus that you search. The results are presented to you as a gopher menu.

Vi

A common **Unix text editor.**

viewers

See **players.**

virus

A program that deliberately does damage to the computer it's on.

.VOC

The audio format for the SoundBlaster sound card.

VRML

Virtual Reality Modeling Language. VRML files usually have a .wrl extension.

VT100

A terminal type, originated by DEC (Digital Equipment Corporation), that has become the standard terminal. If you dial up a **Unix shell,** then your communications program probably emulates a VT100.

w³

An abbreviation for the **Word Wide Web.**

WAN

A wide-area **network.** A computer network spanning a wide geographical area.

warlording

Reposting a **Usenet** article to `alt.fan.warlord` and mocking its **signature** for being too large, ugly, or stupid.

.WAV

Wave format, from Microsoft; perhaps the most widespread sound format on the **Internet.**

Web

The **World Wide Web.**

Web address

A **URL.**

Web browser

A **Web client** program that allows you to view **hypertext page**s and follow **link**s.

Web page

A **hypertext** document on the **Web.**

Web server

A **Web** application that allows you to store **home page**s and make them available via the Hypertext Transfer Protocol. If you lack access to a Web server but have access to an **FTP site,** then you can store your home page there and make sure that **URL**s pointing to it use the ftp:// **protocol** instead of http://.

whisper

A private message to someone in an **IRC** session.

Whois

An **Internet** resource for identifying **e-mail address**es.

WhoWhere?

A **Web site** from which you can look for people.

WinZip

A **compression** program for Windows.

wizard

An expert, usually one willing to help **newbies.**

working directory

The current **directory.** The directory you're "in" right now.

World Wide Web

A collection of **hypertext** documents and associated files, **link**ed together, that spans the **Internet** (and hence, the globe).

worm

A program that duplicates itself, potentially worming its way through an entire **network.**

WRT

With respect to.

WS_FTP

1. An **FTP** program for WindowsWww; 2. A **Unix**-based **Web browser** developed at CERN, the European particle physics laboratory where the Web was invented. It is the original text-based Unix browser for the Web.

WSGopher

A **gopher** program for Windows.

Xmodem

A **protocol** for **download** and **upload** file transfers.

X window
A graphical user interface for **Unix.**

Yahoo
A popular **Web directory.**

Ymodem
A **protocol** for **download** and **upload** file transfers.

YMMV
Your mileage may vary.

zip file
A **compress**ed file.

Zmodem
A **protocol** for **download** and **upload** file transfers.

Index

Note to the Reader: Main level entries are in **bold**. **Boldface** page numbers indicate primary discussions of a topic. *Italicized* page numbers indicate illustrations.

Symbols

& (ampersands), 148
@ (at signs), 237
$0.02 posts, 295
. (periods)
    in e-mail addresses, 237
    for FTP directories, 134, 257
\ / (slashes), 73
:-) (smileys), 295

A

A4 paper size, 147
ABC Radio archive files, 198
About command
    in Internet Explorer, 179
    in True Speech Player, 207, *207*
About Stuffit Expander window, 138
acceptable use guidelines, 296
account names in Exchange client, 242
accounts, 296, 305
Active Content option, **171–172**
ActiveVRML program, 210
ActiveX extensions, 97
activity indicator, 69
Add New File Type dialog box, 206
Add Newsgroups option, 230
add-on programs, **191–193**, *192*

Add profile option, 162
Add/Remove Programs Properties dialog box,
    24–25, *24*, 42
Add Service to Profile dialog box, 240, *240*
Add to Favorites command, 109, 178, 182
Add to Favorites dialog box, 109
Additional options in Advanced tab, **175**
Address Bar, 61, 73, 160, **186**
address books, 296
addresses, 296
    in e-mail, **237**, 306
    in Exchange client, 241
    for news, 220
    in status bar, **62–63**
    TCP/IP for, 4
    in Web pages, **145–146**, *146*
administrivia, 296
Advance One Frame at a Time button, 208
Advance to End option, *196*
Advanced tab, 62, 75, **172–175**, *172–173*
.aiff files, 197, 296
aliases, 296
Alley Oop site, 100, *100*
alt.books.isaac-asimov newsgroup, 229
alt.christnet newsgroup, 229
alt.fan newsgroups, 296
alt.fan.warlord newsgroup, 339
alt.folklore.suburban newsgroup, 337
alt.folklore.urban newsgroup, 337
Alt key, 116–117
alt newsgroup domain, 218, 228–229, 296
alt.religion.kibology newsgroup, 316

AltaVista search site, 84, 292, *292*

Always on Top command, 202

Always Use This Program option, 128

America Online (AOL) service, 297

    news on, **230–232**, *231–232*

    as service provider, **39**

    Winsock version for, 21–22, 39

Amiga computers, 297

Amount of Disk Space to Use setting, 75, 174

ampersands (&), 148

Anarchie program, 297

Andorra page, 15, *15*

animation

    formats for, **207–209**, *208–209*

    options for, 58, 159, 171

anon.penet.fi site, 297

anonymous FTP, 9, 256, 258, 297

Anonymous Login option, 258

anonymous remailer services, 297

answers newsgroups, 297

AOL (America Online) service, 297

    news on, **230–232**, *231–232*

    as service provider, **39**

    Winsock version for, 21–22, 39

API (application programming interface), 34

applications, 297

Archie database, **134–136**, *135–137*, 298

ArchiePlex search engine, **134–136**, *135–137*

Argic, Serdar, 330

Arial font, 61, 160

.arj files, 138

ARPAnet, 298

articles in newsgroups, 10, 298

    browsing, 301

    canceling, 301

    crossposting, 304

    forwarding, **225**

    reading, 219, **221–223**, *223*, **229–232**, *230, 232*

    replying to, 216, **225**, 329

    selecting, 330

    sending, **223–225**, *224*

ASCII (American Standard Code for Information Interchange), 298

ASCII files, 298

associations of file types, **63–64**, *65*, **124–125**

    adding, **128–129**, *128–129*

    changing, **125–127**, *126–127*

    for compressed files, 138

    for sound files, 195, *196*, 206

    viewers for, **129–130**, 167, *168*

asynchronous communication, 298

at signs (@), 237

AT&T backbone, 4

AT&T Business Network site, 285, *285*

AT&T WorldNet, 37

attachments, e-mail, **248–249**, *249*, 252, 298

.au format, 194–195, 197, 298

audio. *See* sound

Audio Properties dialog box, 201

authentication certificates, 171

Auto Disconnect option, 163

autoselect feature, 298

AutoSurf feature, 298

.avi format, 299

B

B1FF, 299

Back button, 184, *184*

Back command, 76, 176, 299

backbones, 4, 299

Background Bitmap option, 61, 160

Background Color feature, 82

background operation with StreamWorks, 204

Background tab, 181, *181*

backgrounds

    color for, 59, 61, 82, 159–160

    copying, 182

    saving, **180**, *180*

    wallpaper, **180–181**, *181*

backslashes (\), 73

Backward Seek button, *200*, 201

bandwidth, 32, 299

Barlow, John, 305

baud, 299

BBS (bulletin board systems), 299, 301

Bcc: line in e-mail, 299

Big Dummy's Guide to the Internet, 299

binaries, 300

binary files, 300

binary transfers, 257, 260, 300

BinHex format, 300

bionet newsgroup domain, 218

bitnet network, 300

bitnet newsgroup domain, 300

bits per second (bps), 301

biz newsgroup domain, 218, 300

blind carbon copies, 299

boldface type

for e-mail messages, 244

for newsgroup articles, 223

bookmarks, 108–109, 300. *See also* Favorites list

'bots, 300

bounced messages, 301

bozo filters, 301

bps (bits per second), 301

Browse for Folder dialog box, 106

browsers, 7, 15, 301, 339

default, 77, **119–120**, *120*, **169**

source documents in, 313

browsing, 301. *See also* Web pages; World Wide Web (WWW)

BTW acronym, 301

bulletin board systems, 299, 301

bulletin boards, 301

C

.ca e-mail domain, 237

cable companies as service providers, 37, 48

calls for votes (CFVs), 302

campus-wide networks, 48

Canadian Broadcasting Corporation archive files, 198

canceling articles, 301

captions for toolbar commands, 61, 160

cascade posts, 302

case sensitivity in searches

in ArchiePlex, 135

in Web pages, 153

catalogs, library, 317

cc:Mail program, 302

Central Search Pages, 302

Certificates options, 171

CFVs (calls for votes), 302

Change Icon dialog box, 112–113, *113*

character-based browsers/readers, 302

character sets, **62**, *63*, 161

in Exchange client, 243

International Globe for, 70

chats, 302

Check for Default option, 169

Check for New Messages option, 248, *249*

Check for Newer Versions of Stored Pages options, 75, 174, *174*

Check Mail command, 251

Check Mail Every _ Minutes option, 251

checkboxes in forms, 91, *92*

Checking Mail Options dialog box, 251, *252*

children, rating options for, 172–173, *173*

clari newsgroup domain, 218

cleaning out Favorites list, **107–108**

client/server applications, 302

clients, **6–7**, 15–16, 302

Clip menu, 203

Clipboard, 151

clocks, synchronizers for, **270–271**, *271*

Close command, 150

clueless newbies, 302

C|net site, 84, *86*, 286, *286*

color options, **59**, 74, 82, **159**

.com e-mail domain, 237, 302

COM ports, 35–36, 303

comic strips, 81, 100, *100*

comm.drv driver, 36

command lines, 303

commands

in Internet Explorer

Edit menu, **151–153**

Favorites menu, **178**

File menu, **143–151**

Go menu, **176–178**

Help menu, **179**

right mouse button, **179–184**

toolbar, **184–186**

View menu, **153–176**

in RealAudio Player, **202–203**

commercial online services, 303

news on, **230–232**, *231–232*

as service providers, **38–41**

comp newsgroup domain, 218, 303

compatibility

of modems, **34**

of Winsocks, **40–41**

compiler for Java, 175

compressed files

downloading, **137–138**

for Internet Explorer, 52

for sound, **197–198**, *199*

RealAudio Player for, **199–203**, *200–201*, *203*

StreamWorks for, **203–204**, *205*

True Speech for, **206–207**, *207*

compressing, 303

compression, 303

CompuServe online service, 303

as service provider, **39–40**

Winsock version for, 21, 40

configuring

Eudora, **250**

Exchange client, **241–243**, *242*

Internet News, **220–221**, *220–221*

Confirm File Open window, 131, *132*

Confirm Open After Download option, 64, 127, 131

conflicts between Winsocks, **40–41**

Connect option in WS_FTP, 258, 260

Connect ➤ Remote System command, 263

Connect through a Proxy Server option, 164–165

Connect To dialog box

for Dial-Up Networking profiles, 43, *45*

in HyperTerminal, 264, *265*

Connect to the Internet as Needed option, 55, 161

Connecting to Internet Mail option, 243

Connection Description dialog box, 264, *265*

connection profiles, **41**, **43–45**, *44–45*, 55, 162, *163*

Connection Properties dialog box, 162, *163*

Connection Statistics dialog box, 202, *203*

Connection tab

in Internet Explorer, 46, *47*, 55, *55*, **161–165**, *162–163*, *165*

in Internet Mail, 243

Connections Properties dialog box, 43, *44*

connections to Internet, **31–32**

alternative, **48**

default, **46**, *47*

Dial-Up Networking, **41–45**, *42*, *44–45*

kinds of, **32**

Microsoft Network, **45–46**

modems for, **32–36**, *35*

service providers for, **36–41**

Windows 3.1, **47–48**

Content Advisor dialog box, 173, *173*

context-sensitive commands, **179–184**, *180–181*

Control Panel

for modem installation, 34

for Volume Control window, 201, *201*

converting Netscape bookmarks, 109

cookies, 171

Copy command, 151

Copy Background command, 182

Copy Shortcut command, 183

copyrights, 303

Courier New font, 62, 161

crackers, 303

Create New Folder option, 105, 130

Create Shortcut command, 111, 150, 182

credit card numbers, 169

crossposting newsgroup articles, 304

Crosstalk program, 262, 266

CRT program, 266

cryptography, 169, 175

Ctrl key, 116–117

CU-SeeMe protocol, 304

cultural values in newsgroups, 217

Custom Options page, 80, 93, *93*

Cut command, 151

CuteFTP program, **261**, *261*

cyberspace, 304

D

&d code, 148

daemons, 304

data bits, 304

dates in headers and footers, 148

Dead Heads, 322

decoding, 304

decrypting, 304

defaults

Dial-Up Networking, 161

home pages, 14

Internet connections, **46**, *47*

Internet Explorer configuration, 58

Internet News and Mail, 167

news servers, 221

search sites, 84, *85*

Start Pages, **78**, *79*

text and background color, 159

Web browsers, 77, **119–120**, *120*, **169**

deities, Internet, 316

DejaNews search engine, 304

Delete command, 56

deleting

Favorites list items, **107–108**

temporary Internet files, 76

delurk, 304

descriptions

for e-mail messages, 243–244

for favorite sites, 109

for file associations, 126, 128

for newsgroup articles, 223, 225

desktop

Internet icon on, 53–54, *54*

shortcuts on, 111, *112*

Details option, 103

diagnostic tools

ping, **267–268**, *268*

traceroute, **268–269**, *269*

WS Ping, **269–270**, *270*

dial-up accounts, 305

Dial-Up Networking, 41

auto disconnections for, **163–164**

connection profiles for, **43–45**, *44–45*, 55, 162–163, *163*

defaults for, 161

with Free Agent, 227

loading, **42**, *42*

Winsock version for, 22

Dial-Up Networking window, 43

digests for mailing lists, 305

Dimension 4 time synchronizer, **270–271**, *271*

Direct-Access ISPs, 305

directories, 305

in FTP archives, 132–134, 257–258, *258*

home, 312

parent, 257, 325

/pub, 134, 328

root, 330

working, 340

Disconnect If Idle option, 55, **163–164**

discussion groups, 305

disk drive space for visited sites, 75, *75*, 174, *174*

Display Properties window, 181, *181*

displaying

images, 183–184

local files, 103

saved Web pages, **130–131**

subscribed newsgroups, **222–223**

distant computing. *See* telnet and telnet clients

documents, HTML, 313

domains

for e-mail, 237, 305

for newsgroups, 218–219

dos2unix program, 318

dots (.)

in e-mail addresses, 237

for FTP directories, 134, 257

downloading files, **123–124**, 305

file type associations for, **124–130**, *126–129*

from FTP archives, **132–138**, *133*, *135–137*, **256–260**, *258–259*, *261*

from gopher servers, **138–140**, *139*

with Internet Explorer, **23–24**, **26–28**

progress indicator for, 70

sources for, **288–289**, *288–289*
with telnet, 264
Trumpet Winsock, 48
Web pages, **130**
from Web Pages, **131**, *132*
drag-and-drop FTP clients, **261**, *261*
drivers
FTP sites for, 9
for messaging services, 239
for modems, 36
drop-down menus in forms, **94**, *94*
dying boy, 331

E

e-mail, **11–12**, **235–236**, 306
addresses in, **237**, 306
attachments in, **248–249**, *249*, 252, 298
clients and servers in, 7
creating and sending messages in, **243**, *244*,
  247–248, *248*, **252–253**, *253*
defaults for, 167
with Eudora, **250–253**, *251–253*
with Exchange, **238–245**, *239–240*, *242*,
  244–245
with Internet Explorer, 238
with Internet Mail, **245–249**, *246–249*
operation of, **236–238**, *236*
receiving and reading messages in, **244–245**,
  245–246, **248**, **251–252**, *252*
shortcuts in, 118
Edit ➤ Copy command, 151
Edit ➤ Cut command, 151
Edit File Type dialog box, 64, 125–127, *127*
Edit ➤ Find (on This Page) command, 152–153,
  153
Edit ➤ Mark All As Read command, 223
Edit ➤ Mark As Read command, 223
Edit ➤ Mark As Unread command, 223
Edit ➤ Paste command, 151
Edit ➤ Select All command, 152, *152*
Editing Action for Type dialog box, 64, *65*, 125

editors
full-screen, 309
for HTML, 109
text, 335
.edu e-mail domain, 237, 305
EFF's Guide to the Internet, 306
EFNet network, 306
elapsed times in RealAudio Player, 202
Electronic Frontier Foundation (EFF), 305
elm mail program, 306
.elmrc file, 306
emacs operating system, 306
embedded sound and video files, **190–191**
emoticons, 306
Empty Folder option, 76
Enable Java JIT Compiler option, 175
Enable Java Logging option, 175
encoding, 306
encrypting, 307
encryption, 169, 175, 307, 325
envelope size, 147
Esc character, 295
etiquette, 322
Eudora Light program, 250
Eudora mail program, **250**, *251*, 307
configuring, **250**
receiving and reading messages in, **251–252**, *252*
sending messages in, **252–253**, *253*
Winsock version for, 47
Eudora Pro program, 250
Every Time You Start Internet Explorer option, 174
EWAN program, 267
Exchange program, 25, **238–241**, *239–240*, 321
configuring, **241–243**, *242*
sending mail in, **243**, *244*
Exit command in RealAudio Player, 202
exiting Internet Explorer, 150
extensions for associations, 63–64, 124
external modems, 33

F

fair use doctrine, 307
FAQs (frequently asked questions), 216, 307

Favorite Links feature, 81
favorite Web pages, **99**
  Favorites list for, **100–109**, *102*, *104*, *106–107*
  hot lists for, **109–110**, *110*
  jumping to, **87**
  shortcuts for, **110–119**, *112–117*, *119*
Favorite Web Pages command, 178, *179*
Favorites ➤ Add To Favorites command, 101, 109, 178
Favorites button, 185, *185*
Favorites ➤ Favorite Web Pages command, 178, *179*
Favorites folder, 103
Favorites list, **100–101**
  adding to, **101**, **104–105**, **109–110**
  appearance of, **103–104**, *104*
  cleaning out, **107–108**
  folders for, **105–106**, *106–107*
  from Netscape Navigator, **108–109**
  opening, **101–102**, *102*
  organizing, **102–103**
Favorites ➤ Organize Favorites command, 102–103, 105, 108, 178
Fetch program, 307
FidoNet, 307
File ➤ Close command, 150, *150*
File ➤ Create Shortcut command, 111, 150
File ➤ Folder command, 246–247
file:// in URLs, 14
File menu in RealAudio Player, 202
File ➤ New command, 118
File ➤ New Window command, 144
File Open button, 207, *207*
File ➤ Open command, 144
File ➤ Page Setup command, **146–148**, *147–148*
File ➤ Print command, **149**, *149*
File ➤ Properties command, 150, *150*
File ➤ Save As File command, 130, **144–146**, *145*
File ➤ Save command, 144
File ➤ Send Message command, 247
File ➤ Send Queued Messages command, 252–253
File ➤ Send To command, 146
File Transfer Protocol. *See* FTP (File Transfer Protocol) archives and clients

File Types tab, 64, 125–126, *126*, 128, 167, 206
files
  ASCII, 298
  associating. *See* associations of file types
  attaching to e-mail messages, **248–249**, *249*, 252, 298
  binary, 300
  compressed. *See* compressed files
  downloading. *See* downloading files
  image, 314
  shareware, 289, *289*, 331
  temporary, 75–76, *75*, **173–174**, *174*
film at 11 tag, 307
Find (on This Page) command, 152–153
Find windows, 152–153, *153*
finding
  Internet Explorer, **23**
  newsgroups, 221, **228–229**, *228–229*
  viewers, **129–130**
  Web page items, 152–153, *153*
finger command, 308
firewalls, 56, 164
fixed-width fonts, 62, 161
flame wars, 308
flamebait, 308
flamers, 308
flames, 308
Flash Sessions, 308
FOAF acronym, 308
folders
  for Favorites list, **105–106**, *106–107*
  for Internet Explorer, 52
  for Internet Mail, 246–247
  for shortcuts, **113**, *114*
  for Web pages, 130
follow-up lines, 309
follow-ups, 308
following links, 308
Font command button, 185, *185*
fonts, 61–62, **153–155**, *154*, **160–161**
Fonts command, **153**, **155**
foreign character sets, **62**, *63*, 161
forms, **89–90**
  checkboxes in, **91**, *92*
  drop-down menus and scrollbar lists in, **94**, *94*

radio buttons in, **93**, *93*

Submit and Reset buttons in, **95–96**, *95*

text fields in, **90**, *91–92*

Forward button, 184, *184*

Forward command

in Internet Explorer, 76, 176

in Internet News, 225

Forward Seek button, *200*, 201

forward slashes (/), 73

forwarding news messages, **225**

FQA acronym, 309

.fr e-mail domain, 237

Free Agent newsreader, **226–227**, *226–227*

free-nets, 309

Free Software Foundation, 310

freeware, 309

frequently asked questions (FAQs), 216, 307

FTP (File Transfer Protocol) archives and clients, 6, **9–10**, **132**, **256–257**, 309

Archie database for, **134–136**, *135–137*

compressed files in, **137–138**

CuteFTP, **261**, *261*

navigating, **133–134**, *133*

WS_FTP, **257–260**, *258–259*

ftp.cdrom.com site, 111

ftp.cso.uiuc.edu site, 138

ftp:// in URLs, 14, 73, 132

ftp.jasc.com site, 130

ftp.microsoft.com site, 23

ftp.NCSA.uiuc.edu site, 208

ftp.synapse.net site, 48

ftp.usma.edu site, 9

FTPmail, 309

full names, 309

Full Newsgroup Access EForm, 229, *229*

full-screen editors, 309

FUQ acronym, 310

FWIW acronym, 310

G

<g> indicator, 310

games, **96–97**, *97*, 321

garbage characters, 310

gardens, 91, *92*

gated lists, 310

gateways, 4, 236, 310

general-interest Web guides, **281–287**, *282–287*

General tab

in Internet Explorer, **58–62**, *59*, 70, **156–161**, *156*

in Internet Mail, 241, *242*

geography, gopher organization by, 139

Gibson, William, 304

GIF (graphic interchange format) images, 310

Global Network Navigator site, 283, *283*

GNNnet

as service provider, 37

Winsock version for, 21

gnu format, 137–138

gnu newsgroup domain, 310

Go ➤ Back command, 76, 176

Go ➤ Forward command, 76, 176

Go menu, history list on, 176, *177*

Go ➤ Open History Folder command, 76, **177–178**, *177*

Go ➤ Product Update command, 273

Go ➤ Search the Internet command, 84, 176

Go ➤ Start Page command, 176

Go To newsgroup option, 222

Go ➤ Today's Links command, 176

gopher:// in URLs, 14, 140

Gopher Jewels site, 140

gopher sites, **12–13**, *13*, **138–140**, *139*, 311

gopherspace, 311

.gov e-mail domain, 237, 311

Graphics feature, 82

Grateful Dead, 322

green-card lawyers, 311

grepping, 316

<grin> indicator, 311

groups, discussion, 305

guides to World Wide Web

general-interest, **281–287**, *282–287*

software, **288–289**, *288–289*

gunzip program, 311

.gz files, 137–138

gzip program, 311

H

^H character, 311
hackers, 312
hacking, 312
hard disk drive space for visited sites, 75, *75*, 174, *174*
Hayes-compatible modems, 312
he who greps, 316
Headers/Footers option, **148**, *148*
headphones, 194
Help menu
    in Internet Explorer, **179**
    in RealAudio Player, 203
Help Topics command, 179
hiding
    icon bars, 223, 246
    images, 58, *60*, 157, *158*
    Internet icon, **56**
    Internet News icon, 225
    status bar, 153
    toolbars, **61**, *62*, 70, 153, **160**
hierarchies, 312
high-speed data services, 48
Highlight a Link When Clicked option, 175
History folder, **76**, 167, **177–178**, *177*
history lists, 176, *177*, 312
Home button
    in Internet Explorer, 185, *185*
    in RealAudio Player, 201
home directories, 312
home pages, 14, 312. *See also* Start pages
$HOME variable, 312
hoohoo.ncsa.uiuc.edu site, 134
hosts, 7, 313
hot links, 14–15, **73–74**, *74*
hot lists pages, **109–110**, *110*, 313
HotJava browser, 313
.htm extension, 130
HTML (Hypertext Markup Language), 124, 313
    editor programs for, 109
    source code for, 155–156, 182, 313

HTTP (Hypertext Transfer Protocol), 14–15, 313
http:// in URLs, 14, 73
HyperACCESS platform, 264
hypermedia, 313
HyperTerminal Private Edition, 264
HyperTerminal program, 262, **264–266**, *265–266*
hypertext documents, 313
hypertext links, 313
Hypertext Markup Language (HTML), 124, 313
    editor programs for, 109
    source code for, 155–156, 182, 313
Hypertext Transfer Protocol (HTTP), 14–15, 313
Hytelnet program, 313

I

IBM Global Network, 37
IBM Internet Connection, 256
    tools in, 47
    Winsock version for, 21
icon bars, hiding, 223, 246
icons
    changing, **111–113**, *113*
    hiding, 56, 225
    Internet icon, **53–57**
idle time counter, 55, **163–164**
images, 314
    for backgrounds, 180, *180*
    displaying, 183–184
    options for, 58, *60*, **157**, *158*
    saving, **145–146**, *145*, 183
    viewers for, 129–130
IMHO acronym, 314
Immediate Send e-mail option, 252–253
Imminent Death of the Net Predicted warning, 314
IMNSHO acronym, 314
IMO acronym, 314
Impact on other users ArchiePlex field, 136
importing bookmarks, **108–109**
inboxes, 314
index files in FTP archives, 133
info addresses, 314

Info & Volume command, 202

Insert ➤ File Attachment command, 248

Install New Modem wizard, 34–36

installing

Internet Explorer, **52–53**, *53*

Microsoft Network, **24–25**, *24–25*

modems, **34–36**, *35*

Integrated Services Digital Network (ISDN), 32

interactive games, **96–97**, *97*, 321

interactive multimedia, 210

interactive search tools, **289–292**, *289–292*

interactive Web pages, **89–96**, *91–95*

internal modems, 33

International dialog box, 62, *63*

international features, **62**, *63*, 70, 161

International Globe, 70

Internet, **3**, 314

clients and servers on, **6–7**

connecting to. *See* connections to Internet

e-mail on, **11–12**

FTP in, **9–10**

gopher on, **12–13**, *13*

newsgroups on, **10–11**

structure of, **4–6**, *5–6*

telnet on, **7–8**, *8*

World Wide Web on, **14–16**, *15*

Internet Center, 228, *228*

Internet Chameleon, 21, 47, 256

Internet Dictionary, 295

Internet E-Mail driver, 239

Internet Explorer, **19–20**, *20*, **51**, 314

with AOL, 39

appearance and performance of, **57–63**, *59–60*, *62–63*

associating file types to programs in, **63–64**, *65*

character sets in, **62**, *63*, 161

color options for, **59**, 159

commands in. *See* commands

with CompuServe, 40

downloading, **23–24**, **26–28**

e-mail with, 238

finding, **23**

fonts in, **61–62**, **160–161**

installing, **52–53**, *53*

Internet icon for, **53–57**, *54–55*, *57*

keyboard shortcuts in, **277–278**

multimedia element options for, **58**

quick links in, **71**, *72*

screen for, **68–70**, *69*

starting, **68**

status bar address format in, **62–63**

text link options in, **60–61**, 159

toolbar options in, **61**, *62*, **70**, **160**

updating, 20, **273–274**

versions of, **21–22**

World Wide Web with. *See* Web pages; World Wide Web (WWW)

Internet Explorer command, 68

Internet Explorer Should Check to See Whether It is the Default Browser option, 169

Internet Guide, 306

Internet icon, 53–54, *54*

hiding, **56**, *57*

properties for, **54–56**, *55*

renaming, 56

Internet in a Box, 21, 47

Internet Mail, **245–247**, *246–247*

attaching files in, **248–249**, *249*

defaults for, 167

sending and receiving messages in, **247–248**, *248*

Internet Mail dialog box, 241, *242*

Internet Mail window, 246, *247*

Internet News, **219–220**

configuring, **220–221**, *220–221*

defaults for, 167

forwarding messages in, **225**

hiding icons for, 225

reading messages in, **221–223**, *223*

replying to messages in, **225**

sending messages in, **223–225**, *224*

viewing subscribed newsgroups in, **222–223**

Internet Over The Microsoft Network driver, 239, 241

Internet Phone protocol, 314

Internet Properties dialog box, 54–56, *55*, **156–161**, *156*

Internet Protocol (IP), 315

Internet Relay Chat (IRC), 315
Internet Resources Meta-Index, 315
Internet service providers (ISPs). *See* service
 providers
Internet Shortcut tab, 112, 116–117, *117*
Internet Tools folder, 52
internetMCI
 for downloading Internet Explorer, 27–28
 as service provider, 37
InterNIC site, 315
**interrupt request line (IRQ) numbers for
 modems**, 36
invalid site certificates, 171
investments, 81–82
IP (Internet Protocol), 315
IRC (Internet Relay Chat), 315
Ircle program, 315
**IRQ (interrupt request line) numbers for
 modems**, 36
Is-IR files, 134
ISDN (Integrated Services Digital Network), 32
ISPs (Internet service providers). *See* service
 providers

J

Java programming language, 97, 175, 315
JIT (Just In Time) compiler, 175
joining newsgroups, **221–222**, *222*
JPEG format, 315
Jughead index, 315
Junod, John, 257
Just In Time (JIT) compiler, 175

K

k12 newsgroup domain, 218, 316
Kapor, Mitch, 305
Kermit protocol, 264, 316
keyboard shortcuts, **115–117**, *117*, **277–278**
keys, encryption, 316

keywords, 90, 316
Kibo, 316
kibology, 316
killfiles, 316
kilobits per second (kps), 316–317
KING-FM site, 192, *192*, 195
Knowbots, 316
KPIG radio station, 204, *205*
kps (kilobits per second), 316–317

L

Landscape orientation option, 147
languages, character sets for, **62**, *63*, 70, 161
LANs (local-area networks), 317
 connections to, 32, 48
 firewalls for, 56, 164
legends, urban, 336–337
lharc program, 317
libraries, catalogs for, 317
line-at-a-time programs, 317
Link Central page, 71
links, 14–15, 313, 317
 appearance of, **59–61**, **159**
 in ArchiePlex, 136
 copying, 183
 following, 308
 in gopher servers, 140
 highlighting, 175
 opening, 183
 quick links, 68–69, **71**, *72*, 166, **186**, *186*
 saving. *See* favorite Web pages
 targets of, 183
Links toolbar, 61, 71, 160
List option for Favorites list, 103
List Topics option, 230
lists in forms, **94**, *94*
Listservs, 317
live sound connections, 193–194
loading
 Dial-Up Networking, **42**, *42*
 Web pages, 144

local-area networks (LANs), 317
    connections to, 32, 48
    firewalls for, 56, 164
local files, displaying, 103
local service providers, **38**
logging off, 318
logging on, 317
login names in anonymous FTP, 9, 256, 258
logins, 317
logs for Java, 175
LOL acronym, 318
.lst files, 260
Lucida Console font, 62, 161
lurkers, 318
lurking, 318
LView program, 130
Lynx browser, 318
.lzh files, 138

M

^M character, 318
Magellan Internet Guide site, 287, *287*
mail. *See* e-mail
mail boxes, 318
Mail ➤ Move To command, 247
Mail ➤ Options command, 248
mail readers, 319
mail reflectors, 319
mailing lists, 318
.mailrc file, 318
main window, 69, *69*
majordomo program, 319
MAKE.MONEY.FAST chain letter, 319
Make New Connection wizard, 43
MAPI (Messaging Application Program Interface),
    238, 244
Margins option, 148
Maximized keyboard shortcut option, 117
MCI
    backbone of, 4
    for downloading Internet Explorer, 27–28

menu bar, 68, *69*
menus. *See also* commands
    in forms, **94**, *94*
    in gopher, 12–13, *13*, **139–140**, *139*
Message ➤ Attach File command, 252
message formats in Exchange client, 242
Message Handling Service (MHS), 236
Message ➤ New Message command
    in Eudora, 252
    in Internet Mail, 247
**Message ➤ New Message to Newsgroup
    command**, 224
messages, 319. *See also* e-mail; news and newsgroups
Messaging Application Program Interface (MAPI),
    238, 244
Messaging Subsystem, 239, *240*
MHS (Message Handling Service), 236
Microsoft Download Service, **26–27**, *27*
Microsoft Exchange dialog box, 25
Microsoft Exchange program, 25, **238–241**,
    239–240, 321
    configuring, **241–243**, *242*
    sending mail in, **243**, *244*
Microsoft Network (MSN), 282, *282*
    for downloading Internet Explorer, 23–24
    installing, **24–25**, *24–25*
    for Internet connections, **45–46**
    Link Central page in, 71
    as newsreader, **227–230**, *228–230*
Microsoft Network dialog box, 46
Microsoft On The Web command, 179
Microsoft Plus! package, 20
Microsoft Product Update Web site, 20
Microsoft quick link, 71
**MIDI (Musical Instrument Digital Interface)
    format**, 319
.mil domain, 319
MIME (Multipurpose Internet Mail Extensions),
    319
    associations for. *See* associations of file types
    in Exchange client, 242
Minesweeper game, 96, *97*
mIRC program, 319

mirror sites, 319
misc newsgroup domain, 218, 320
mjablecki.extern.ucsd.edu site, 111
Model 3270 terminal emulation, 262
modems, **32–33**, 320
 choosing, **33–34**
 compatibility of, **34**
 for StreamWorks, 204
 with Windows 3.1, **36**
 with Windows 95, **34–36**, *35*
Modems Properties dialog box, 34–36, *35*
moderated mailing lists, 320
moderated newsgroups, 217, 320
moderators, 320
more program, 320
Mosaic browser, 320
MOTAS acronym, 320
Mother Gopher, 12, 140
MOTOS acronym, 320
MOTSS acronym, 320
motto! posts, 320
.mov files, 209
Move Folder option, 76, 174
Movie Link feature, 81
moving
 Favorite list items, 106
 shortcuts on Start menu, 115
 toolbars, 70
moving around. *See* navigating
moving pictures, **207–209**, *208–209*
MPEG format, **208**, *208*, 320
MPEGPLAY program, 208, *208*
MSN. *See* Microsoft Network (MSN)
MSN Start Page, **78–83**, *79–80*
MSN Today feature, 81
MUDs, 321
multimedia, **189–190**, *190*
 embedded files for, **190–191**
 interactive, **210**
 options for, **58**, *60*, **157–159**, *158*
 plug-in and add-on programs for, **191–193**, *192*
 sound. *See* sound video, **207–211**, *208–211*
multiple windows, **76–77**, 183

Multipurpose Internet Mail Extensions (MIME),
 319
  associations for. *See* associations of file types
  in Exchange client, 242
MUSE (multiuser simulation environment), 321
Music Clip feature, 81
music on Start Page, 82–83
My Newsgroups list, 230
my two cents tag, 321

N

names
 in anonymous FTP, 9, 256, 258
 in e-mail addresses, 237
 in Exchange client, 241–242
 for Favorites list items, 108
 for folders, 105, 113
 full, 309
 for Internet icon, 56
 for news servers, 221
 for newsgroups, 218
 in profiles, 43
 for quick link sites, 71
 real, 328
 for shortcuts, 150
 text fields for, 90
 for wallpaper files, 181
National Public Radio archive files, 198
national service providers, **37**
navigating, **72**
 with favorite pages, **87**
 FTP archives, **133–134**, *133*
 Go menu for, **176–178**, *177*
 History folder for, **76**, 167
 hot links for, **73–74**, *74*
 multiple windows for, **76–77**, 183
 Start pages in, **77–83**
 URL addresses for, **73**
 visited sites, **75–76**
Navigation tab, **166–167**, *166*
 for quick links, 61, 71
 for Search page, 85, *86*
 for Start pages, 78, *79*, **166–167**

Ncftp program, 321

NCSA (National Center for Supercomputing Applications), 321

NCSA Mosaic browser, 20, 321

NCSA What's New Page, 321

Net, 321

net.celebrities, 322

net.cops, 322

.net domain, 322

net.gods, 322

net.personalities, 322

net.spewers, 323

Netcom
    backbone of, 4
    as service provider, 37

NetCruiser browser, 22, 322

Netfind resource, 322

netheads, 322

netiquette, 322

netizens, 322

.netrc file, 322

Netscape Navigator, 20, 323
    importing bookmarks from, **108–109**
    plug-ins for, 192
    Winsock version for, 47

NetTerm program, 266–267

network information centers (NICs), 324

network interface devices, 48

Network News Transfer Protocol (NNTP), 10, 219

networking protocols, 4, 327

networks, 4, 299, 323
    campus-wide, 48
    local-area, 32, 48, 56, 164, 317
    wide-area, 339

New Action dialog box, 64, *65*, 206

New File Type dialog box, 64, 206

New ➤ Folder command, 113

New Message command
    in Eudora, 252
    in Internet Mail, 247
    in Internet News, 224

New Message window
    in Internet Mail, 247, *248*
    in Internet News, 224–225, *224*

New Program Object dialog box, 118

New Window command, 144

newbies, 302, 323

news and newsgroups, **10–11**, **215–216**, 323
    AOL for, **230–232**, *231–232*
    forwarding messages in, **225**
    Free Agent for, **226–227**, *226–227*
    Internet News for, **219–225**, *220–224*
    joining, **221–222**, *222*
    MSN for, **227–230**, *228–230*
    operation of, **216–218**
    organization of, **218–219**
    reading messages in, 219, **221–223**, *223*, **229–232**, *230*, *232*
    replying to messages in, **225**
    sending messages in, **223–225**, *224*
    viewing, **222–223**

News ➤ Choose Newsgroups command, 225

News feature, 81

news newsgroup domain, 218

News ➤ Newsgroups command, 221

News ➤ Options command, 220

News ➤ Reply to Newsgroup command, 225

News Server Properties dialog box, 220–221, *221*

News Xpress newsreader, 323

newsfeeds, 323

newsgroups. *See* news and newsgroups

Newsgroups dialog box, 221, *222*

.newsrc file, 323

newsreaders, 11, 219, 301, 323
    Free Agent, **226–227**, *226–227*
    Internet News, **219–225**, *220–224*
    MSN, **227–230**, *228–230*
    threaded, 335

NewsWatcher newsreader, 323

Next Clip command, 203

NFS protocol, 324

NICs (network information centers), 324

Nn newsreader, 324

NNTP (Network News Transfer Protocol), 10, 219

nodes, 324

noise, 217, 324, 331

Normal safety level, 172

Normal Window option, 117

NSF (National Science Foundation), 324
NSFNet, 325
nudity, rating options for, 172–173, *173*
Number of Copies option, 149

O

Ob prefix, 324
Object Linking and Embedding (OLE), 238
offline readers, 324–325
offline status, 324
OLE (Object Linking and Embedding), 238
Once Per Session option, 75
Online ➤ Get New Groups command, 227
Online ➤ Refresh Groups List command, 227
online services, 303
    news on, **230–232**, *231–232*
    as service providers, **38–41**
online status, 324
Open button, 208
Open command, 144, 183
Open dialog box, 144, *144*
Open File command, 202
Open History Folder command, **177–178**, *177*
Open in New Window command, 77
Open Location dialog box, 202
Open Recent command, 202
Open Start Page button, 77
Open With dialog box, 128–129, *129*
opening Favorites list, **101–102**, *102*
operating systems, 4
Options dialog box
    in Eudora, 250–252, *252*
    in Internet Explorer
        Advanced tab in, 62, 75, **172–175**,
          172–173
        Connection tab in, 46, *47*, 55, *55*,
          161–165, *162–163*, *165*
        File Types tab in, 64, 125–126, *126*, 128,
          167, 206
        General tab in, **58–62**, *59*, 70, **156–161**

    Navigation tab in, 61, 71, 78, *79*, 85, *86*,
        166–167, *166*
    Programs tab in, 64, *65*, 125, **167–169**,
        168
    Security tab in, **169–172**, *170*
    in Internet Mail, 248, *249*
    in Internet News, 220, *220*
.org domain, 325
Organize Favorites dialog box, 102–105, *104*, 108
Organizing Favorites command, 178
Orientation option, 147

P

&p code, 148
package tracking, 90, *91*
padlock indicator, 169, *170*
page numbers, 148
Page Setup command, 146
Page Setup dialog box, **146–148**, *147–148*
pager program, 325
pages. *See* Web pages
Paint Shop Pro program, 130
papa.indstate.edu site, 261
Paper Size option, 147
Paper Source option, 147
parent directories, 257, 325
parity, 325
Parry, James F., 316
passwords
    in anonymous FTP, 9, 256, 258
    in Exchange client, 242
    with news servers, 221
    in profiles, 43
    security for, 169
    text fields for, 90
Paste command, 151
patches, FTP sites for, 9
pathfinder.com site, 284, *284*
Pause button
    in audio player, *197*
    in RealAudio Player, 199, *200*

PCMCIA (PC Card) modems, 33, 36

Pegasus Mail, 325

Perform System Security Check Before Dialing option, 56, 164

periods (.)
in e-mail addresses, 237
for FTP directories, 134, 257

Personal Info feature, 82

pgp program, 325

phrases, searching for, 152–153, *153*

Pico editor, 325

pictures. *See* images

Pine mail program, 325

ping tool, **267–268**, *268*, 326

Pipeline USA, 22

pkunzip program, 326

pkzip program, 326

Plain Old Telephone Service (POTS), 32

.plan files, 326

platforms, 326

Play option
in audio player, *197*
in MPEGPLAY, 208
in RealAudio Player, 199, *200*
in Sound Recorder, *196*
in True Speech Player, 207, *207*

Play Sounds option, 58, 157

Play Videos option, 58, 159

player programs, 326

playing sound, **195–197**, *196–197*

plebiscites, 326

***plonk* posts**, 326

Plug and Play specification, 34

plug-in programs, 191–193, *192*, 326

Point-to-Point Protocol (PPP), 36, 327

pointing at clients, 326

POP (points of presence), 327

POP (Post Office Protocol) servers, 327

POP3 servers, 236, 239, 246

Portrait orientation option, 147

ports, 35–36, 303

Post Office Protocol (POP) servers, 236, 239, 246, 327

postcard champion, 331

posting, 10–11, 327

Postmasters, 327

POTS (Plain Old Telephone Service), 32

PPP (Point-to-Point Protocol), 36, 327

Preferences command, 202

Previous Clip command, 203

Print button, 185, *185*

Print command, 149

Print dialog box, 149, *149*

Print Range option, 149

Printer option, 148

printing, **149**
headers and footers for, 148
margins for, 148
orientation for, 147
page setup for, 146, *147*
paper source for, 147

privacy, **169–171**, *170*

private keys, 327

ProComm program, 262, 266

Prodigy online service, 40

Product Update Site, 20, *20*

Product Updates quick link, 71

profiles, connection, **41**, **43–45**, *44–45*, 55, 162, *163*

Program Files folder, 52

Program Item Properties dialog box, 118–119, *119*

Program Manager, shortcuts in, **118–119**, *119*

programs
associating. *See* associations of file types
on Favorites list, 104
plug-in and add-on, **191–193**, *192*, 326

Programs tab, 64, *65*, 125, **167–169**, *168*

progress indicator for downloads, 70

.project files, 327

propagation, 327

Properties option for connections, **162**

Properties windows and dialog box, 150, *150*
for Internet icon, **54–56**, *55*
for keyboard shortcuts, 116–117, *117*
for shortcut icons, 112–113
for wallpaper, 181
for Web pages, 182–183

proportional fonts, 61, 160

protocols, 4, 327
providers. *See* service providers
Proxy option, 56
proxy servers, 56, **164–165**, *165*
Proxy Settings dialog box, 165, *165*
PSInet
    backbone of, 4
    as service provider, 37
/pub directory, 134, 328
public data networks, 328
public keys, 328
public telnet hosts, 8

Q

QModem program, 262
.qt files, 209
queries, 328
queues, 328
quick links, 68–69, **71**, *72*, 166, **186**, *186*
QuickMail, 328
quicktime.apple.com site, 208
QuickTime format, **208–209**, *208*, 328
QuickTime Movie Player program, *208*, **209**

R

radio buttons, **93**, *93*
radio station sites, 192, *192*, 195
Radio Telefis Eireann (RTE), 198, *200*
Ratings option, **172–173**, *173*
Ratings tab, 173, *173*
Read My Newsgroup option, 230
Read tab, 248, *249*
reading
    e-mail messages, **244–245**, *245–246*, **248**,
      251–252, *252*
    news articles, 219, **221–223**, *223*, **229–232**, *230*,
      232
readme files, 133
real names, 328

real-time, 328
RealAudio format, 191–192, 194, 198, 328
RealAudio page, 198, *199*
RealAudio Player
    controls for, **199–202**, *200–201*
    menu commands in, **202–203**, *203*
rec.music.folk newsgroup, 229, *230*
rec newsgroup domain, 218, 329
receiving e-mail messages, **244–245**, *245–246*,
    248, **251–252**, *252*
Record option, *196*
Recreational Software Advisory Council (RSAC),
    173
Refresh button, 75, 185, *185*
Refresh command, **155**, 182
registered file types, 64, 124
relative addresses in Web pages, **145–146**, *146*
reloading Web pages, **155**, 182
remailer services, 297
remote computing. *See* telnet and telnet clients
remote logins, 329
Remote Mail feature, 243
Remote System file list, 260
Rename command, 150
renaming
    Favorites list items, 108
    Internet icon, 56
    shortcuts, 150
Reply to Author command, 225
Reply to Group command, 225
replying to messages, 216, **225**, 329
reposting, 329
-request addresses, 329
Requests for Comments (RFCs), 329
Requests for Discussion (RFDs), 329
Reset buttons in forms, **96**
Restrict the number of results field, 136
Restrict the results to a domain field, 135
Return to Start option, *196*
revisiting sites. *See* favorite Web pages
Rewind button, 208
RFCs (Requests for Comments), 329
RFDs (Requests for Discussion), 329
Rich Text Format (RTF), 118

right mouse button commands, **179–184**, *180–181*
Rlogin program, 329
Rn newsreader, 330
roboposters, 330
role-playing games, 321
root directory, 52, 330
ROTFL acronym, 330
RSAC (Recreational Software Advisory Council), 173
RTE (Radio Telefis Eireann), 198, *200*
RTF (Rich Text Format), 118
RTFM acronym, 330
Run field for keyboard shortcuts, 117

S

Safety Level option, 171–172
Save command
  in Internet Explorer, 144
  in WS_FTP, 260
Save As File command, **144–146**, *145*
Save Background As command, **180**, *180*
Save It to Disk option, 131
Save Picture As command, 146, 183
Save Target As command, 183
saving
  backgrounds, **180**, *180*
  images, **145–146**, *145*, 183
  site links. *See* favorite Web pages
  Web pages, **130**, **144–146**, *147*
sci newsgroup domain, 218, 330
scrambling messages, 307
screen in Internet Explorer, **68–70**, *69*
script files, 48
scrollbar lists, **94**, *94*
scrolling options, 175
Search button, 84, 185, *185*
search.com search tool, 84, *86*, 96, 290, *290*
Search for field, 134–135
Search Forms feature, 81
Search page, 84–85, *85–86*, **166–167**
Search the Internet command, 84, 176

search tools, 330
  forms for, 90, *92*
  for World Wide Web, **83–86**, *85–86*, **289–292**, *289–292*
searching
  for Internet Explorer, **23**
  for newsgroups, 221, **228–229**, *228–229*
  for viewers, **129–130**
  in Web pages, 152–153, *153*
secondary newsgroup domains, 219
Security tab, **169–172**, *170*
Seek to End button, 207, *207*
Seek to Start button, 207, *207*
Select All command, 152, *152*, 182
Select Network Component Type dialog box, 42, *42*
selecting
  news articles, 330
  text, 151–152, 182
semi-anonymity, 330
Send and Receive button, 248
Send Message command, 247
Send on Check option, 252–263
Send To command, 146
sending
  e-mail messages, **243**, *244*, **247–248**, *248*, **252–253**, *253*
  news messages, **223–225**, *224*
  shortcuts to other users, **118**
Sending Mail dialog box, 252
Sending Mail icon, 252
Serial Line Internet Protocol (SLIP), 332
Server Tab, 220, *220*
Server Types dialog box, 43, *44*
servers, **6–7**, 331
  for Exchange client, 241
  proxy, 56, **164–165**, *165*
  in World Wide Web, 15–16, 339
service providers, 315, 331
  for Internet connections, **36–41**
  local, **38**
  national, **37**
  for news setup information, 220
  newsreaders from, 219

online services, **38–41**
Winsocks from, 48
Services quick link, 71
Services tab, 241
Session Profile dialog box, 258, *259*
Set As Wallpaper command, **180–181**, *181*
Set Up Page option, 80
Settings dialog box, 75, *75*, 174, *174*
Settings ➤ Taskbar command, 115
Setup wizard, 46, 53, *53*
sex, rating options for, 172–173, *173*
shareware.com site, 289, *289*
shareware files, 331
shell accounts, 331
shell environments, 331
Shergold, Craig, 331
Shockware format, 210
shortcuts, 87, **110–111**
to attached files, 249, *249*
changing, **111–113**, *113*
copying, 183
creating, **111**, *112*, 150, 182
on Favorites list, 104–105
folders for, **113**, *114*
in History folder, 76
keyboard, **115–117**, *117*, **277–278**
renaming, 150
sending to other users, **118**
on Start menu, **114–115**, *115–116*
to URLs, 60
in Windows 3.1, **118–119**, *119*
Shortcuts printing option, 149
Show Friendly URLs option, 62–63, 175
Show Picture command, 183–184
Show Pictures option, 58, 157
.sig files, 331
Sign In window, 46
signal-to-noise ratio, 331
signature files, 331–332
Simple Mail Transfer Protocol (SMTP), 11, 236, 239, 246, 332
site certificates, 171
sites, 332
Sites menu, 203

size
of fonts, **153–155**, *154*
of paper, 147
Ski Reports feature, 81
slashes (/), 73
SLIP (Serial Line Internet Protocol), 332
SlipKnot program, 332
smileys, 295, 332
smooth scrolling option, 175
SMTP (Simple Mail Transfer Protocol), 11, 236, 239, 246, 332
snail mail, 332
SO acronym, 333
soc newsgroup domain, 218, 333
software sources on World Wide Web, **288–289**, *288–289*
Sort by field, 135
sound
compressed files for, **197–198**, *199*
RealAudio Player for, **199–203**, *200–201, 203*
StreamWorks for, **203–204**, *205*
True Speech for, **206–207**, *207*
embedded files for, **190–191**
options for, 58, **157**
playing, **195–197**, *196–197*
requirements for, **193–194**
sound clips and live connections for, **193–194**
on Start Page, 82–83
sound cards, 193
sound clips, **193–194**
Sound Recorder applet, 195, *196*
SoundBlaster cards, 193
Sounds option, 194
source code for Web pages, 155–156, 182, 313
Source command, 155–156
spamming, 333
speakers, 193–194
spewing, 333
Sports Scores feature, 81
Spry Mosaic, 22
SPRYnet, 37
stand-alone programs, 333
Standard toolbar, 61, 160, **184–185**, *184–185*

starbase.neosoft.com site, 267

Start and Search Pages dialog box, 84, 166

Start menu, shortcuts on, **114–115**, *115–116*

Start Menu Programs tab, 115, *116*

Start Page command, 176

Start Page link, 80

Start pages, 54, **77–78**

    changing, **78**, *79*, **167**

    choosing, **78**, 166

    customizing, **78–83**, *79–80*

starting Internet Explorer, **68**

Statistics command, 202

status bar, *69*, **70**

    address formats in, **62–63**

    hiding, 153

    security indicator in, 169, *170*

Status Bar command

    in Internet Explorer, 153

    in RealAudio Player, 202

stock information, 81–82

stop bits, 333

Stop button

    in audio player, *197*

    in Internet Explorer, 155, 184, *184*

    in MPEGPLAY, 208

    in RealAudio Player, *200*, 201

    in Sound Recorder, *196*

    in True Speech Player, 207, *207*

Stop command, 155

streaming, 333

StreamWorks format, 194

    for audio, **203–204**, *205*

    for video, 211

StreamWorks Player, **203–204**, *205*

StreamWorks window, 204, *205*

strong language, rating options for, 172–173, *173*

Stuffit Expander program, 138

style sheets, 175

subdirectories, 333

subdomains, 333

subfolders for Favorites list, **105–106**, *106–107*

subject, gopher organization by, 139

Submit buttons

    in ArchiePlex, 136

    in forms, **95–96**, *95*

subscribed newsgroups, viewing, **222–223**

Subscribed tab, 222

subscribing to newsgroups, 222, 333

SuperHighway Access, 22

support from local service providers, 38

surfing, 334

synchronizers, time, **270–271**, *271*

synchronous communication, 334

sysadmins, 334

sysops, 334

system administrators, 334

system operators, 334

T

&t code, 148

talk newsgroup domain, 218, 334

talk program, 334

tar program, 334

targets of links, 183

TCP (Transmission Control Protocol), 334

TCP/IP (Transmission Control Protocol/Internet Protocol), 4, 334

TCP/IP Settings option, 43

tech support from local service providers, 38

telephone companies as service provider, 37, 48

telephone numbers in profiles, 43

telnet and telnet clients, **7–8**, *8*, **262**, 335

    HyperTerminal, **264–266**, *265–266*

    in Windows 3.1, **266–267**

    in Windows 95, **263–264**, *263*

telnet:// in URLs, 14

Temporary Internet Files folder, 75–76, **173–174**

terminal emulation programs, 262, 338

test newsgroups, 335

text

    color for, 59, 82, 159

    in forms, **90**, *91–92*

    transferring, 257, 260, 335

Text Color feature, 82

text editors, 335

text files, 257, 260, 335

Text Labels toolbar, 61, 160

text link options, **60–61**, **159**

theft of data, 169

thelist.com site, 38

This Server Requires Me to Logon option, 221

threaded newsreaders, 335

threads in newsgroups, 216, 335

time

in headers and footers, 148

in RealAudio Player, 202

synchronizers for, **270–271**, *271*

Time-Life Garden Encyclopedia, 91, *92*

time outs, 335

Times New Roman font, 61, 160

Tin newsreader, 335

title bar, 68, *69*

titles in headers and footers, 148

TN3270 program, 262

Today's Links command, 176

Today's Links quick link, 71

Toolbar command, 153

toolbars, 68–69, *69*

commands on, **184–186**, *184–186*

hiding, **61**, *62*, 70, 153, **160**

options for, **61**, *62*, **70**, **160**

Tools ➤ Options command

in Eudora, 250, 252

in Internet Mail, 241

Tools ➤ Services command, 240

topics for newsgroups, 218–219

traceroute tool, **268–269**, *269*

tracking packages, 90, *91*

transferring files. *See* downloading files

Transferring Internet Mail option, 243

Transmission Control Protocol (TCP), 334

travel, national service providers for, 37

Trn newsreader, 335

trolling, 336

True Speech format, 194, **206–207**, *207*

TrueSound format, 336

Trumpet Winsock

downloading, 48

Winsock version for, 22

.tsp files, 206

TUCOWS site, 256, 288, *288*

for HTML editor programs, 109

for stock information, 82

for telnet programs, 267

TurboGopher program, 336

TV feature, 81

Tweak UI program, 56, *57*, 225

.txt files, 260

type fonts, 61–62, **153–155**, *154*, **160–161**

Type of search field, 135

U

&u code, 148

ULs (urban legends), 336–337

uncompressing, 336

uncompression, 336

Underline Links option, 61, 159

Undernet server, 336

Uniform Resource Locators (URLs), 14, 337

address field for, **186**

entering, **73**

format options for, 62–63, 175

in headers and footers, 148

printing table of, 149

in searches, 83

shortcuts to, 60

United Parcel Service (UPS) Package Tracking page, 90, *91*

Unix operating system, 336

Unix to Unix Copy (UUCP), 215, 337

unmoderated groups, 337

unselecting articles, 337

unsubscribing, 337

untarring, 337

Unviewed Links Color feature, 82

Unvisited Links option, 61, 159

upgrades

FTP sites for, 9

for Internet Explorer, 20, **273–274**

uploading files, 337

urban legends (ULs), 336–337

URLs. *See* Uniform Resource Locators (URLs)

Use Current option, 167

Use Custom Colors option, 159

Use Smooth Scrolling option, 175

Use Style Sheets option, 175

Use the Following Dial-Up Networking Connection option, 161–162

Use These Colors Instead of Windows Desktop Colors option, 59, 159

Usenet newsgroups, 323, 337. *See also* news and newsgroups

user IDs for profiles, 43

usernames, 337

UUCP (Unix to Unix Copy), 215, 337

uudecode program, 338

UUENCODE message format, 242

uuencode program, 338

UUnet, 4

V

V.32bis modem standard, 34

V.34 modem standard, 34

vacation program, 338

VDOLive Video format, **210**, *211*

Veronica index, 338

versions

 of Internet Explorer, **21–22**, **273–274**

 of Winsock, **21–22**, 39–40

Vi editor, 338

video, **207–208**

 embedded files for, **190–191**

 MPEG players for, **208**, *208*

 options for, 58, 159

 QuickTime format for, **208–209**, *208*

 Shockware format for, **210**

 StreamWorks format for, 211

 VDOLive Video format for, **210**, *211*

 VRML format for, **209–210**, *210*

View Files option, 76, 174

View ➤ Fonts, **153–155**, *154*

View ➤ Icon Bar command, 223

View menu in RealAudio Player, 202

View option in WS_FTP, 260

View ➤ Options command. *See* Options dialog box

View ➤ Refresh command, 75, **155**

View ➤ Source command, 155–156, 182

View ➤ Status Bar command, 153

View ➤ Stop command, 155

View ➤ Toolbar command, 153

View ➤ Unread Messages Only command, 223

Viewed Link Color feature, 82

viewers, 338

 finding, **129–130**

 options for, 167, *168*

viewing

 images, 183–184

 local files, 103

 saved Web pages, **130–131**

 subscribed newsgroups, **222–223**

violence, rating options for, 172–173, *173*

Virtual Garden, 91, *92*

Virtual Reality Modeling Language (VRML) format, **209–210**, *210*

viruses, 169, 171, 338

Visited Links option, 61, 159

visited sites, returning to. *See* favorite Web pages

.VOC format, 338

Volcano Coffee page, 190, *190*

volume control in RealAudio Player, *200–201*, 201

Volume Control window, 201, *201*

VRML (Virtual Reality Modeling Language) format, **209–210**, *210*, 338

VT-100 terminals, 262, 338

W

&w code, 148

wallpaper, 180–181, *181*

WANs (wide-area networks), 339

warlording, 339

Warn Me About Invalid Site Certificates option, 171

Warn Me Before Accepting "Cookies" option, 171

Warn Me Before Crossing Zones option, 171
Warn Me Before Sending options, 171
.wav format, 190–191, 193–194, 339
wave table synthesis, 193
Weather Information feature, 81
Web browsers, 7, 301, 339
    default, 77, **119–120**, *120*, **169**
    for multimedia, 15
Web Map site, 78
web.nexor.co.uk site, 134
Web pages, **99**, 325, 339
    addresses in, **145–146**, *146*
    character sets for, **62**, *63*, 161
    color options for, **59**, **159**
    downloading files from, **131**, *132*
    editing, **151**
    Favorites list for, **100–109**, *102*, *104*, *106–107*
    fonts for, **61–62**, **153–155**, *154*, **160–161**
    forms for, **89–96**, *91–95*
    Go menu for, **176–178**, *177*
    hot lists for, **109–110**, *110*
    interactive games on, **96–97**, *97*
    jumping to, **87**
    loading, 144
    multimedia in. *See* multimedia; sound
    properties of, 150, *150*
    rating options for, **172–173**, *173*
    reloading, **155**, 182
    saving, **130**, **144–146**, *147*
    searching in, 152–153, *153*
    shortcuts for, 87, **110–119**, *112–117*, *119*
    source code for, 155–156, 182, 313
    Start pages, 54, **77–83**, *79–80*
    stopping transmission of, 155
    temporary files for, 75–76, *75*, **173–174**, *174*
    viewing, **130–131**
Web Picks feature, 81
Web Tutorial quick link, 71
Welcome feature, 82
Well service, 114, 140
What's New Page, 321
whispers, 339
white space in printing, 148

Whois gateway, 340
Whole Internet Catalog site, 78, 283
WhoWhere search engine, 340
wide-area networks (WANs), 339
Win32 programs, 22
winbm2fv.exe program, 109
WinCIM 2.01 program, 39–40
WinComm program, 262
windows, multiple, **76–77**, 144, 183
Windows 3.1
    Internet connections in, **47–48**
    modems with, **36**
    shortcuts in, **118–119**, *119*
    telnet clients for, **266–267**
    Winsock version for, 22
Windows 95
    modems with, **34–36**, *35*
    telnet client in, **263–264**, *263*
Windows Display Properties dialog box, 159
Windows for Workgroups, 22
Windows Setup tab
    for Dial-Up Networking, 42
    for Internet Explorer, 24, *24*
Winsocks
    for AOL, 39
    for CompuServe, 40
    conflicts with, **40–41**
    for multiple applications, 68
    32-bit vs. 16-bit, **21–22**
    for Windows 3.1, 47
WinZip program, 138, 340
wizards, 340
words, searching for, 152–153, *153*
working directories, 340
World Wide Web (WWW), **14–16**, *15*, **67**, 340. *See also* Web pages
    downloading Internet Explorer from, **23**
    general-interest guides to, **281–287**, *282–287*
    navigating, **72–77**, *74–75*
    search tools for, **83–86**, *85–86*, **289–292**, *289–292*
    software guides to, **288–289**, *288–289*
worms, 340

WRT acronym, 340
WS_FTP program, 9, **257–258**, *258*, 340
    connecting to servers with, **258–259**, *259*
    downloading files with, **260**
ws_ftp32.zip file, 9
WS Ping tool, **269–270**, *270*
WSGopher program, 340
WWW. *See* Web pages; World Wide Web (WWW)
www.aladdinsys.com site, 138
www.altavista.digital.com site, 84, 292, *292*
www.bnet.att.com site, 285, *285*
www.bu.edu site, 96
www.cnet.com site, 286, *286*
www.coast.net site, 48
www.dspg.com site, 206
www.eff.org site, 306
www.forteinc.com site, 226–227
www.gnn.com site, 78, 283, *283*
www.hilgraeve.com site, 262, 264
www.ipswitch.com site, 257, 270
www.king.org site, 192, *192*
www.macromedia.com site, 210
www.mckinley.com site, 287, *287*
www.microsoft.com site
    for e-mail driver, 239
    for Internet Explorer, 20, 23
    for Internet Mail, 245
    for Internet News, 219
    for multimedia, 190, *190*
    for Netscape bookmark conversion program, 109
    for Tweak UI program, 56, 225
    for version updates, 273
    for VRML player, 210
www.msn.com site, 78–80, *79*, 84, 282, *282*
www.netscape.com site, 212
www-ns.rutgers.edu site, 134
www.qualcomm.com site, 250
www.search.com site, 84, *86*, 290, *290*
www.shareware.com site, 130, 289, *289*

www.thinkman.com site, 270
www.tucows.com site, 256, 288, *288*
    for HTML editor programs, 109
    for stock information, 82
    for telnet programs, 267
www.unitedmedia.com site, 100, *100*
www.vandyke.com site, 266
www.vdolive.com site, 210
www.winzip.com site, 138
www.xingtech.com site, 203–204
www.yahoo.com site, 291, *291*
www.zdnet.com site, 78

X

X window interface, 341
.xdm files, 203
.xdma files, 203
Xibo, 316
Xmodem protocol, 264, 340

Y

Yahoo site, 291, *291*, 341
YAWTEL program, 267
YMMV acronym, 341
Ymodem protocol, 341

Z

zip format, 137–138, 341
Zmodem protocol, 264, 341